IMAGES
of America

SHAPLEIGH AND ACTON

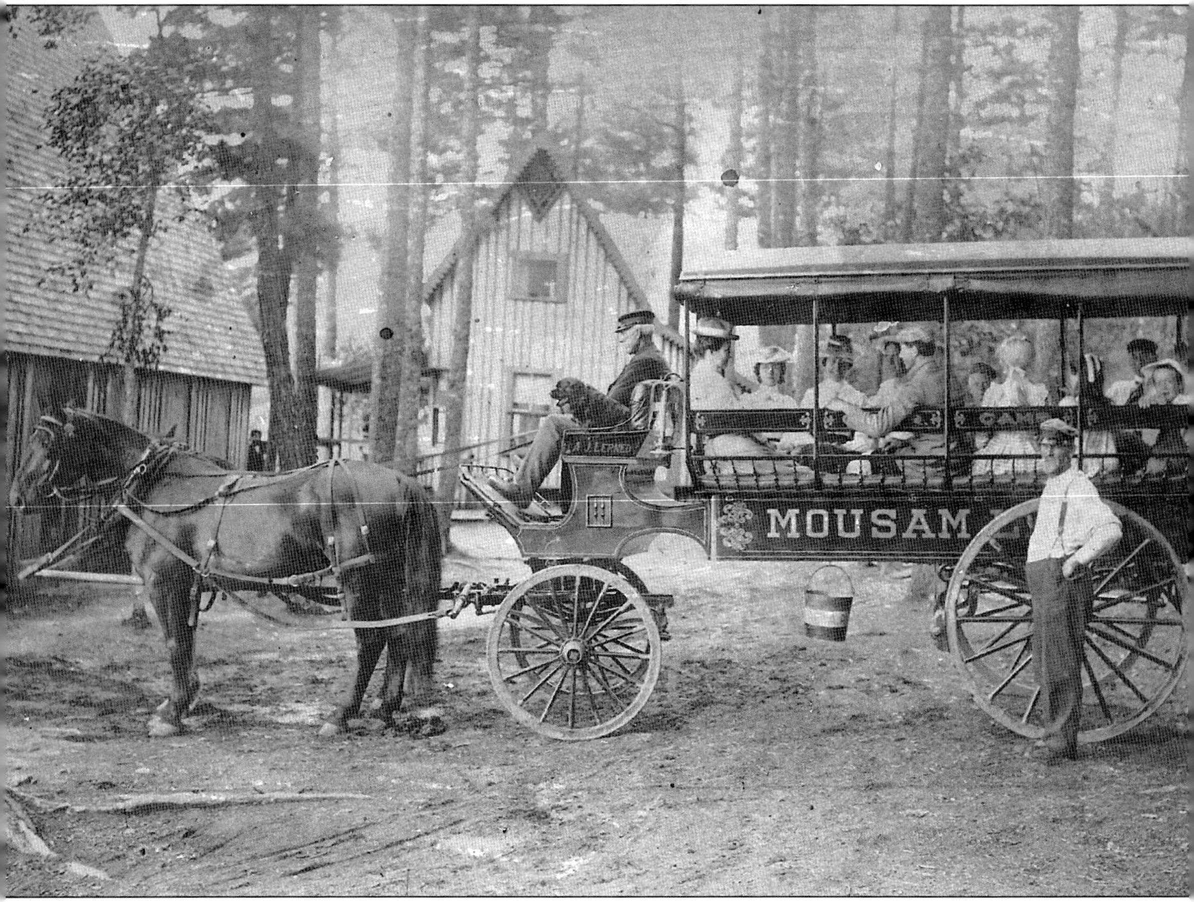

On the Cover: Asa Lerned (standing) built and operated the Grand American Republic (G.A.R.) camps on Mousam Lake in Shapleigh. Guests were transported in this "carry-all" from the Springvale train depot at noon every day for the 5-mile trip to the camps. Read more about Mousam Lake and the G.A.R. camps in Chapter Two: The Lakes Region. (Courtesy of the Acton-Shapleigh Historical Society.)

IMAGES
of America

SHAPLEIGH AND ACTON

Debbie Petersen

ARCADIA
PUBLISHING

ISBN 978-0-7385-7306-9

Published by Arcadia Publishing
Charleston SC, Chicago IL, Portsmouth NH, San Francisco CA

Printed in the United States of America

Library of Congress Control Number: 2009941377

For all general information contact Arcadia Publishing at:
Telephone 843-853-2070
Fax 843-853-0044
E-mail sales@arcadiapublishing.com
For customer service and orders:
Toll-Free 1-888-313-2665

Visit us on the Internet at www.arcadiapublishing.com

Dedicated to all those who came before me, those here with me now, and those yet to be.

Contents

ACKNOWLEDGMENTS

Established in 1964, the Acton-Shapleigh Historical Society is a nonprofit organization providing members and the general public with a glimpse to its past by actively preserving the history of these two towns. The vast majority of donations are from families who lived and/or continue to live in this area. All royalties earned from the sales of this book will benefit the Acton-Shapleigh Historical Society. These proceeds will allow the historical society to continue its mission of "Preserving Our Heritage" for future generations. Unless otherwise noted, all images appear courtesy of the Acton-Shapleigh Historical Society and/or the author. I would like to thank all those generous citizens who welcomed me into their homes and entrusted me with their treasured photographs. As president of the Acton-Shapleigh Historical Society, I would like to extend a thank-you to my fellow officers—Norma Evans, Melissa Conner, Patricia Dunn, Joy Clark, Shirley Sheesley, Fred Webber, and Steve Parello—for supporting me in this endeavor. Finally, to my husband, Dana, and my daughter, Chelsea, a special thank-you for your love, encouragement, and especially your understanding during this venture.

INTRODUCTION

In the winter of 1661, Francis Small began keeping a trading house somewhere in the vicinity of what is now Limington and Cornish. Many local Native Americans became largely indebted to him, promising him furs and other valuables in the spring. These same Native Americans later plotted an easier way to rid their debt and conspired together to surround and burn his house down on a particular night. After learning about the plot, Captain Sunda, a chief of the Ossipees, secretly informed Small so that he was able to make a timely escape. Small at first regarded this as a sly set-up to deprive him of his property, but Captain Sunda openhandedly promised to compensate him with the conveyance of lands if this plan went through. On the night before the scheduled attack, Small left his house and retired to a neighboring hill, where he watched the flames of his business light up the forest. Later that night, Small left the region and returned to Scarborough, his original home.

In 1663, Captain Sunda, faithful to his promise, met Small in Saco and deeded him the Ossipee tract, now the towns of Cornish, Parsonsfield, Newfield, Limerick, Limington, and Shapleigh, to indemnify him for his loss. Afterward, it was established that Maj. Nicholas Shapleigh, of Kittery, was in partnership with Small in the trading house enterprise. Due to this fact, Small deeded Major Shapleigh an undivided half of all the lands conveyed by Captain Sunda. In 1770, Small's family located the original unrecorded deed from Captain Sunda to Francis Small. Nicholas Shapleigh's heirs knew they had an interest in the deed and in 1772 appointed a committee "to go up and possess the land." In May 1773, this committee, accompanied by a surveyor and two chainmen, went out into the wildernesses and marked what eventually became the towns' original boundaries. Later that year, through the Supreme Court of Massachusetts, Small's heirs took possession of Cornish, Limington, Newfield, and half of Limerick, while Major Shapleigh's heirs took possession of the other half of Limerick, Parsonsfield, and Shapleigh.

Because of several large bodies of water at its center, Shapleigh was divided into an east and a west parish. In 1830, the west parish was incorporated as the Town of Acton. As was common for the times, smaller villages grew within townships. Shapleigh has Emery Mills, Shapleigh Corner, Ross Corner, and North Shapleigh, while Acton has South Acton, Acton Corner, and Acton–Milton Mills. Nestled between the rocky Maine coastline and the New Hampshire White Mountain region, settlers of Shapleigh and Acton built homes and communities from their surroundings and built a lifestyle that can still be found here today. Please join me in celebrating their proud heritage.

One

Shapleigh and its Villages

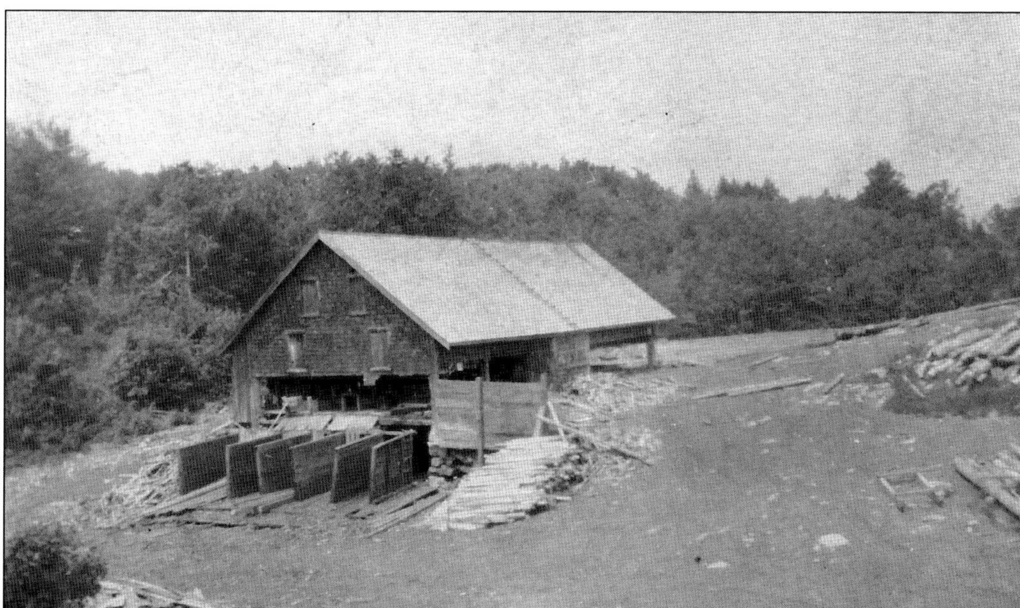

Emery Mills was the first and, for many years, the main business center in Shapleigh. The area's timber was a major attraction for early settlers. Pictured is B. C. Jordan's sawmill, which is believed to be one of the earliest in the town. Jordan also owned a steamboat that was used to tow log booms to the foot of Mousam Lake, where they would then break the boom and float the logs down to his sawmill.

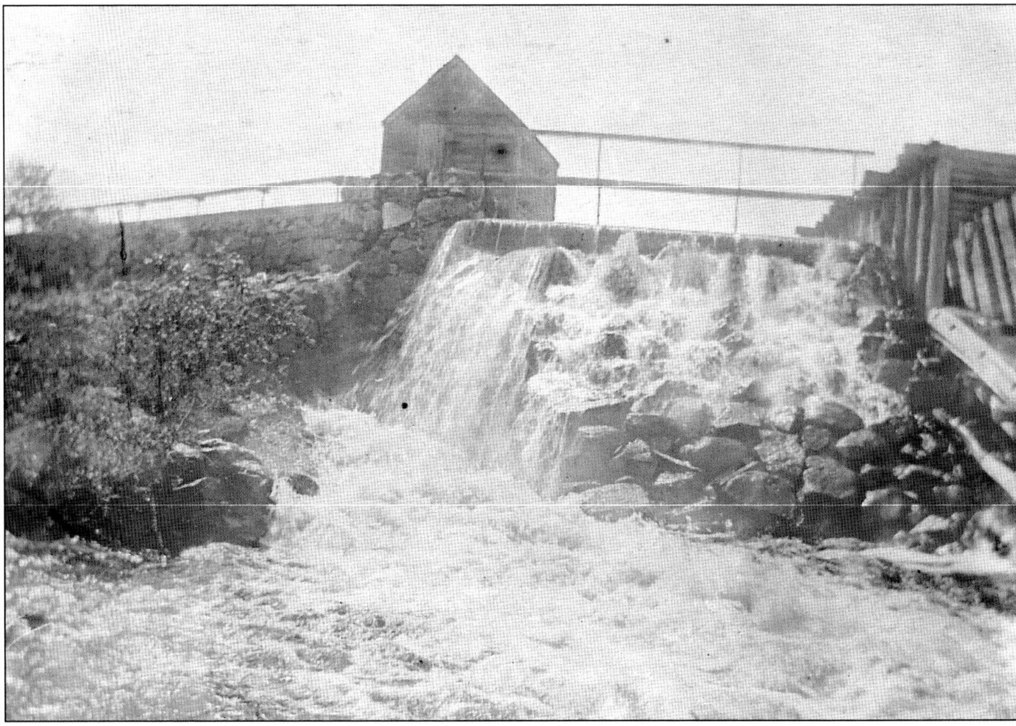

The first dam was built in 1772 by Simon Emery, Emery Mills' namesake. The top photograph was taken in 1895, at a time when the water from this dam was used to supply power to several sawmills in town. The bottom picture is the second dam, which was built in 1899 and located just above the original one. The granite used in the building of the dam was obtained from the Tattle Street area of Emery Mills. Simon Emery also built the first sawmill and first gristmill on record in town. (Both, courtesy of Fred Thyng.)

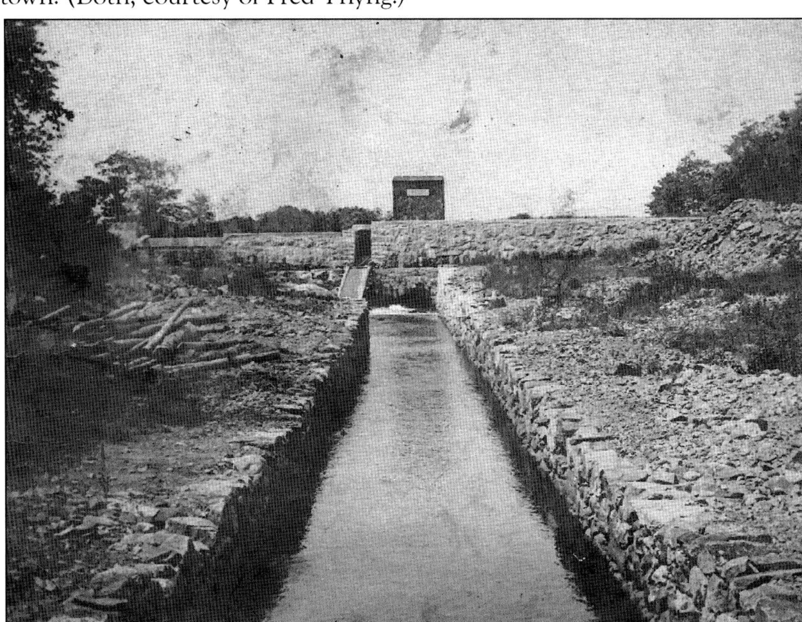

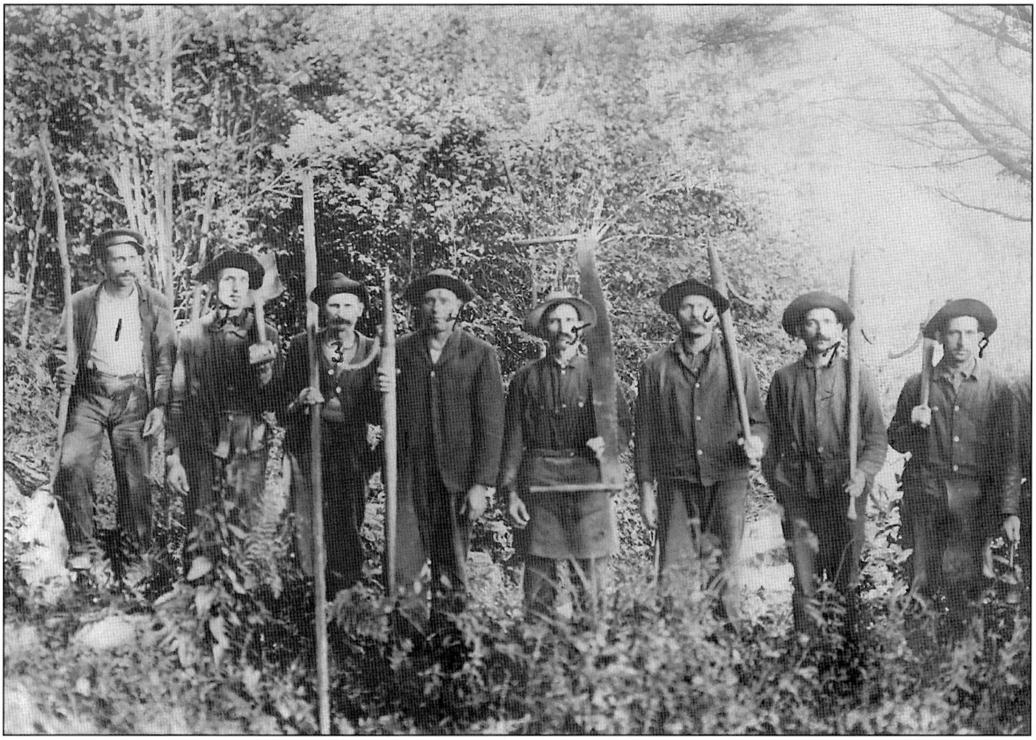

Workers from a local sawmill are pictured. They are, from left to right, Ulysses Ham, Ellsworth Murray, Herman Johnson, Joseph Muchmore, Joseph Grondin, Lester Horne, Edward Grondin and Frank Grondin. Here the proud lumbermen are armed with pike poles, peaveys, and a two-man saw—typical tools of the trade. (Courtesy of Fred Thyng.)

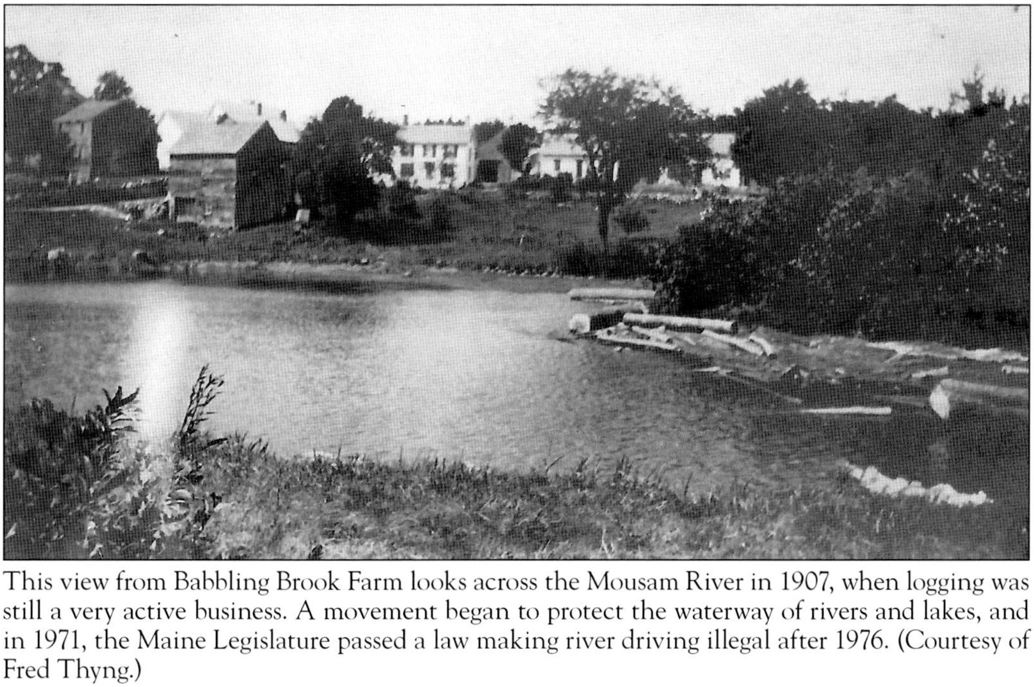

This view from Babbling Brook Farm looks across the Mousam River in 1907, when logging was still a very active business. A movement began to protect the waterway of rivers and lakes, and in 1971, the Maine Legislature passed a law making river driving illegal after 1976. (Courtesy of Fred Thyng.)

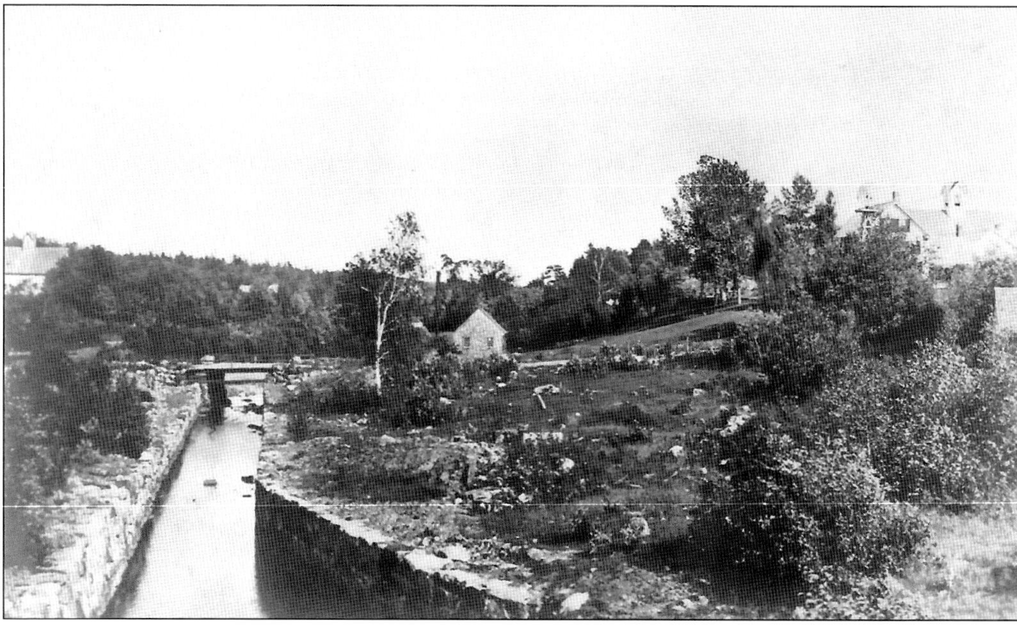

The top photograph is the view from the gatehouse of the Emery Mills Dam, looking along the flume towards Babbling Brook Farm in 1899. The small building in the center was a threshing mill. The bottom photograph, also taken in 1899, shows Babbling Brook Farm.

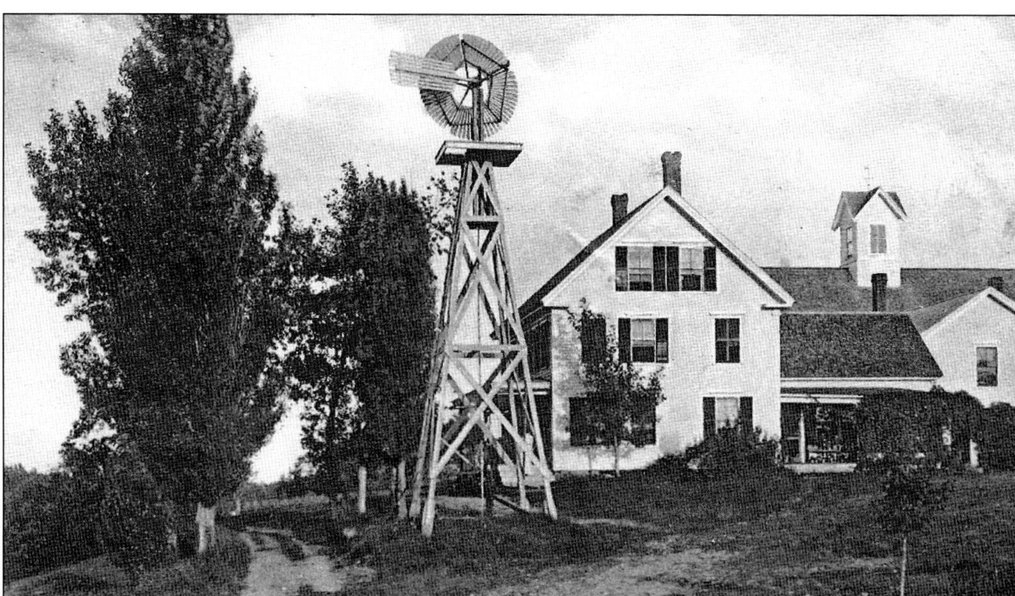

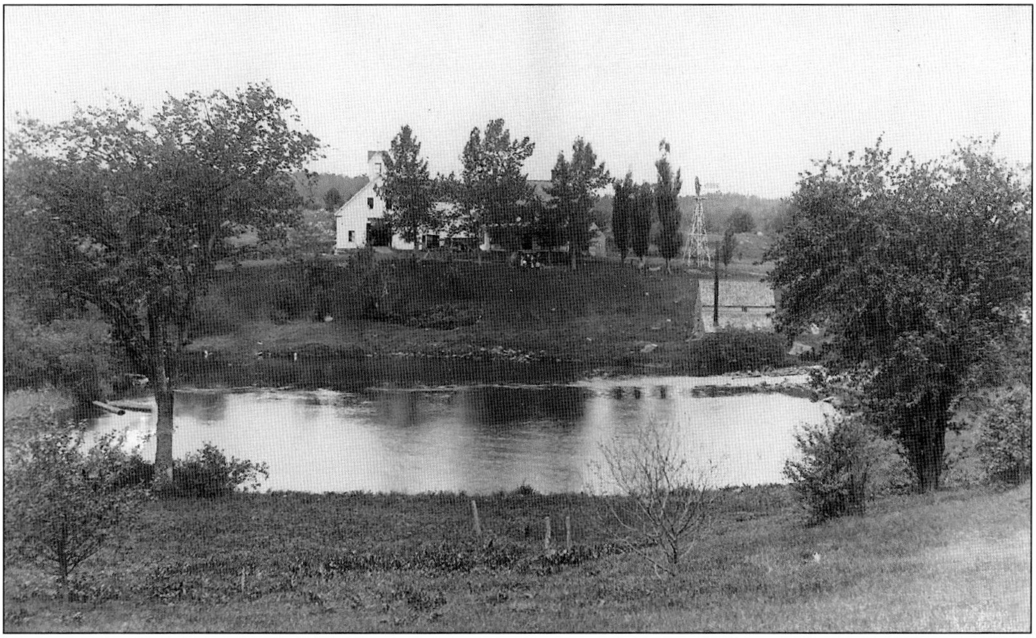

Pictured here is a view of Babbling Brook Farm from what is now Route 109.

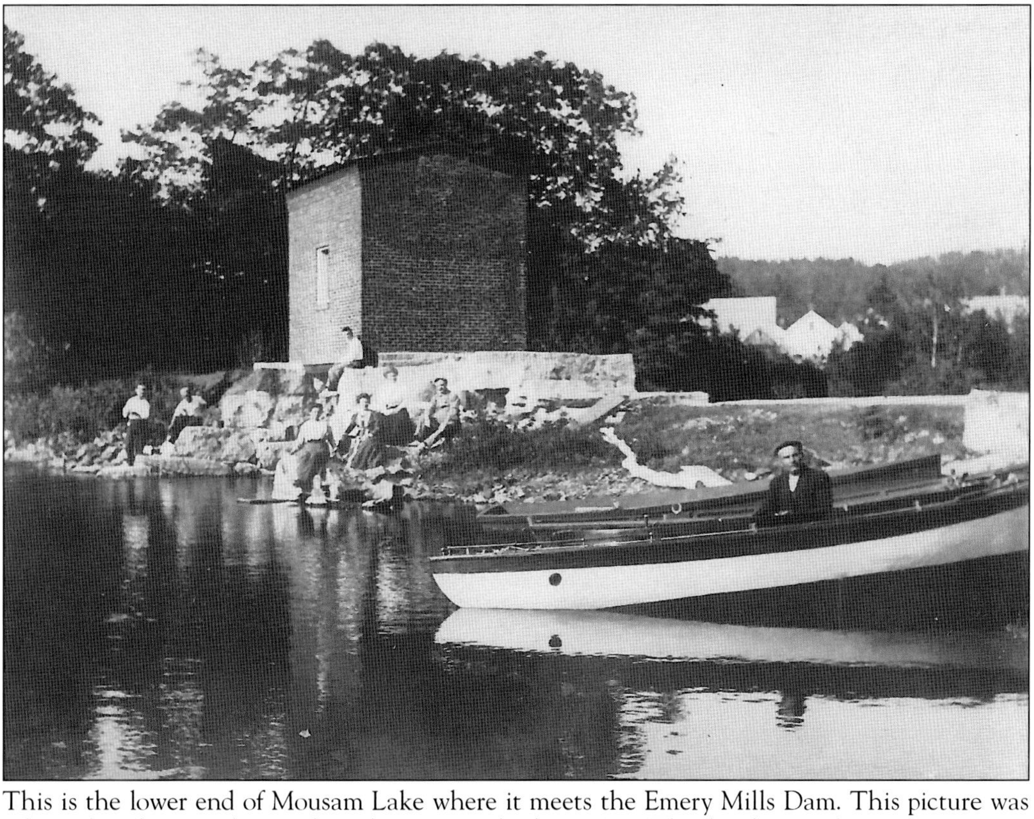

This is the lower end of Mousam Lake where it meets the Emery Mills Dam. This picture was taken after the new dam and gatehouse were built in 1899. This has been a favorite swimming spot for many years.

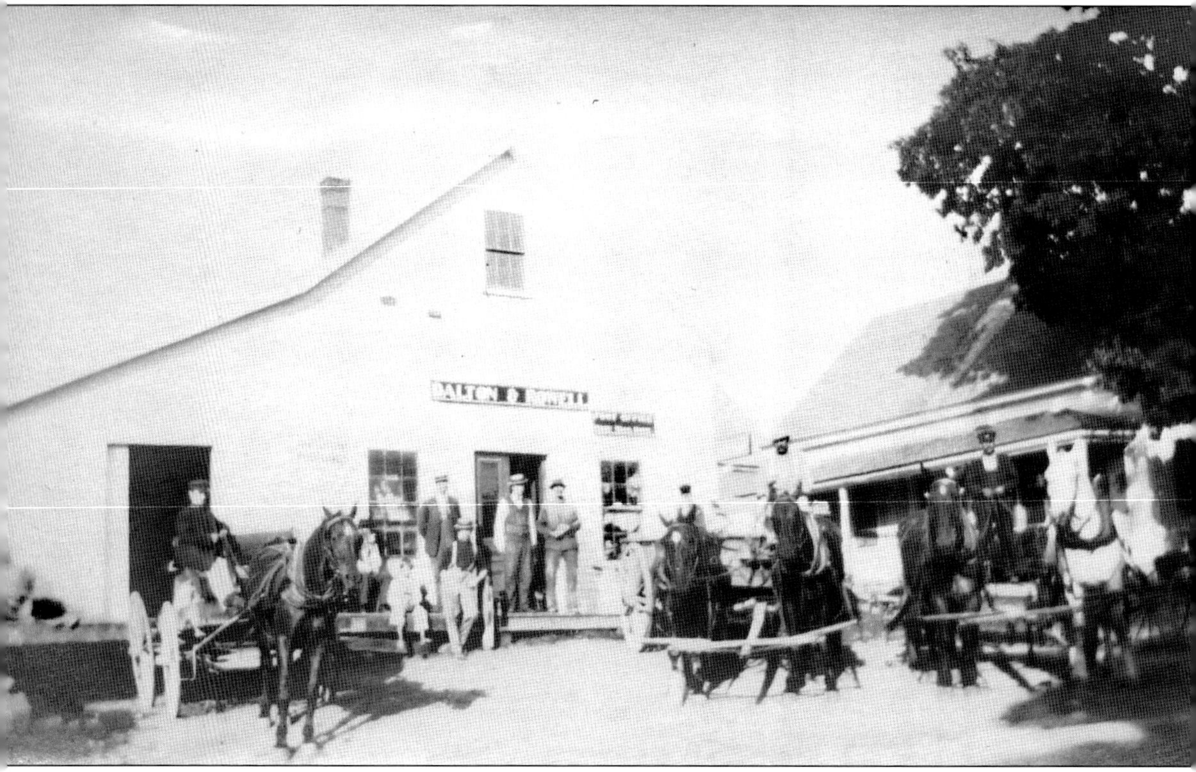

The general store was more than just a purveyor of goods; it held an important and vital place in most towns' histories. More often than not, it was home to the post office and acted as a gathering place for townsfolk to meet and share local events. Pictured here are various townspeople, merchants, and farmers who have gathered to purchase and/or sell merchandise. Unlike today, when traveling to the store is quick and convenient, at the time of this photograph it was sometimes an all-day event just to go into town and back. In 1902, the owner of this store was A. J. Brackett, who later sold it to Dalton and Rowell. This building, one of the oldest stores in Shapleigh, is still standing and currently houses the One Earth Natural Food Store.

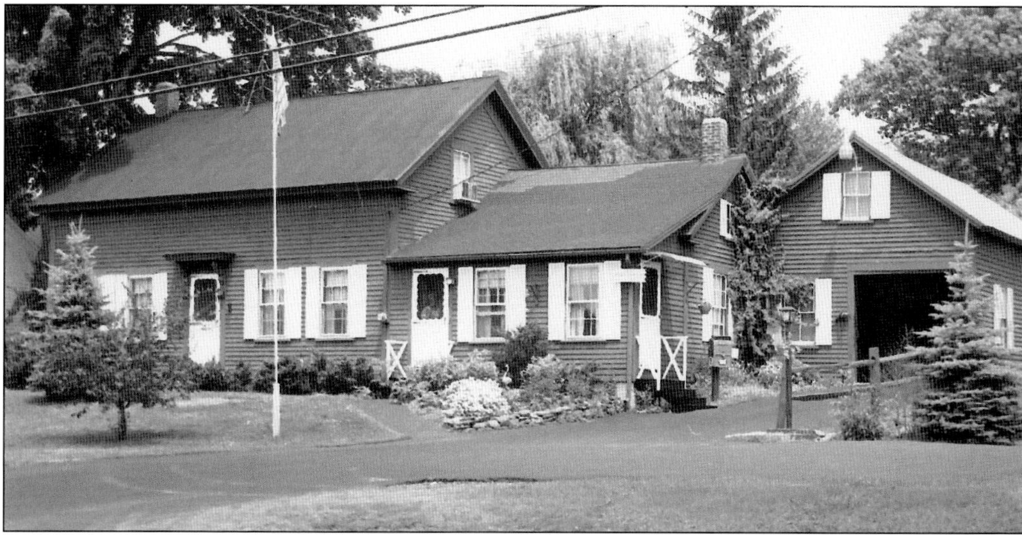

In 1976, the Emery Mills post office (zip code 04031) was in the home of Clinton Guinard. The number of U.S. post offices peaked in 1901 at 76,945; the number sharply declined in the ensuing decade, due to the spread of rural free delivery. By the end of 2005, the number of independent post offices had decreased to 27,385. Postal services were suspended here on December 29, 1988, and the post office officially closed on May 30, 1992, with mail being transferred to the Shapleigh Post Office.

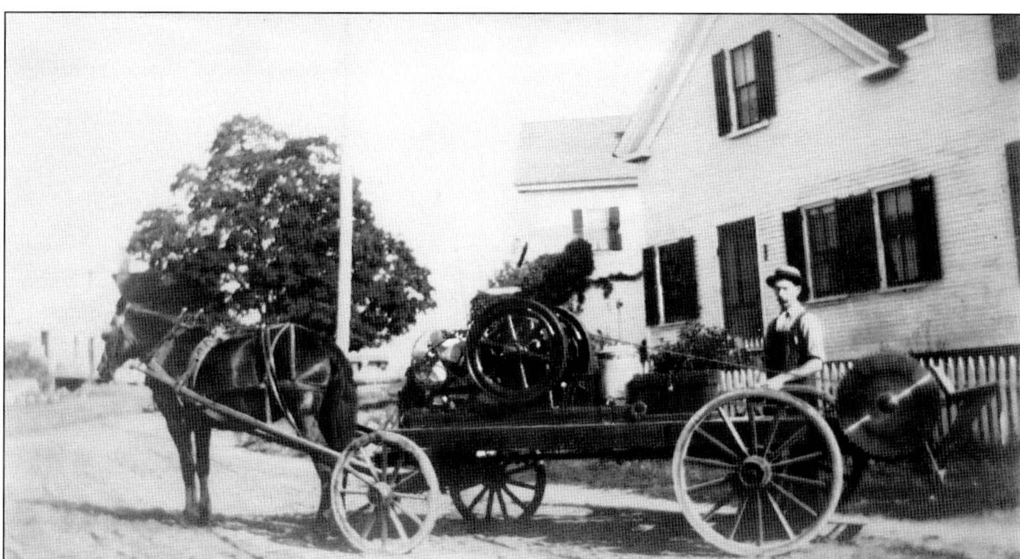

A portable sawmill is at the ready in Emery Mills. Coal-fired, locomotive-type boilers and large steam engines were used for power.

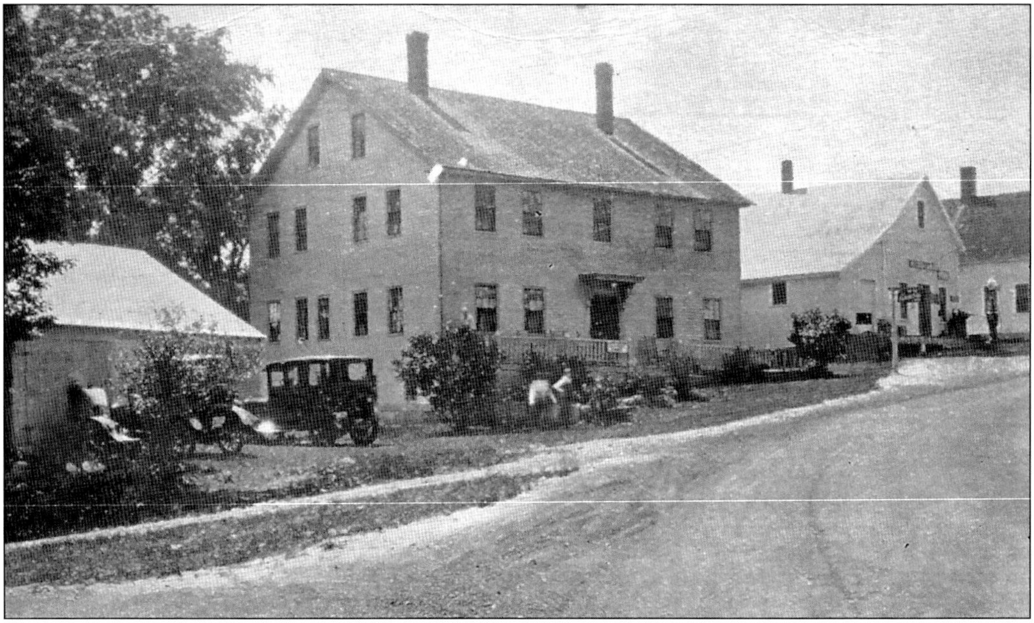

This is the heart of Emery Mills. These two photographs show Emery Mills as it looked in the early 20th century and midway through. The large, two-chimney building is the Elmwood Inn. A popular spot, the Elmwood Inn was also a great place to go for local gossip and later on was known as the "beehive." In the basement was a large barroom that faced the river and provided patrons with a beautiful view of Mousam River. The beehive was later torn down.

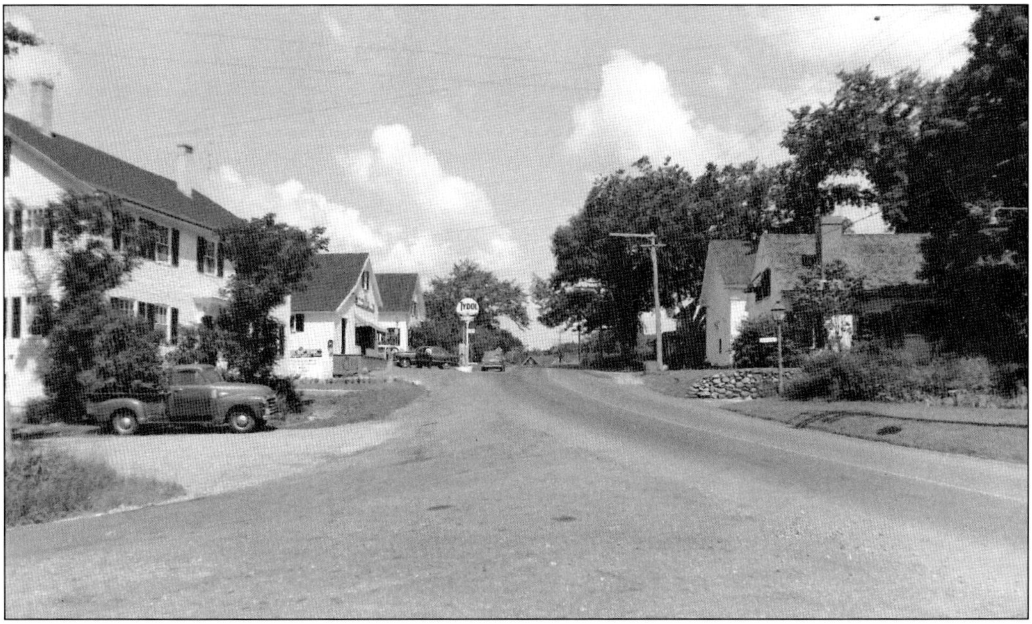

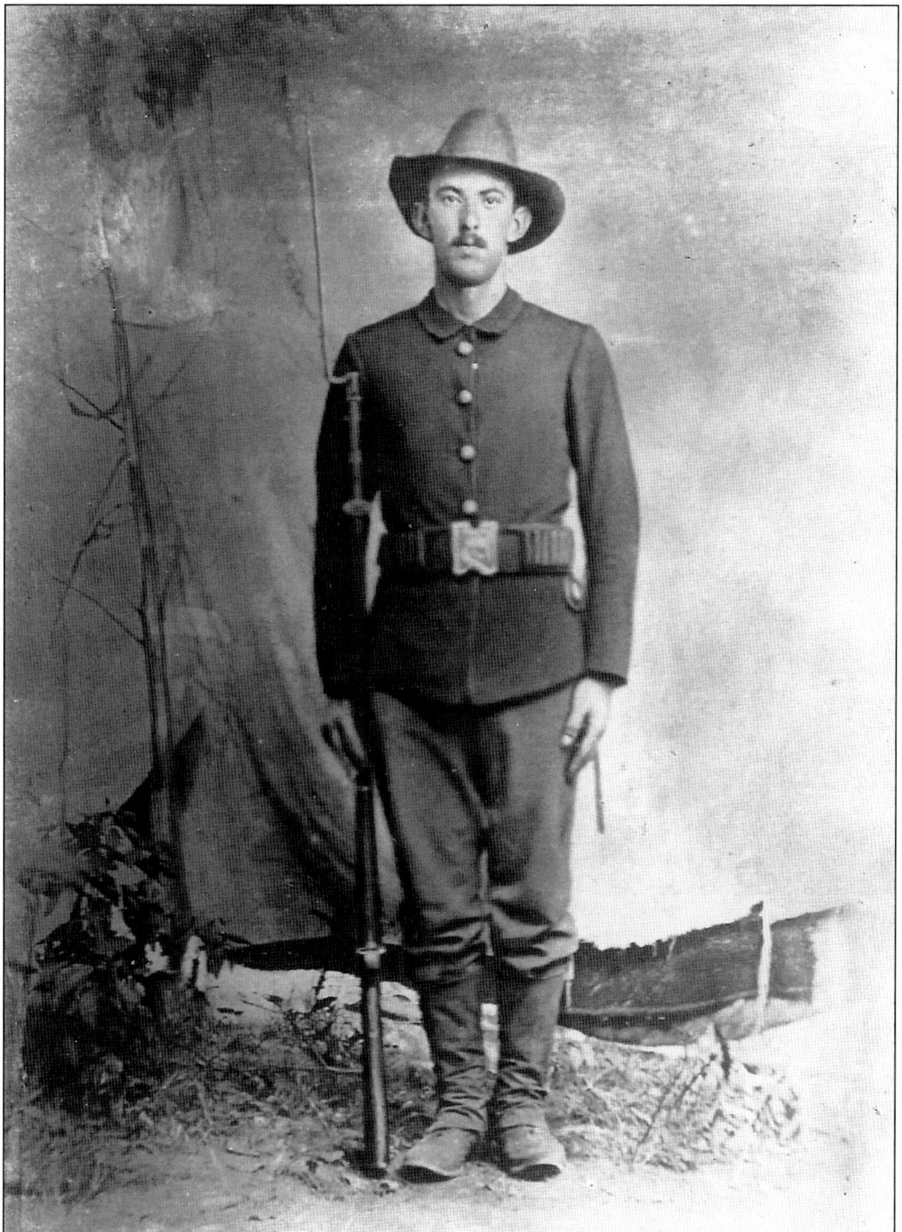

Emery Mills native Leon Murray entered the U.S. Army and served during the Spanish-American War in 1898. Murray's enlistment with Company M of the 1st Rhode Island Volunteer Infantry was from 1879 through 1911. The 1st Rhode Island was mustered into service in May 1898 at Quonsett Point, Rhode Island. At that time, the unit consisted of 46 officers and 958 enlisted men. This regiment was the only infantry regiment raised in Rhode Island during the war. Throughout its term of service, the unit lost 11 enlisted men to disease and one who died as the result of an accident. Thirty-five more enlisted men were discharged for disability. Interestingly, the regiment also had 13 enlisted men who were court-martialed and 89 who deserted. As part of Shapleigh's bicentennial celebration in 1985, a memorial to all war veterans was unveiled and dedicated. The monument is located in front of the Shapleigh Town Hall. (Courtesy of Earl Murray Jr.)

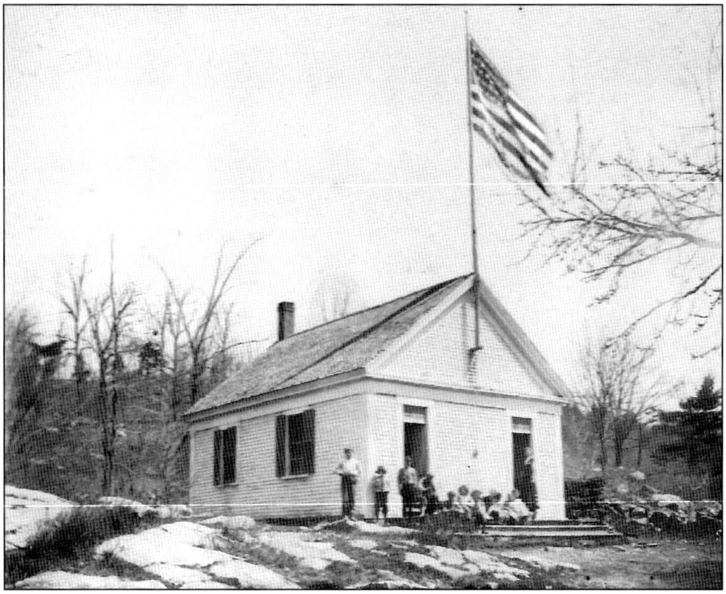

Emery Mills School, pictured around 1920, was the first school in Emery Mills. At one time, there were as many as 50 pupils attending this one-room schoolhouse. The school was located on a rise of land that is now part of Ted's Fried Clams. By 1872, Shapleigh had 10 school districts, each with its own one-room schoolhouse. In 1889, town records state the Emery Mills School, if not the best in town, was ranked among the very best.

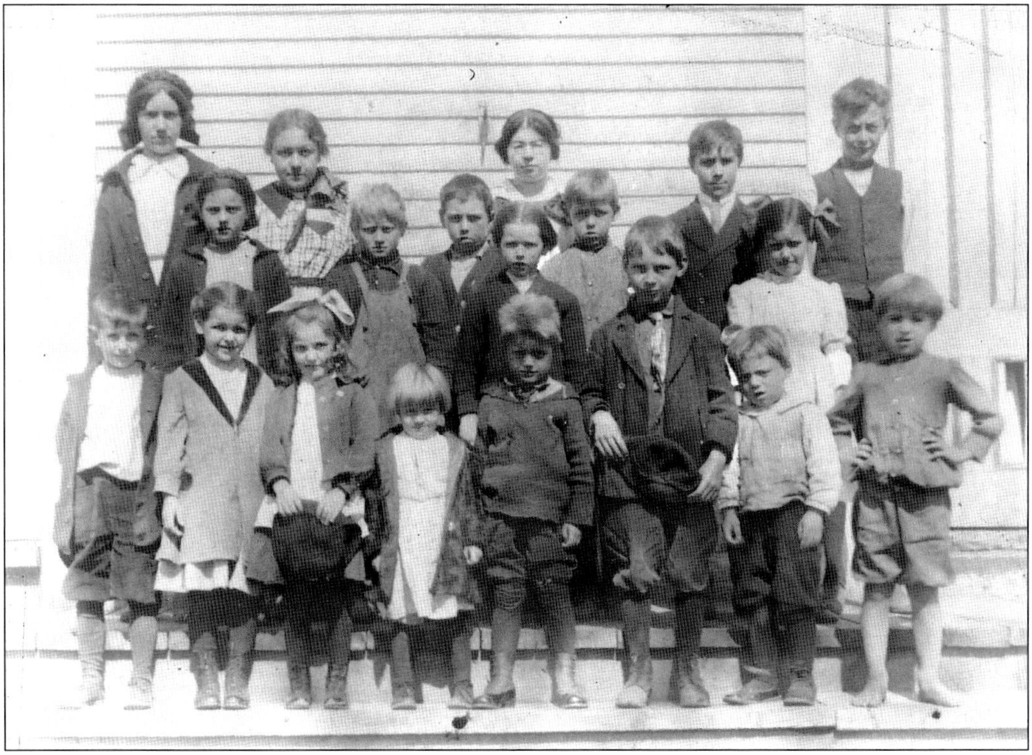

Pictured here are students of the Emery Mills School in 1914. From left to right are (first row) Milford Wescott, Theodora Hobbs, Irene Boothby, Mana Gallant, Jedediah Gallant, Charles Boothby, Kenneth Jellison, and Dorian Griffin; (second row) Gladys Palmer, Donald Muchmore, Edward Muchmore, Jessie Hobbs, Raymond Cousins, and Eleanor Murray; (third row) Pearl Muchmore, Adeline Merrill, Elodia Pray (teacher), Isaiah Ridley and Guy Horn.

Mousam Lake School in Emery Mills was built in 1923 after the closing of the Emery Mills School. It was discontinued in 1949 and seldom used afterward. In 1965, the town of Shapleigh deeded it to the Acton-Shapleigh Historical Society with the condition that it revert back to the town if the society ever disbanded. The Acton-Shapleigh Historical Society is located at 122 Emery Mills Road, a quarter-mile north of Ted's Fried Clams.

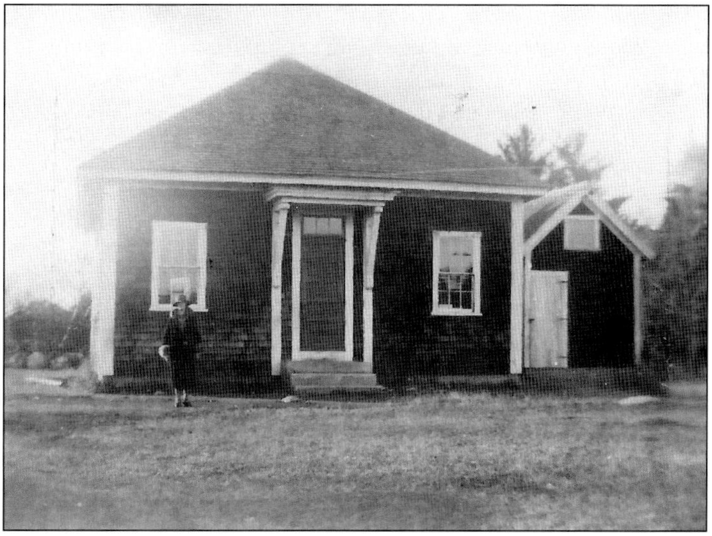

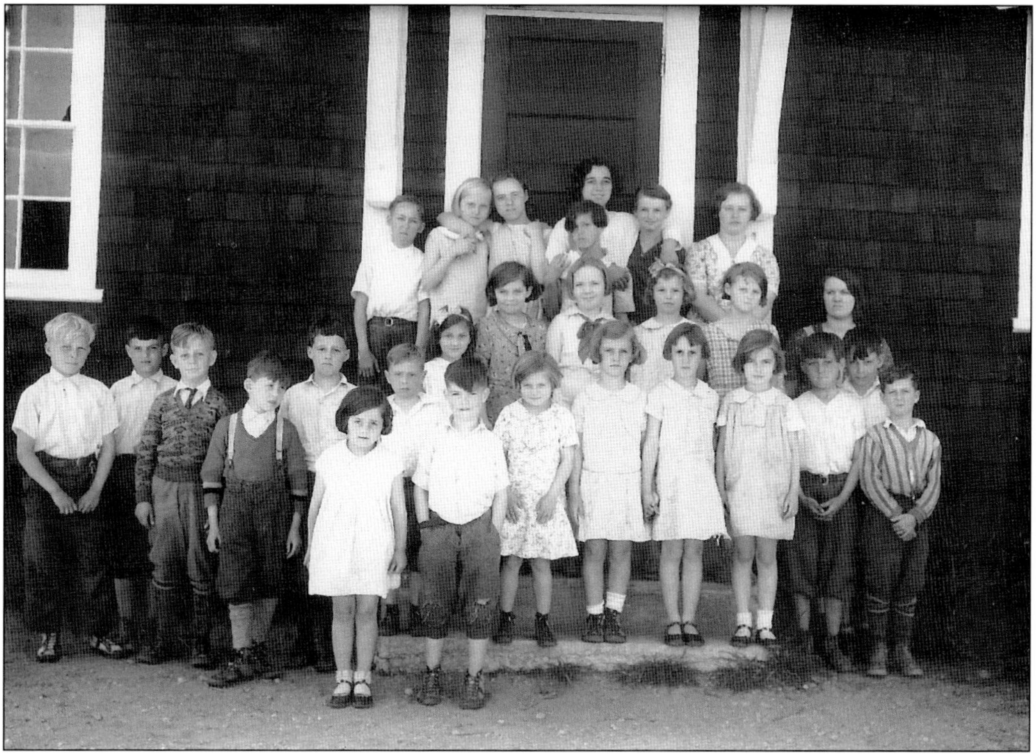

Here are the students of Mousam Lake School in 1932. From left to right are (front) Hazel Goodwin and Elwyn Morrow; (left of doorway) Jedediah Vachon, Robert Morrow, Stanley Hussey, Gordon Weyland, and John Griffin; (bottom step) Willard Wright, Shirley Muchmore, Pearl Vachon, Hazel Muchmore, and Constance Gallant; (right of doorway) Lawrence Vachon, Wallace Ryan, Kenneth Driscoll, and Stella Horn (Teacher); (middle step) June Zellhoefer, Wilhemina Zellhoefer, Marjorie Boothby, Gloria Wright, and Irene Driscoll; (top step) Raymond Vachon, Geraldine Vachon, Phyllis Griffin, Wanda Griffin, Doris Driscoll, Jean Gallant, and Mary Griffin.

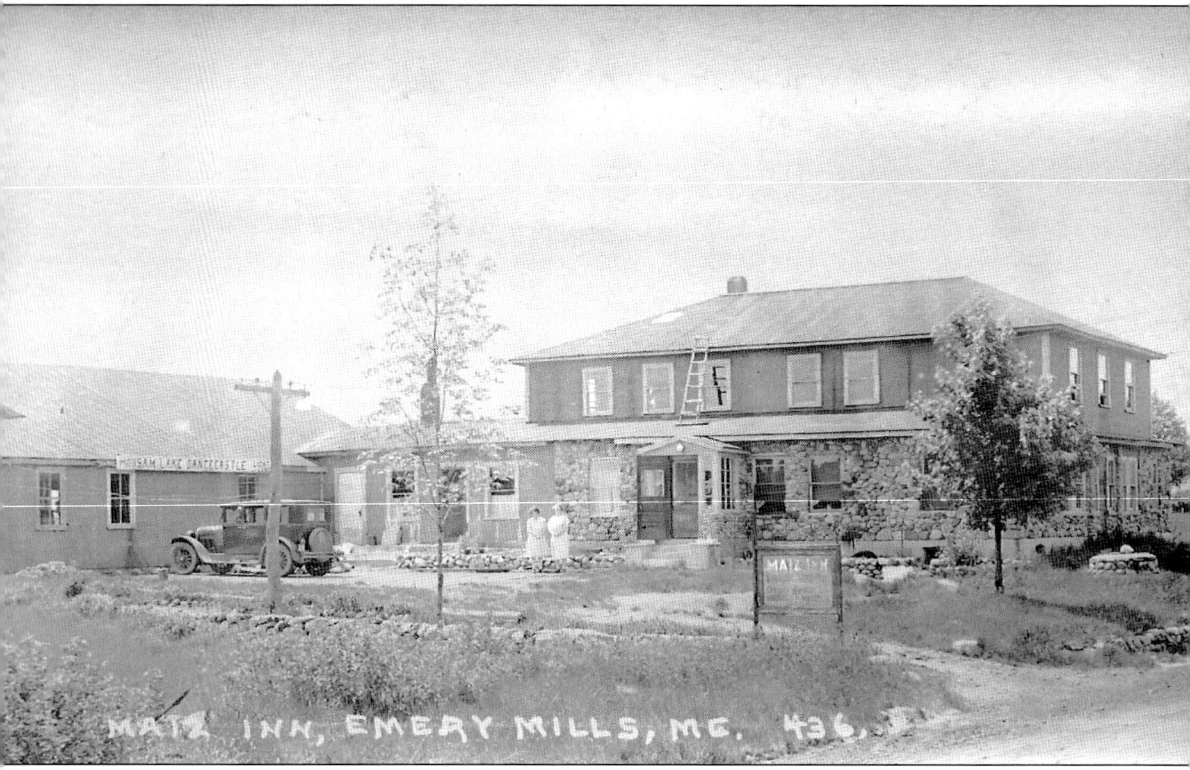

The Maiz Inn and Boys' Camp was located just north of Emery Mills on Lower Mousam Lake. This establishment was owned and operated by Mary S. Regan of Emery Mills. A brochure states, "Just an ideal place for your boy to spend his vacation days. So healthful and restful. Wholesome food. New clean beds. Electric lights. Sanitary septic tank sewage and 100% analyzed water. Counselors to care for and plan all recreation for boys. Registered doctor in attendance. Fishing, boating and bathing. Located on lake seven miles long. We also have year- round reservations for adults. Season of nine weeks $225." The inn attracted boys from as far away as Boston with a one-way train fare costing only $2.98. Lakeside Sport and Marine is currently at this location.

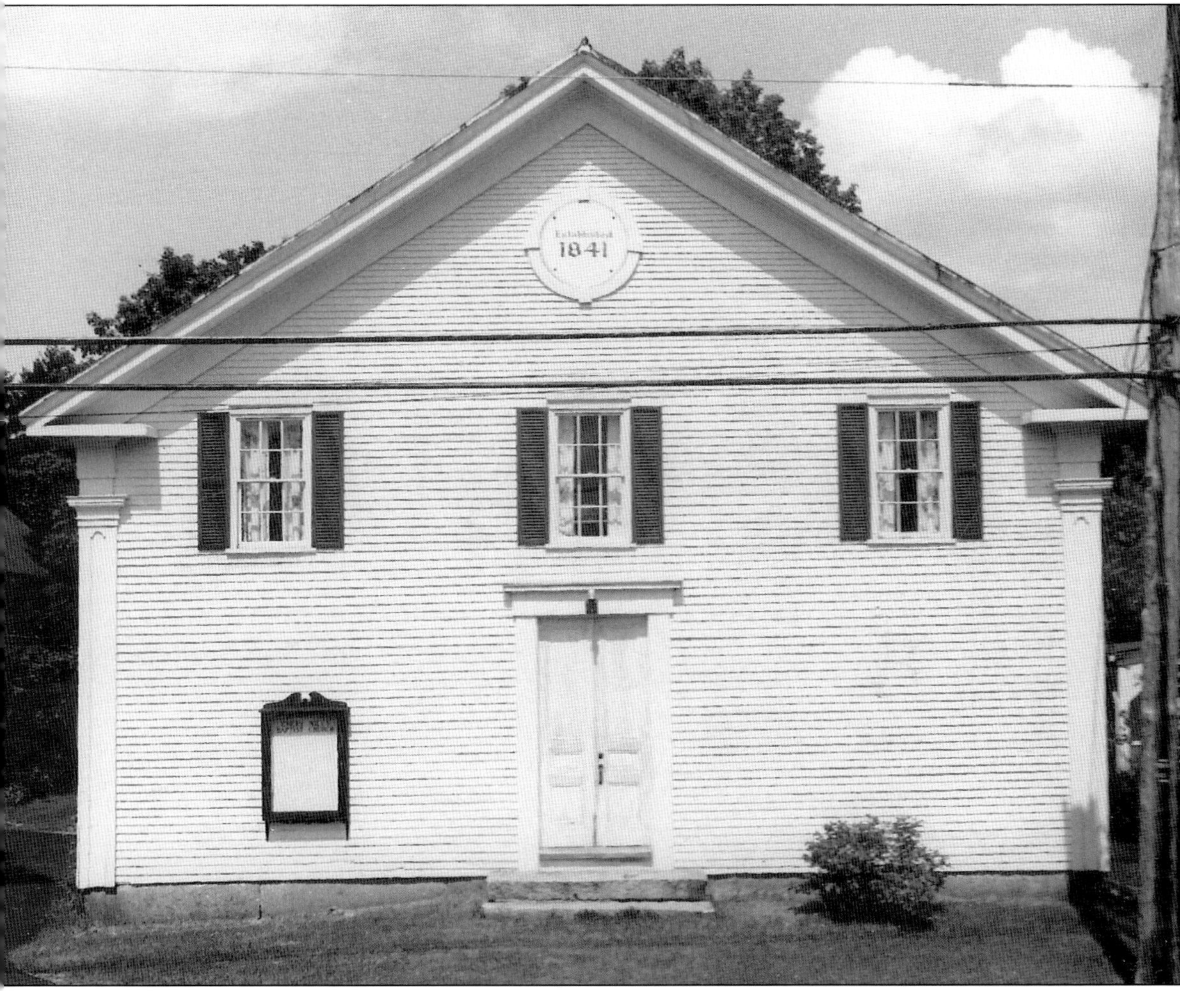

Religion was then, as it is today, the glue of many communities. Like the general store, church was a meeting place where families came together to practice their faith, socialize, and aid each other. Pictured here is the Methodist meetinghouse in Emery Mills, built in 1828. By 1844, village businesses declined, causing members to move away and reducing attendance so much that the Methodists ceased to hold public meetings here and sold the building to the Free-Will Baptist Society. The religious denomination changed several times since the church was built, but regular services were held until the 1970s, when its doors closed and the building was again sold, this time to a private owner. Currently vacant, it is located directly across the street from the One Earth Natural Food Store.

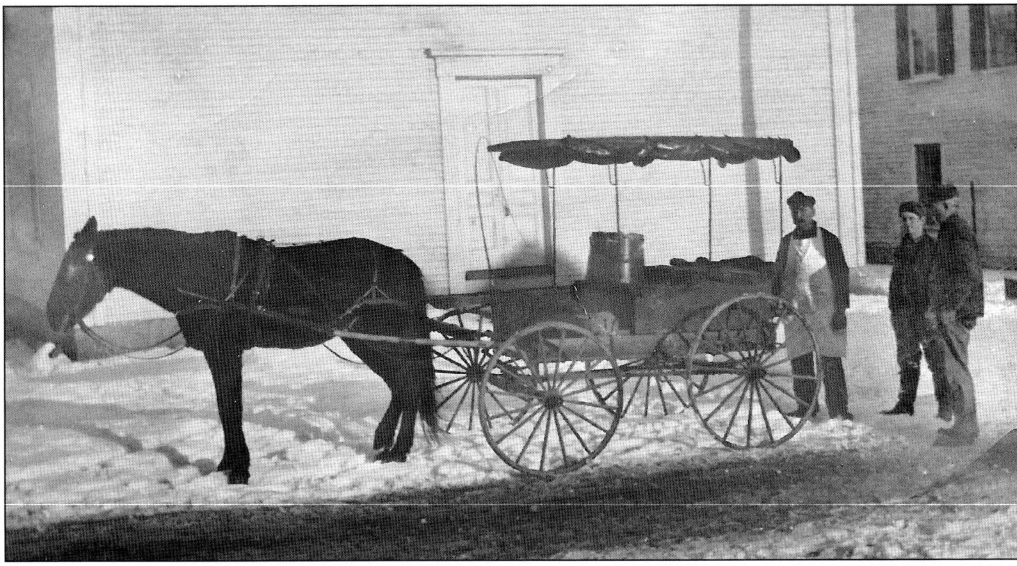

In front of his store, Charles Rowell and friend Andrew Austin confer with a salesman. Peddlers traveling throughout the area were a common site. They often dispensed wisdom with their wares. (Courtesy of Fred Thyng.)

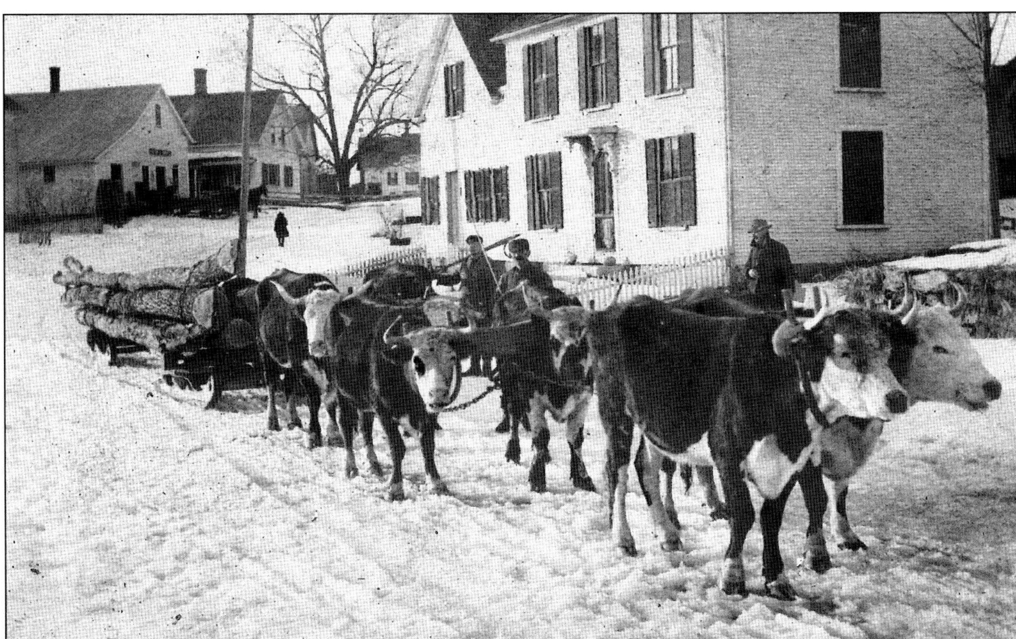

Around 1910, Truman Pillsbury and Sidney Gordon lead three teams of oxen. They are pulling a heavy load of timber through the village of Emery Mills.

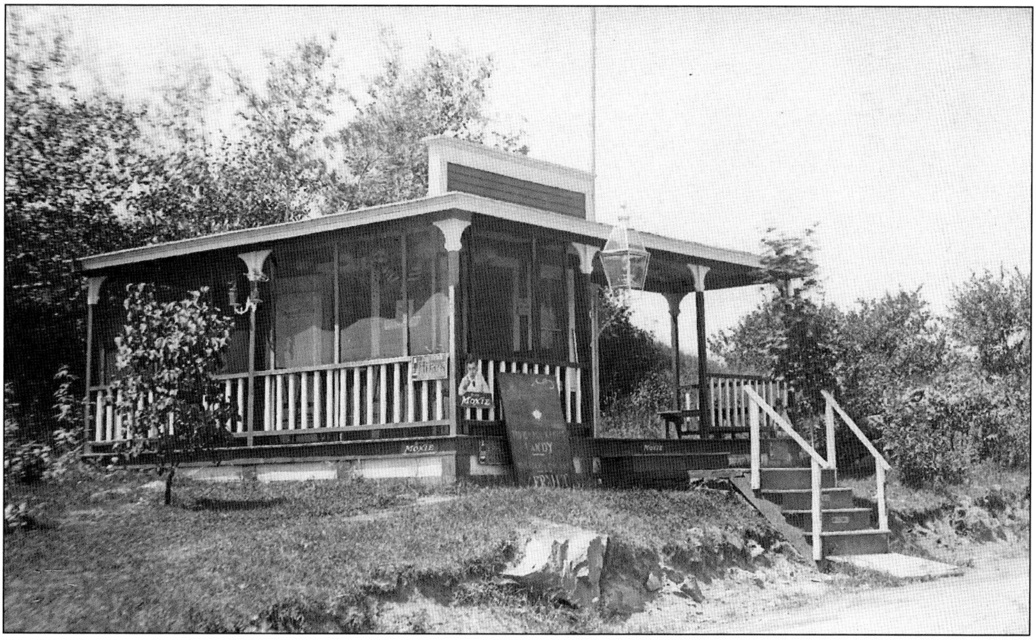

In 1915, George Bowden's Restawhile Ice Cream Parlor advertises "Moxie, Hires Root Beer, tonic—all kinds, candy, tobacco, cigars and fruit." Patrons could sit on the small porch while enjoying their purchase. Invented in 1876 by Maine native Dr. Augustin Thompson, Moxie was the nation's first mass-produced soft drink. In 2005, Moxie was designated as Maine's official soft drink. Restawhile was located just around the corner heading north from the Emery Mills general store.

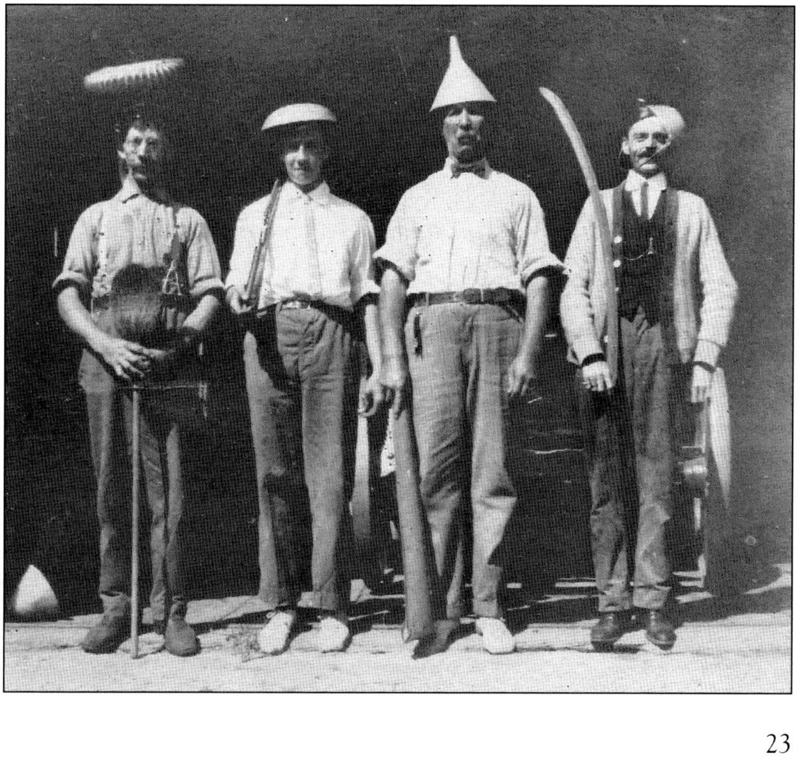

George Bowden, owner of Restawhile Ice Cream Parlor, was also well known for his humor. Three unidentified men join George (far right) in a comical use of household items.

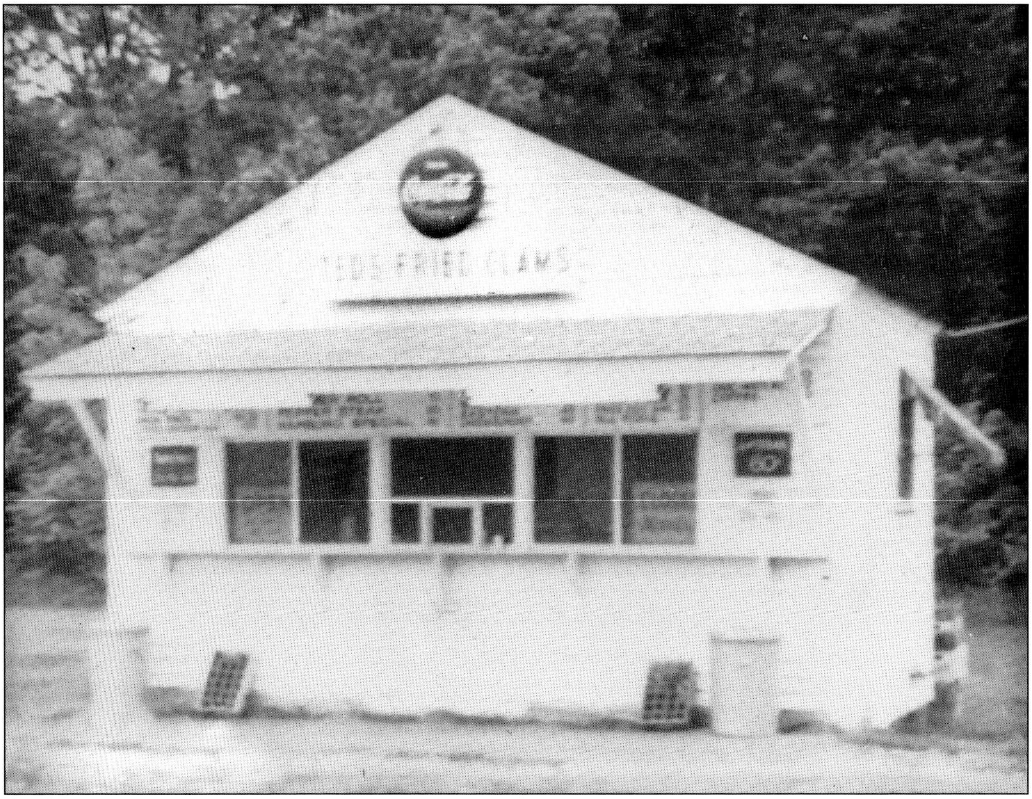

Theodore Mavrakos opened Ted's Fried Clams in May 1950 as a way to keep busy during retirement and strictly as a summer business. Serving great tasting fried seafood, grilled items, and lobster rolls, Ted's quickly became well known to travelers. Sadly, Mavrakos died after only three years of a successful seafood takeout business. (Courtesy of John Mavrakos.)

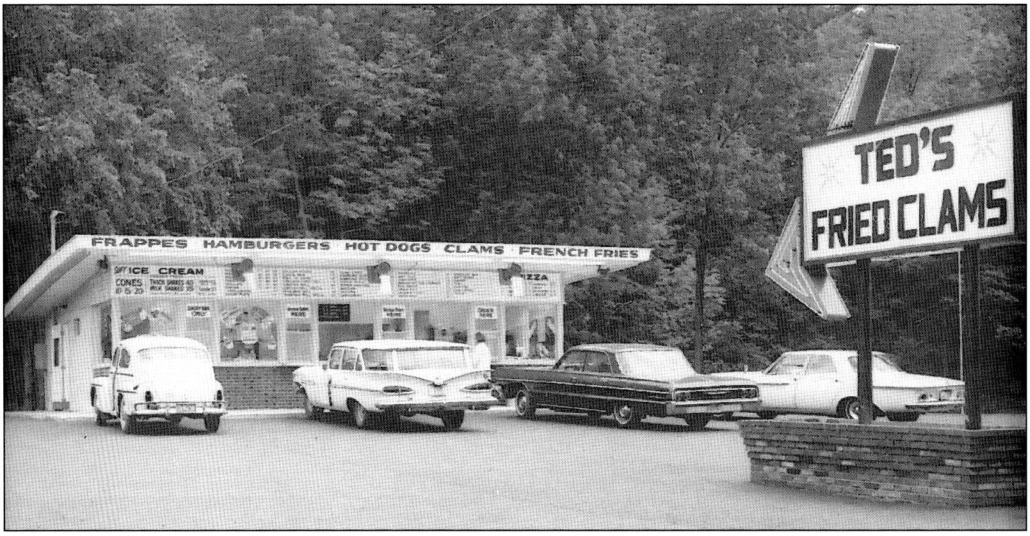

After his father's death in 1953, Harry Mavrakos took over the business (Ted's Fried Clams). The first expansion was in May 1964. Menu choices now included pizza, frappes, and soft serve ice cream. (Courtesy of John Mavrakos.)

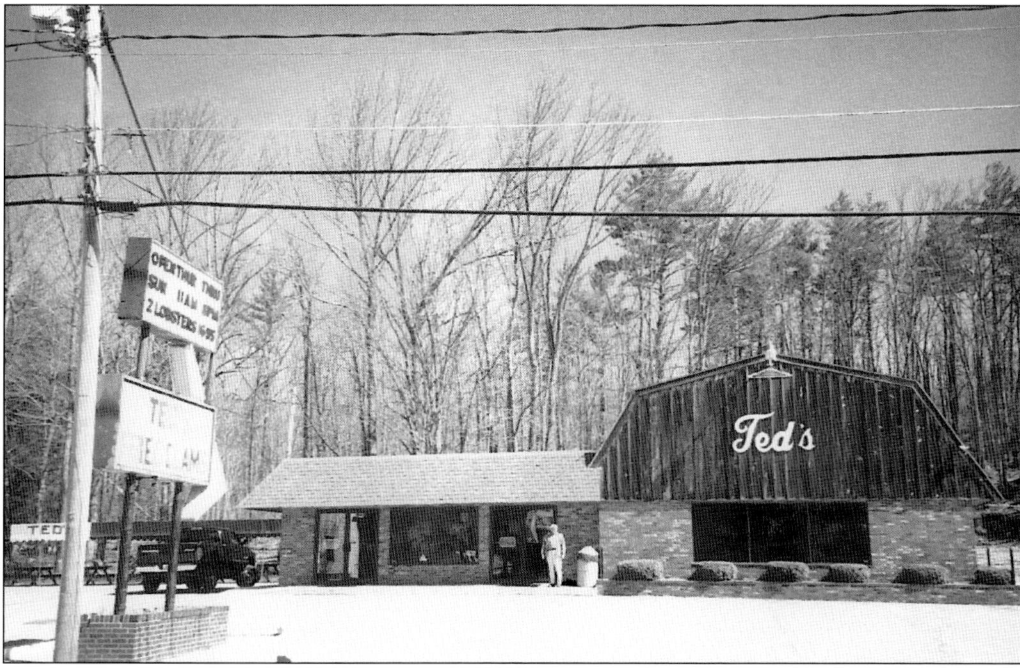

The second expansion took place in 1976 and included indoor dining for over 100 patrons. Pictured is owner Harry Mavrakos standing outside the entrance to Ted's Fried Clams. (Courtesy of John Mavrakos.)

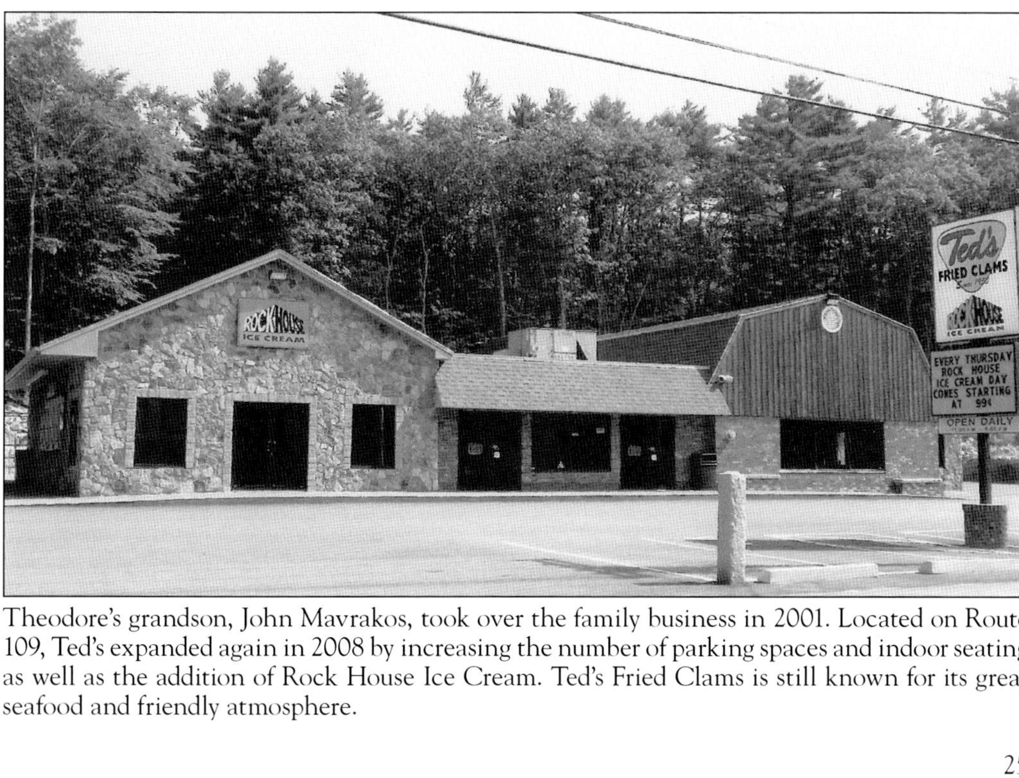

Theodore's grandson, John Mavrakos, took over the family business in 2001. Located on Route 109, Ted's expanded again in 2008 by increasing the number of parking spaces and indoor seating as well as the addition of Rock House Ice Cream. Ted's Fried Clams is still known for its great seafood and friendly atmosphere.

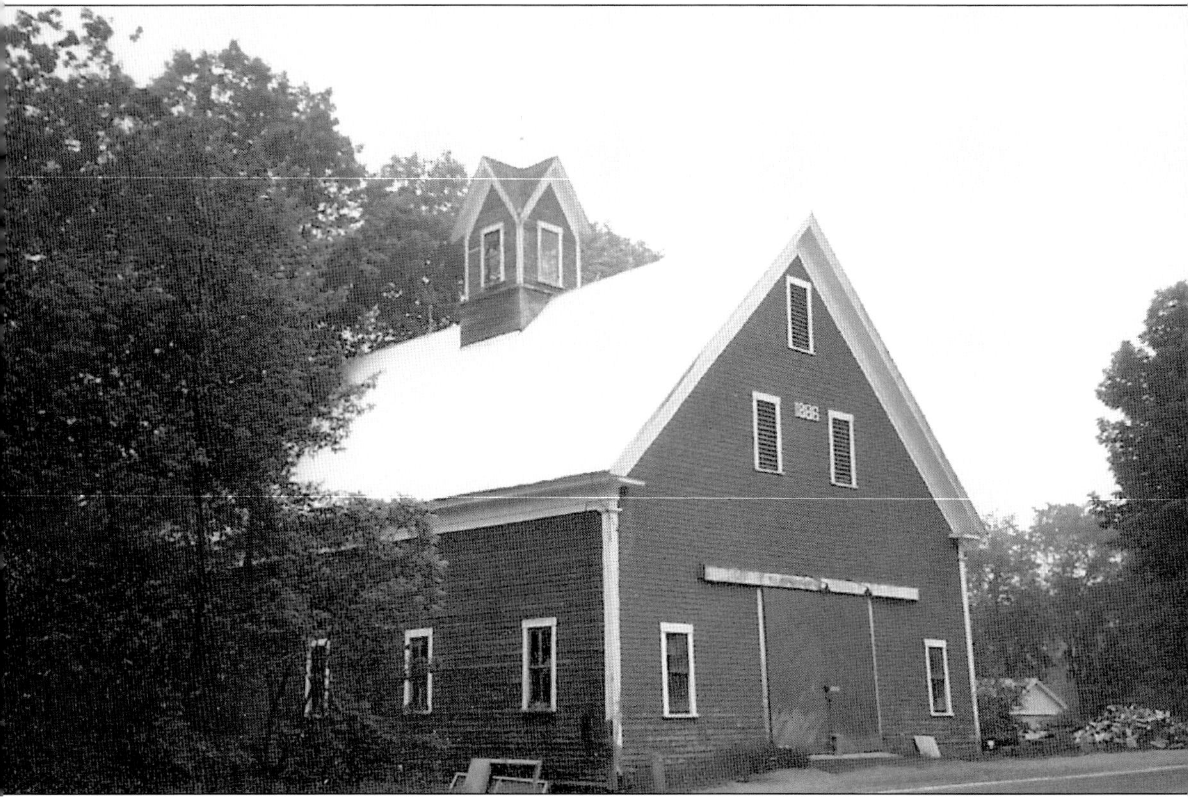

Conveniently located on the main road, this barn was used for horses and oxen that were utilized primarily for hauling logs to the nearby sawmills. The barn was later home to the only playhouse/theater ever known to be in Emery Mills. The second floor was transformed into a stage with raised seating around the perimeter. Theatre in the Round, as it was known, held performances by young Broadway hopefuls during the summers of 1950 and 1951. Colleen Dewhurst is the most noteworthy actor to have performed here. Dewhurst was known as "the Queen of Off-Broadway" and returned to the area in 1991 for what would be her final film, *Bed and Breakfast*. The barn, erected in 1886, is still standing today on Route 109 across from Ted's Fried Clams.

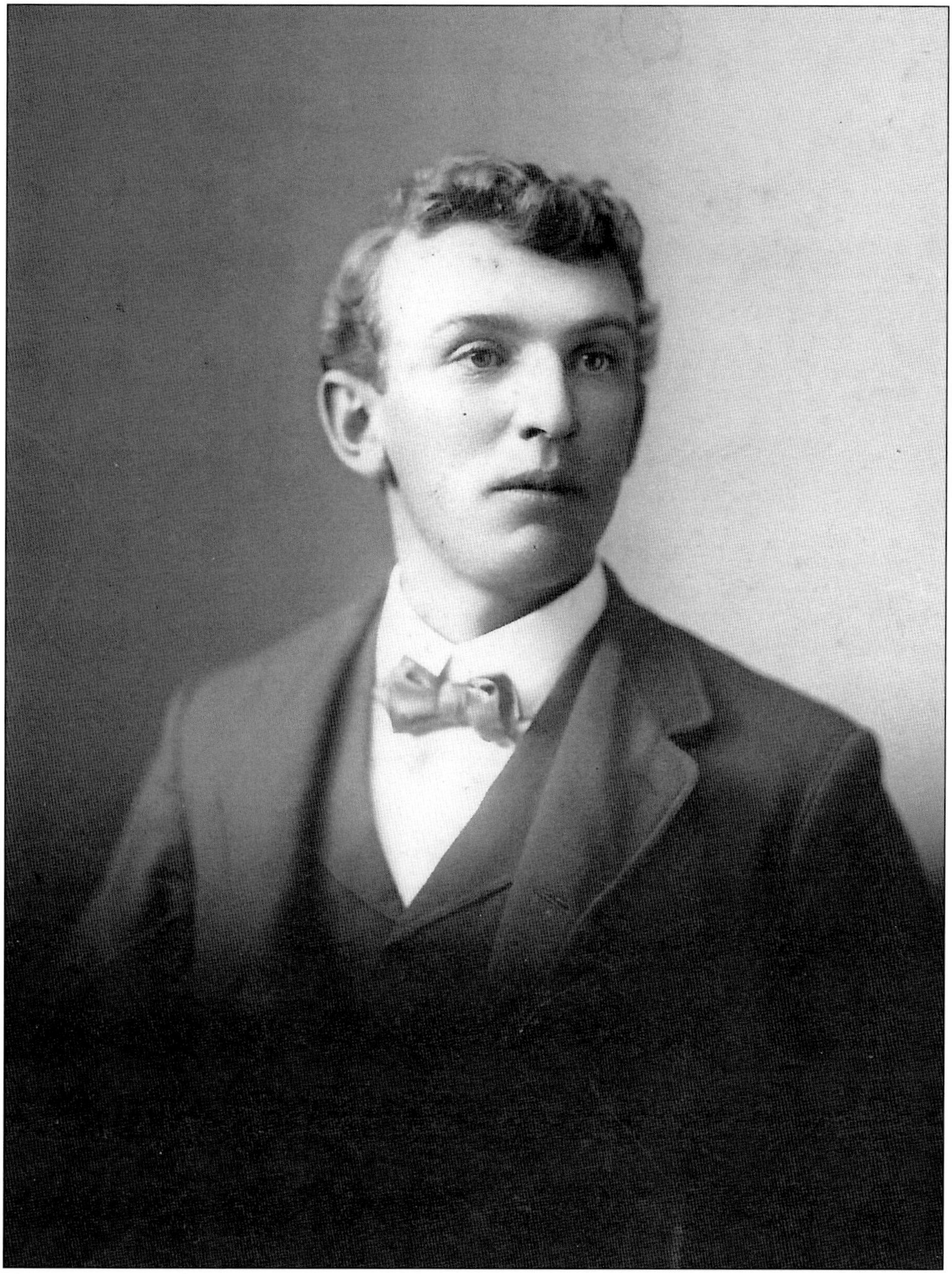

Arthur Murray was born and grew up in Shapleigh and attended the Emery Mills School in the 1890s. Murray lived to be 97 years old and worked on the building of the Emery Mills dam and at some of the early sawmills when the town was just beginning to take root. An entrepreneur, he went into business for himself in 1920, when he opened Murray's Poultry Farm, which grew from a small local business to eventually sell to out-of-state clientele. After retiring from and selling the poultry business, Murray took up strawberry farming and was known to be in the field working by 5:00 in the morning, every day—even at the age of 95. The Murray name has long been associated with Emery Mills. (Courtesy of Fred Thyng.)

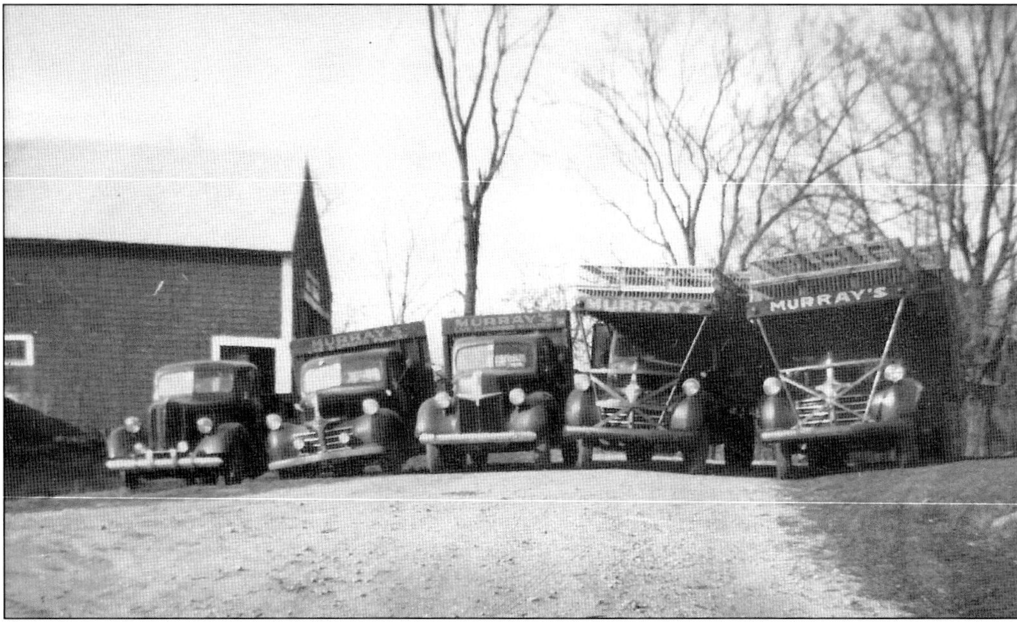

Throughout its 60-year operation, Murray's Poultry Farm sold eggs, chickens (live or dressed), turkeys, and capons to businesses from Bangor to Boston. Here is a fleet of vehicles used to transport the variety of poultry to its final destination. The business was located on the family farm off Deering Ridge Road. (Courtesy of Earl Murray Jr.)

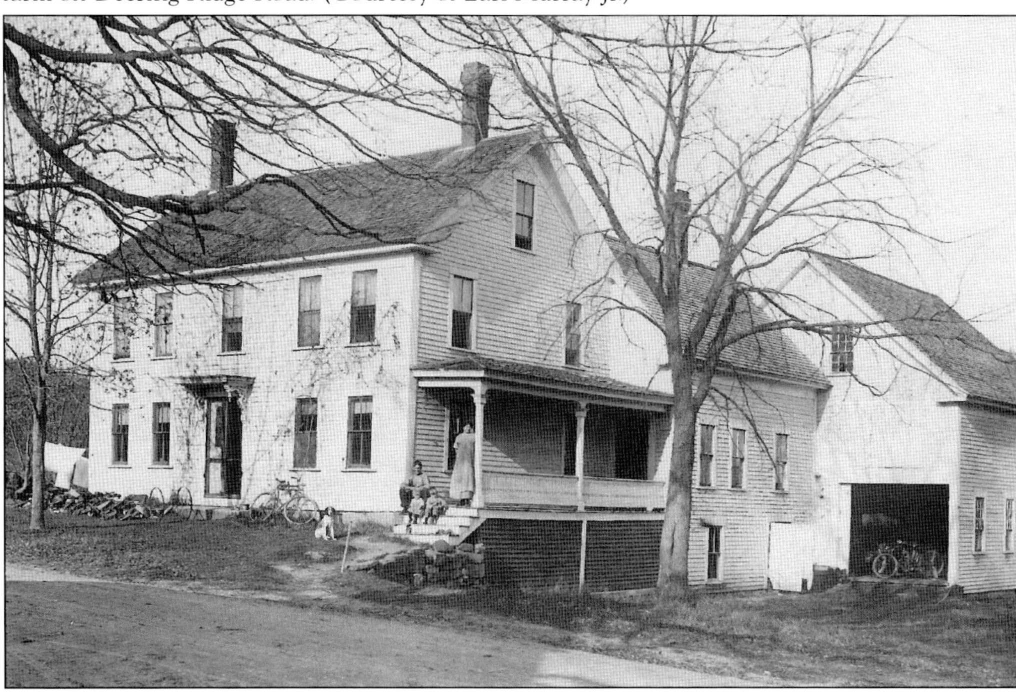

The Gallant home, across the street from the general store, is one of the oldest and largest homes in Emery Mills. Visible on the porch are Everett and Ina Gallant with their children, Mana and Jedediah. With the exception of an enclosed porch, the home has changed little over the past 100 years and still remains in the Gallant family. (Courtesy of Fred Thyng.)

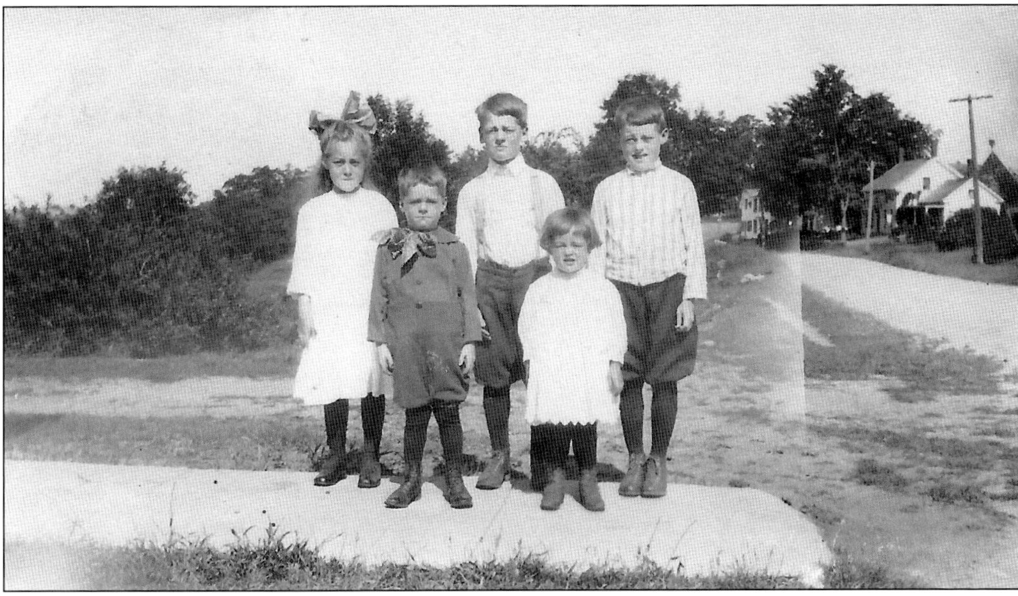

Five of the seven Griffin children—(left to right) Hazel, Jessie, Virgil, Mildred, and Elmer—are pictured in front of their home in Emery Mills, across the street from the Emery Mills School. For over 40 years, Mildred owned and operated Griffin's Variety, which included a lunch counter, gas station, and garage. Griffin was well known for her coconut cream pie and a good story or two while customers waited. (Courtesy of Earl Murray Jr.)

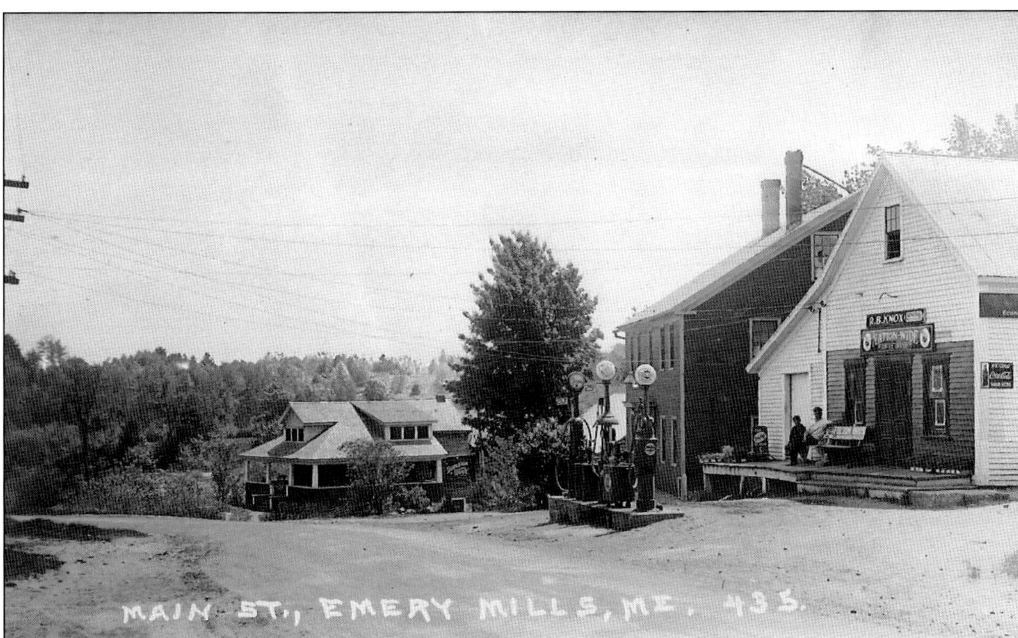

By 1929, Raymond Knox was the owner of the Nation-Wide general store in Emery Mills, and the Elmwood Inn was called the Shapleigh Lodge. Shown here, Knox and his son, Harley, rest on a bench outside his store.

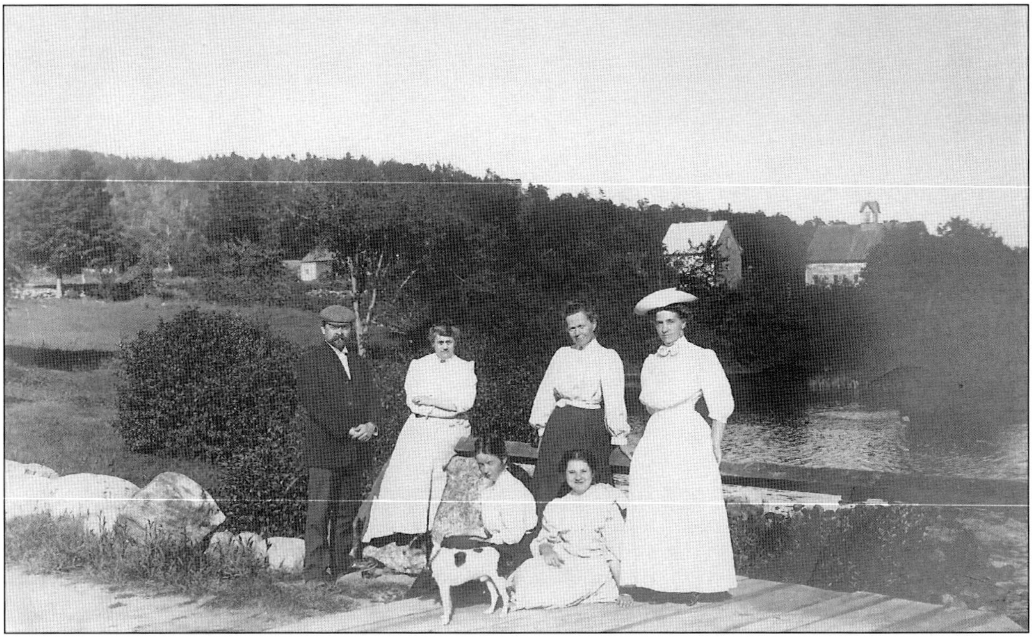

A local family stops at the bridge in Emery Mills for a photograph taken in 1908. In the background, the large barn with cupola and the backside of the Griffin home are located on Route 109. Both are still standing today.

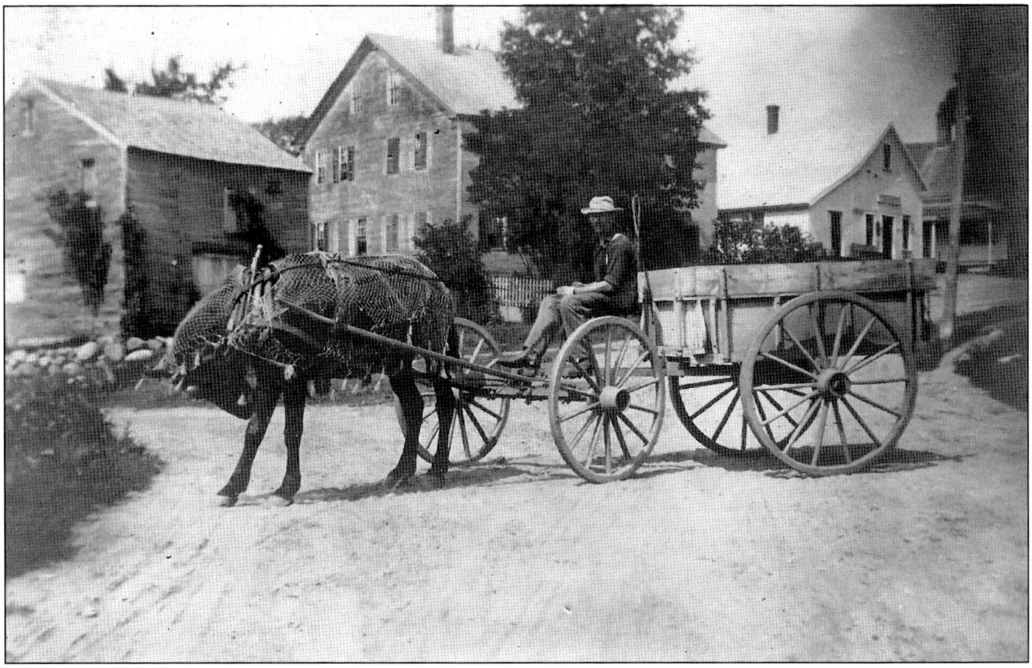

The typical mode of transportation was by horse and carriage. Farmers would make weekly trips to town for food, supplies, and mail.

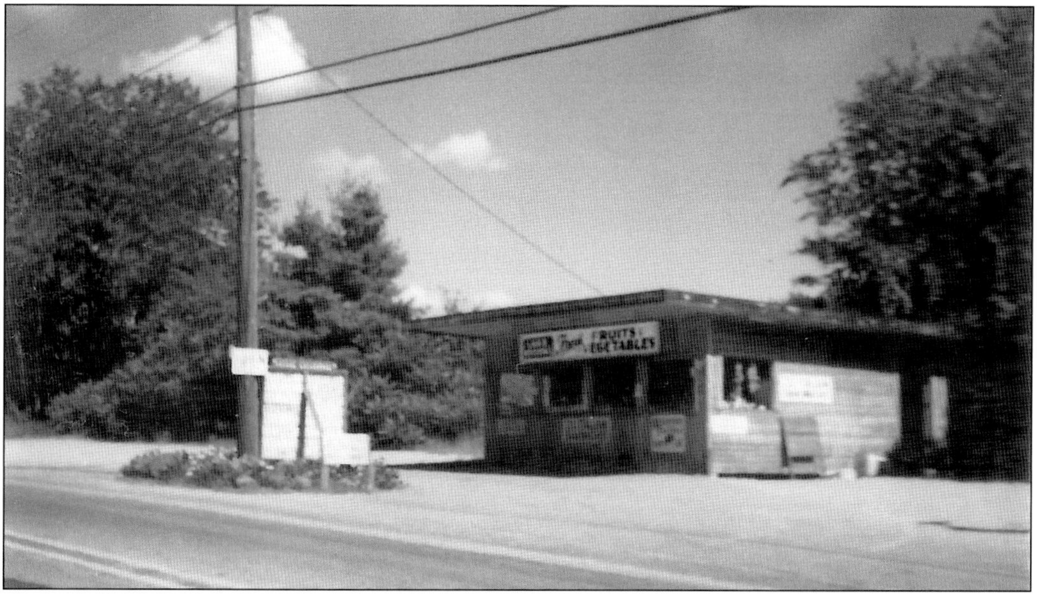

For several years in the 1970s, Ruth Gallant sold fresh fruits, vegetables, and home baked goods from this roadside stand. Gallant lived next door to the stand and was well known in the area for her baking skills. (Courtesy of Fred Thyng.)

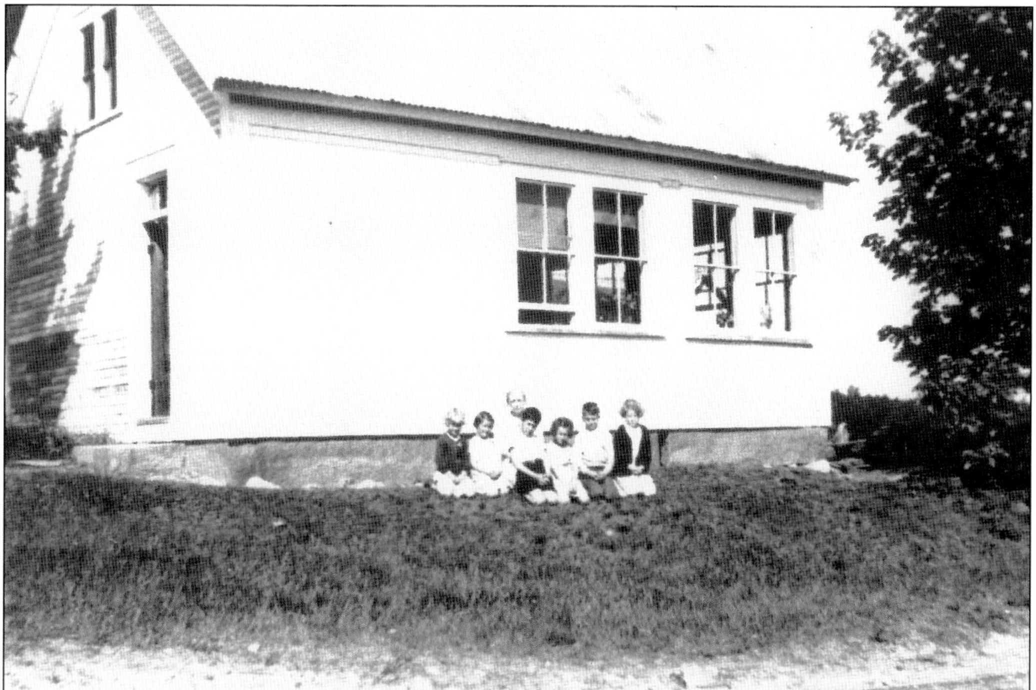

Pictured here are students at Highland School in 1936. Located on Deering Ridge Road, the Highland School has since been converted into the home of Thomas Penney. From left to right are Edith Webber, Carlene Grant, Raymond Grant, Pauline Camire, Warren Farwell, and Norma Webber; in the second row is their teacher, Mable J. Goding.

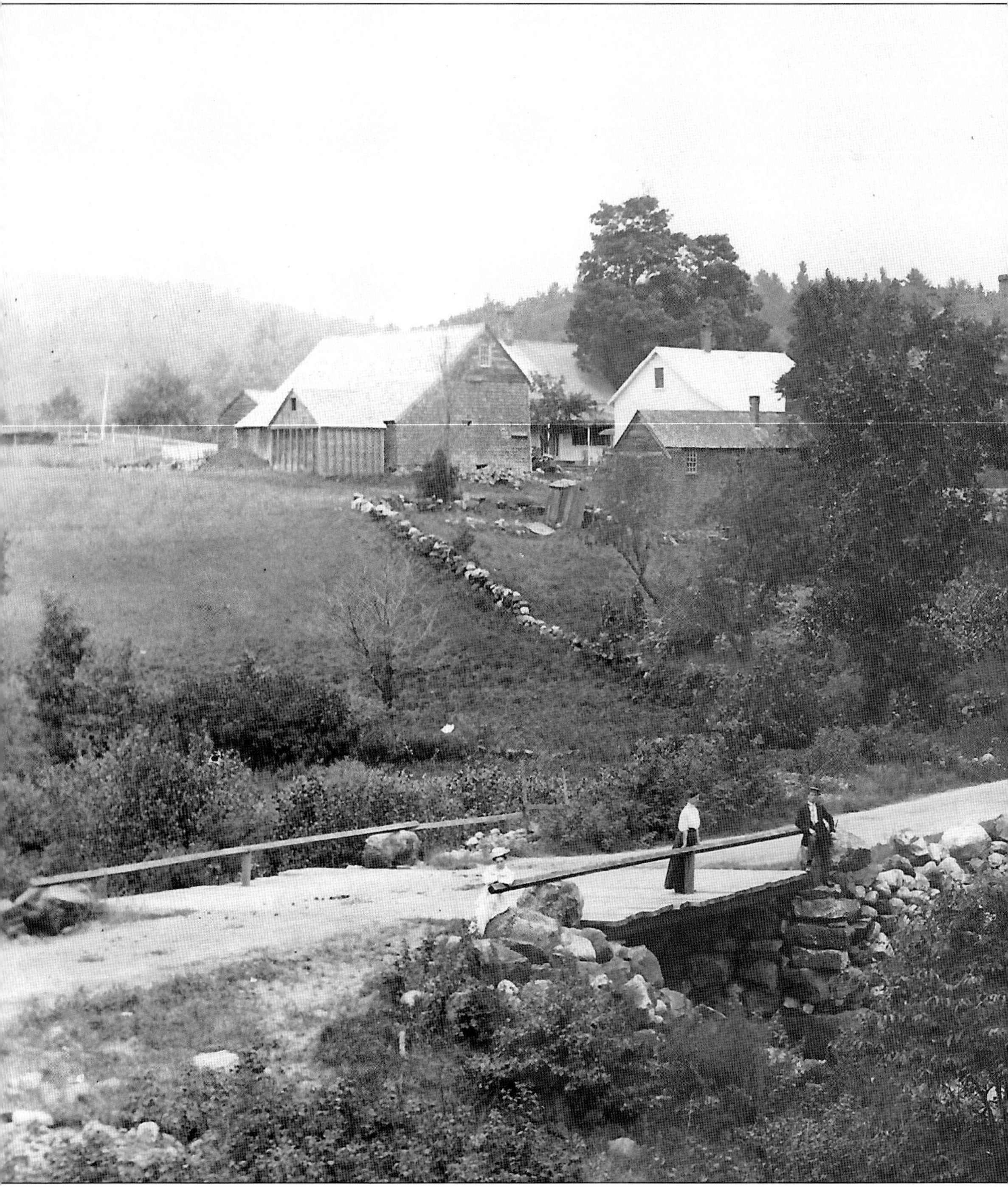

This view is of Emery Mills looking north from Babbling Brook Farm in 1908. In the early winter of 1773, Joseph Jellison and his 12-year-old daughter brought a load of household items to settle into their new home in Emery Mills. The next morning, Jellison left his daughter alone with the family dog, plus a few provisions, and returned to North Berwick for the remainder of the household. He fully intended to return the next day. But during the night, a heavy snowstorm

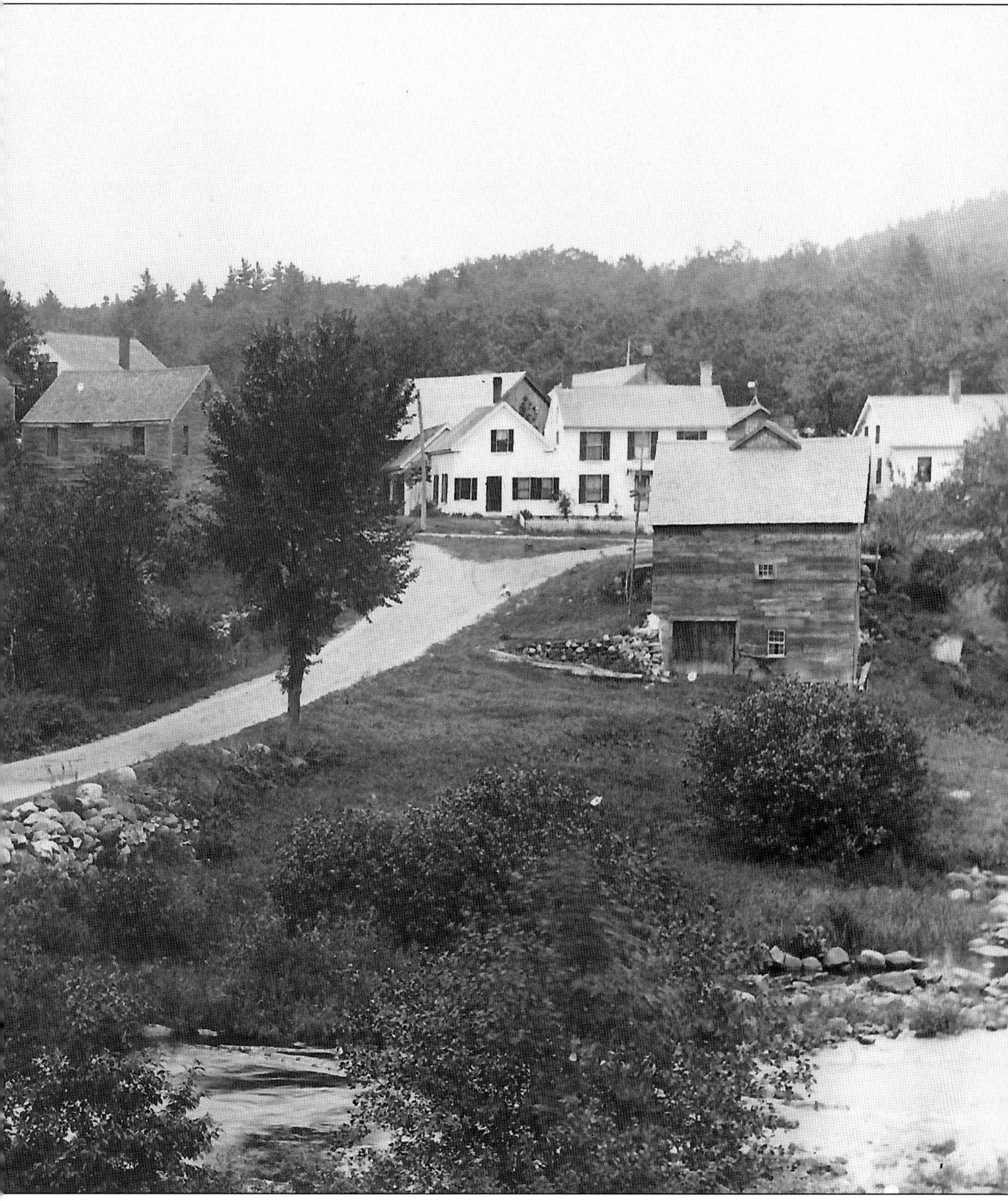

arrived and made traveling impossible. After two long weeks, family and friends were able to make passage from North Berwick to Emery Mills. Jellison is credited with being the first settler, but his daughter should at least be given an honorable mention. The barn on the right, before the fork in the road, is believed to have been built on the location of the old Jellison home.

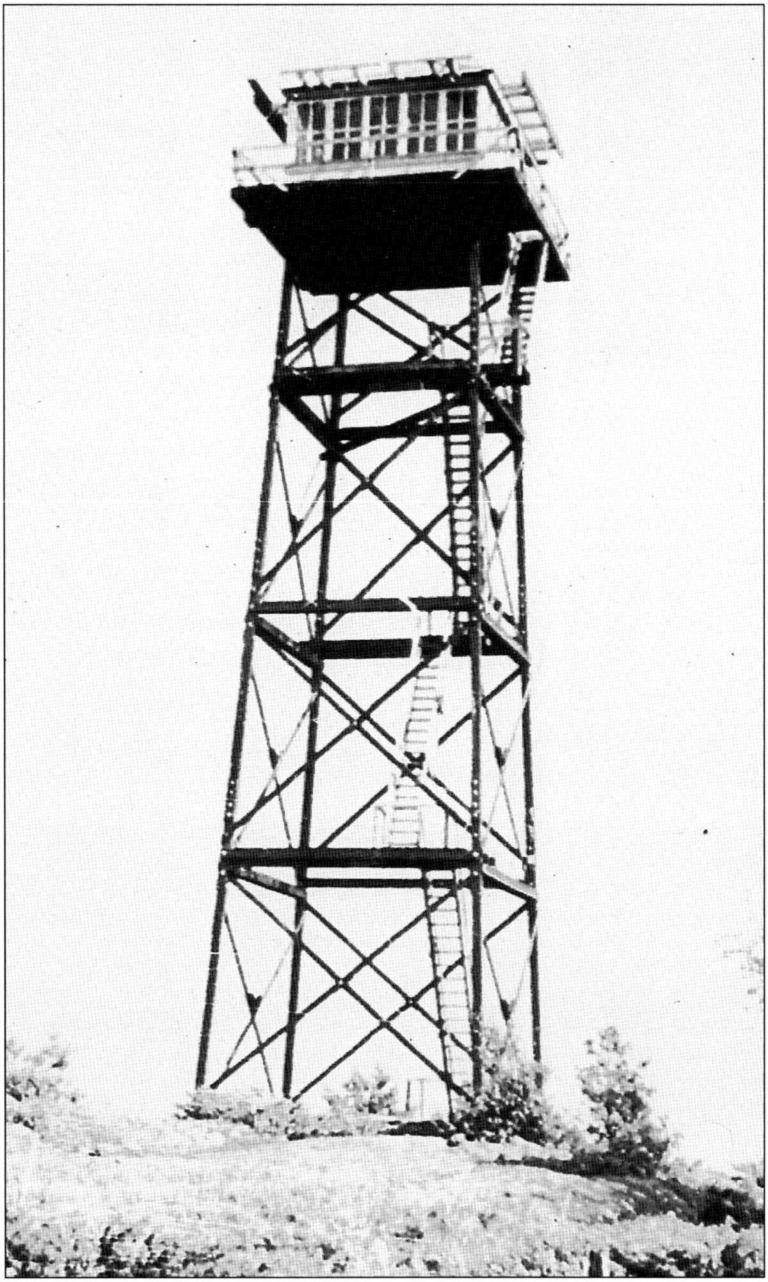

Fire towers were built so watchmen could spot a fire in its early stages and then direct local firemen to its site to contain it. At an elevation of 740 feet, this 66-foot wooden fire tower was built in 1942 by the Maine Forest Service on Ridley Hill in Shapleigh. The cabin at the top measured 14 feet by 14 feet on the outside, with a 3-foot catwalk and 33-inch railing. Ridley Hill Fire Tower was in direct contact with the Springvale Fire Department via telephone and hand radio. Many acres of woodland have been saved from possible destruction by fire in this area, mainly because the watchman in the Ridley Hill Fire Tower had a sharp eye and worked quickly. Harold Clark of North Shapleigh was the watchman in 1943–1944 and again from 1959 to 1962. This fire tower was discontinued and dismantled in 1963.

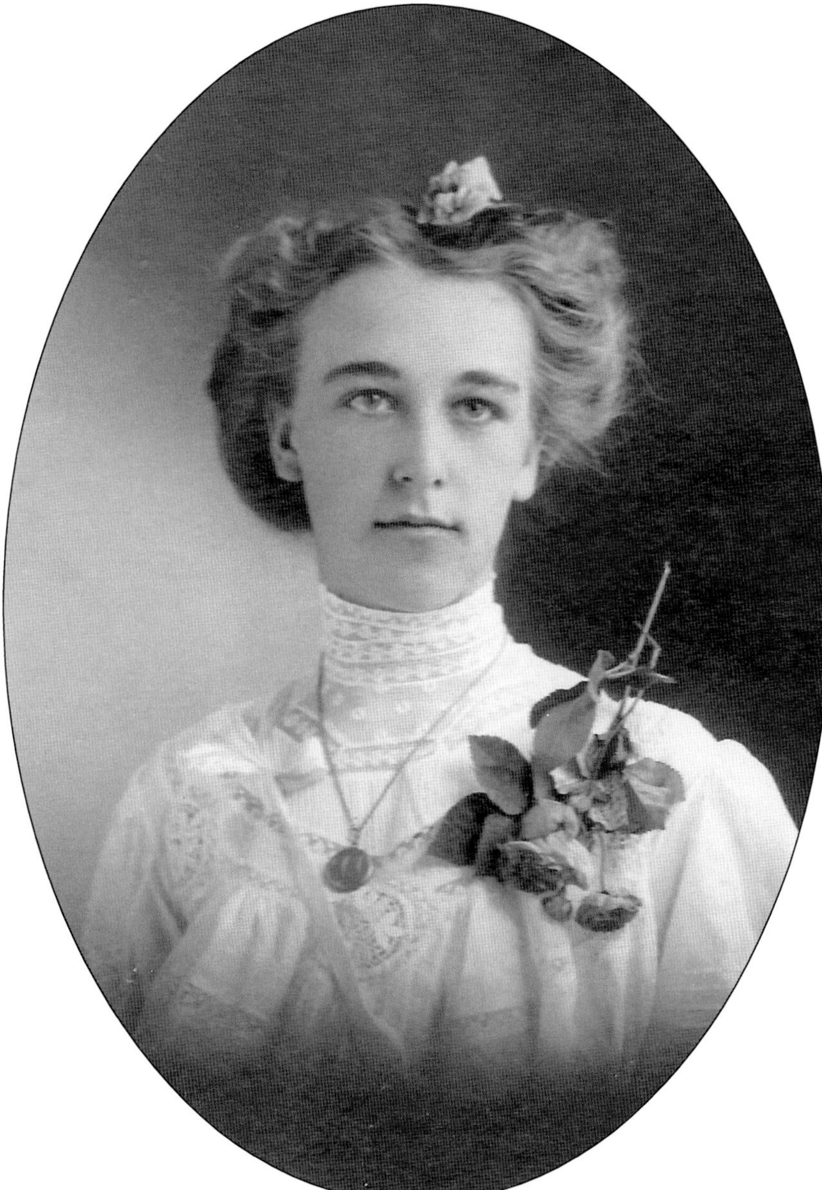

Although she was born in Boston on January 19, 1889, Gladys Ridley moved to Shapleigh in 1912, shortly after her marriage to Edward Ridley, and thereafter called it home. Gladys was a lifetime member of the Mousam Lake Grange (1922) as well as a charter member of the Acton-Shapleigh Historical Society (1962). In 1983, at age 92, Gladys was awarded the Boston Post Cane Award. The Boston Post Cane was originally a gimmick to increase the circulation of the *Boston Post* newspaper. It started in 1909, when 431 canes were distributed throughout New England to be presented to the oldest male citizen of the community. When a recipient was chosen, his biography and a photograph were published in the newspaper, hopefully increasing sales. In 1930, women were allowed to be considered for the honor. The canes were made from African ebony and topped off with a 14-karat gold head. Gladys lived to 100 years of age and left behind 1 daughter, 7 grandchildren, 18 great-grandchildren, and 17 great-great-grandchildren.

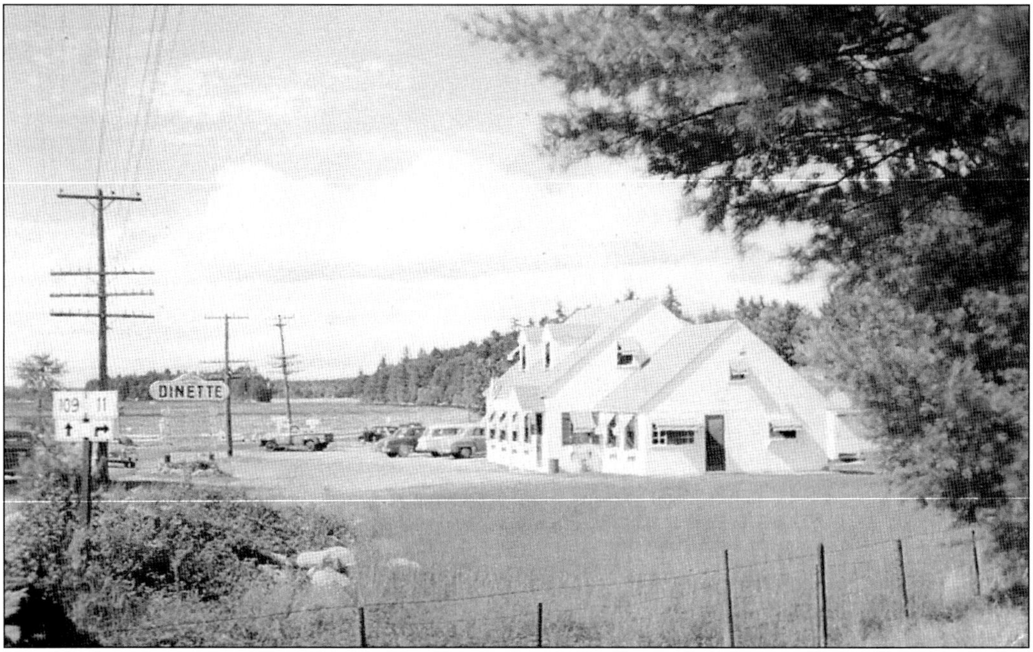

A home-cooked meal with plenty of tasty desserts was always on the menu at the Mousam Lake Dinette in 1958. By 1970, the restaurant had closed. Key Real Estate took over the building and is still conducting business at this location at the intersection of Routes 109 and 11.

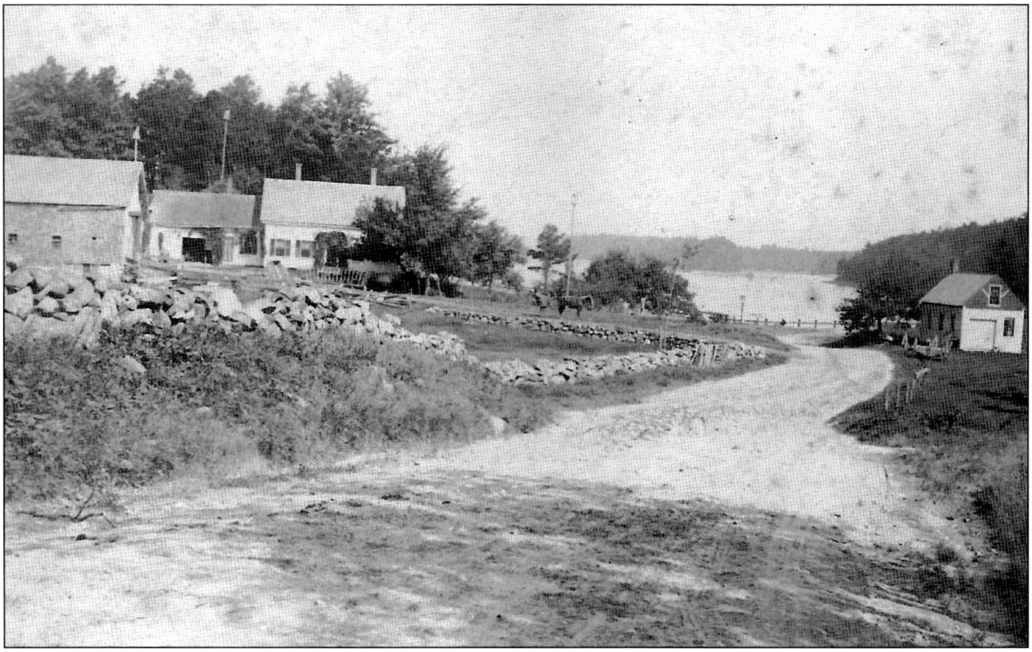

The view was taken of the foot of Mousam Lake around 1900. The small building on the right was a blacksmith shop until it was moved to Springvale, where it still stands. Blacksmiths in early American settlements were responsible for making just about everything. They repaired farm equipment, made weapons, building materials such as nails, and kitchen items such as cookware, and were responsible for shoeing horses.

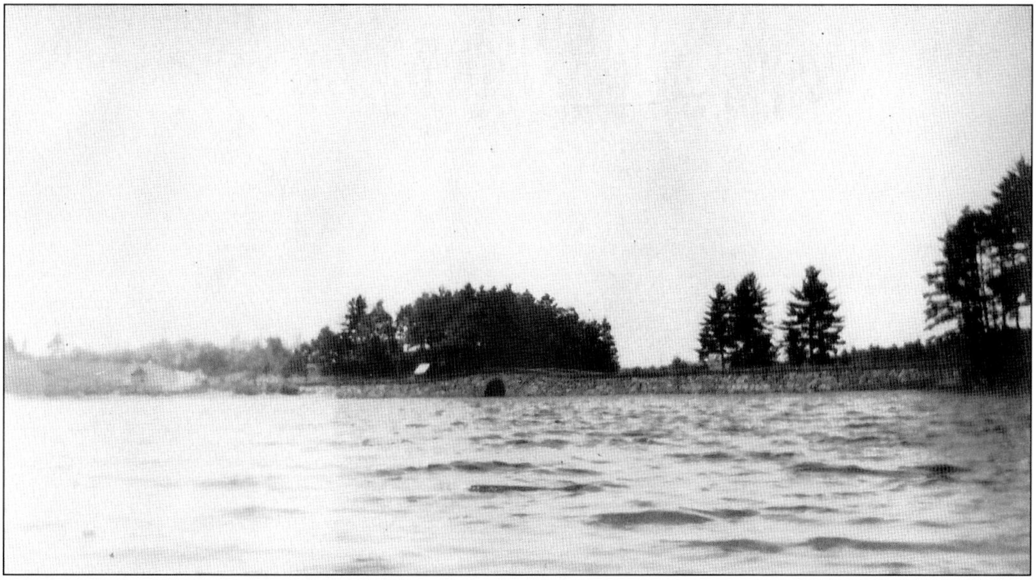

Taken from the water, this is a view of the foot of Mousam Lake towards Emery Mills. Although this picture is quite faded, one can see the same blacksmith shop from the previous picture on the left. (Courtesy of Herman Abbott.)

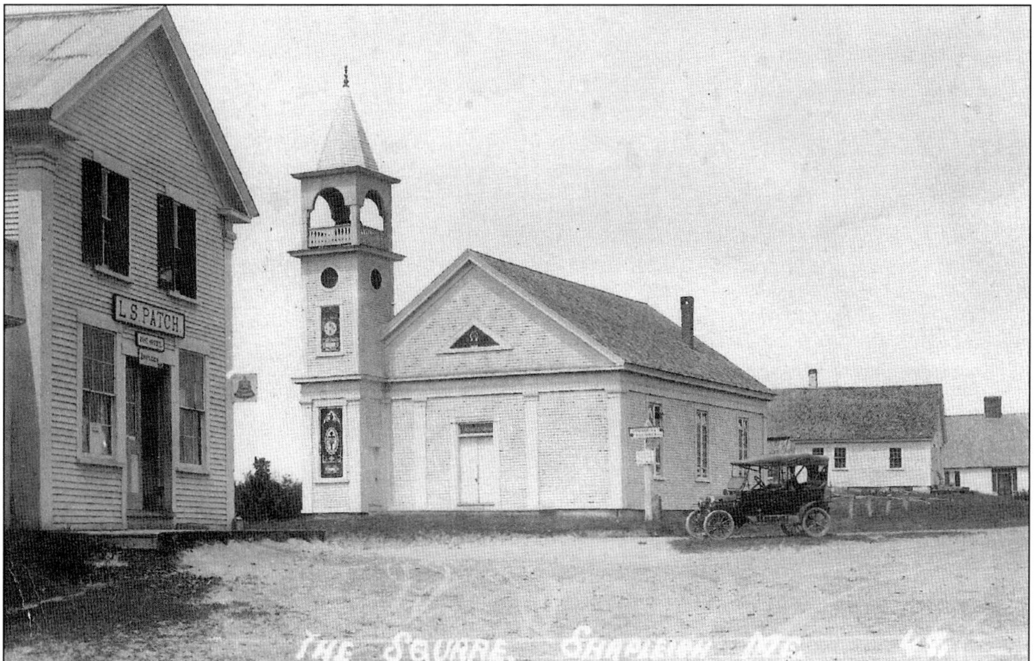

Since 1841, this church has been known as the First Baptist Church of Shapleigh. Previous to the division of the town, the Acton church was called the "First" and this church was called the "Second." It was erected at a cost of $1,500 and organized in 1802. In 1900, the replacement of old windows with stained-glass memorial windows and the addition of the steeple added to its beauty. Electric lights replaced kerosene lamps in 1935. This photograph was taken in 1925. (Courtesy of Christy Fisher.)

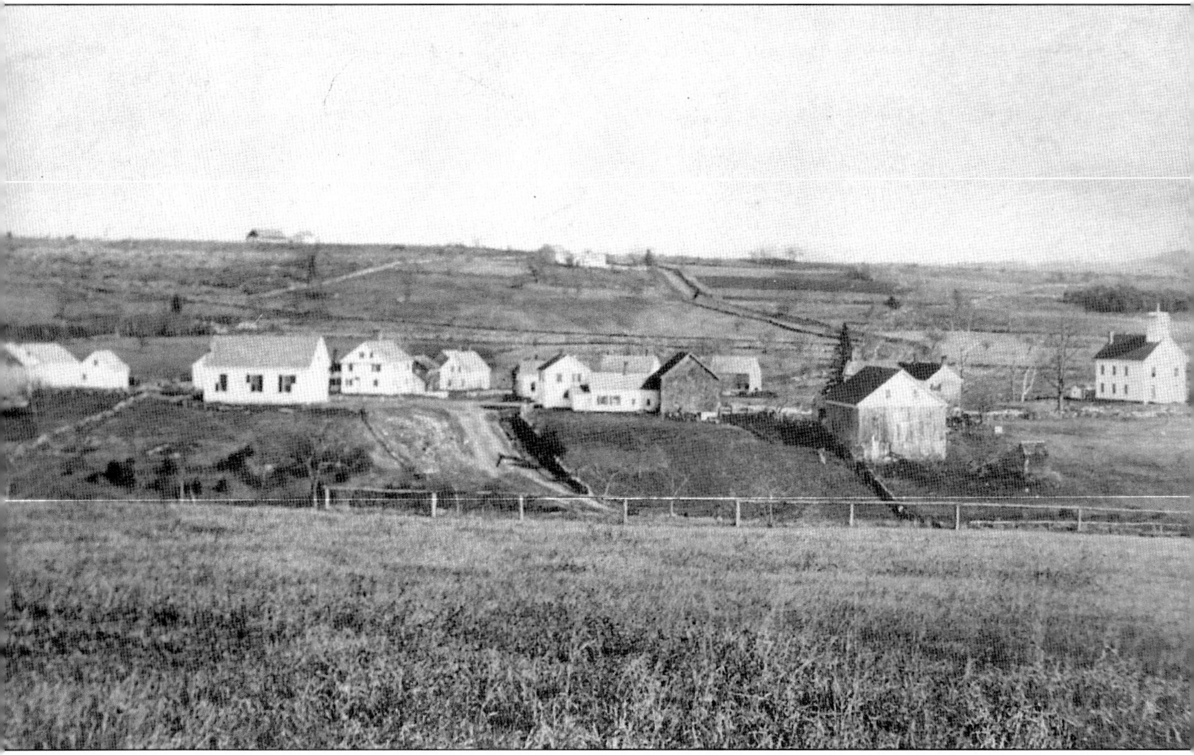

This is one of the earliest known views of Shapleigh Corner, taken some time between 1877 and 1899. The presence of the Lindsey High School (built in 1877) and the lack of the First Baptist Church steeple (erected in 1900) are telltale indicators of the time frame. The Crediford farm can be seen at the top of the hill, and the Ham farm is also visible to its right. One of the four principle settlements and the most central village, Shapleigh Corner is the seat of town government. The town of Shapleigh was incorporated in 1785 and named in honor of its original proprietor, Maj. Nicholas Shapleigh. It was previously known by the name of Hubbardstown, having taken that name from Joshua Hubbard, one of Major Shapleigh's heirs and a leading proprietor. Shapleigh was the 35th town incorporated in the district of Maine, as it was called while still a part of Massachusetts. (Courtesy of Lista Staples.)

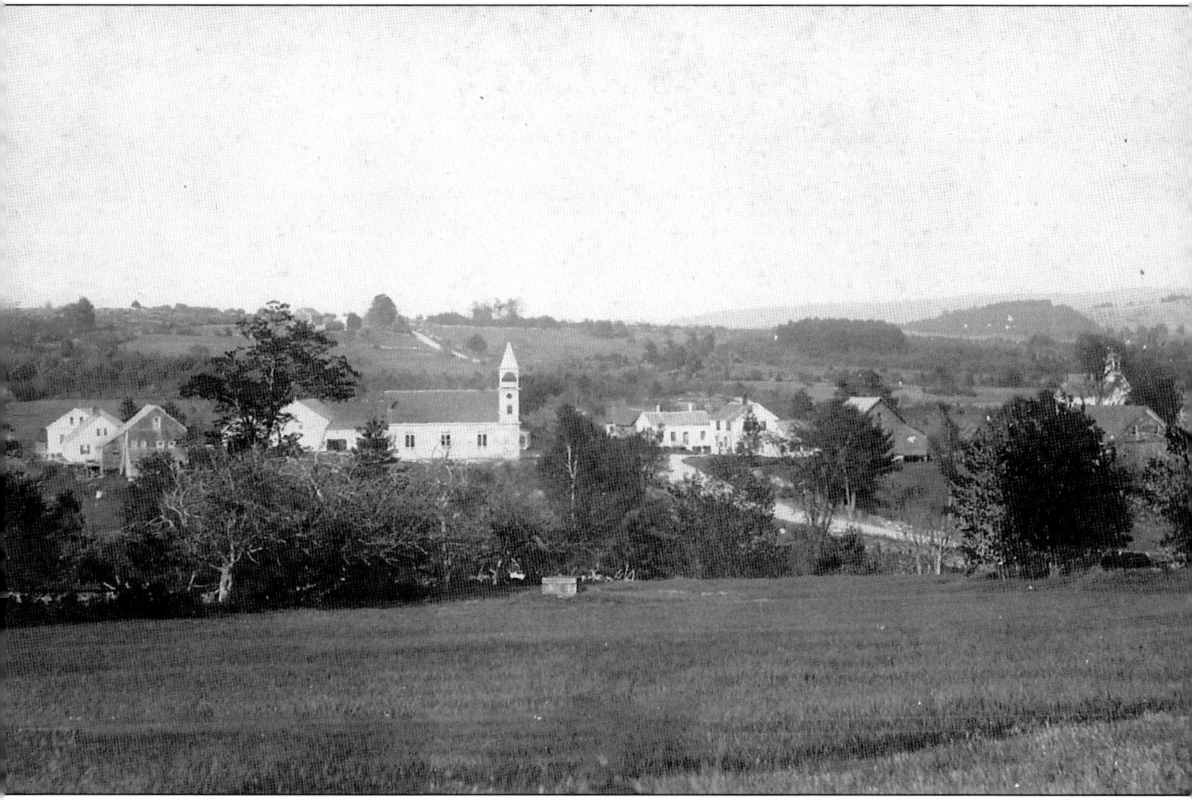

Although the trees have grown, this bird's-eye view of Shapleigh Corner clearly shows some of the same buildings that are in the previous picture. The First Baptist Church has its steeple, and both farms at the top of the hill are harder to see through the tall trees. The eastern ridge has been traditionally known as Fort Ridge, though no fort has ever been connected with its history. In the early days of mast cutting by the British, a short turn in the road was necessary. A brow was erected from the earth and in connection with a swing or derrick, the long pieces of timber were raised and swung around a difficult bend in the road. The timber was then replaced in the correct direction to follow the turn in the road. This brow was thought to resemble a fort, hence the name Fort Ridge.

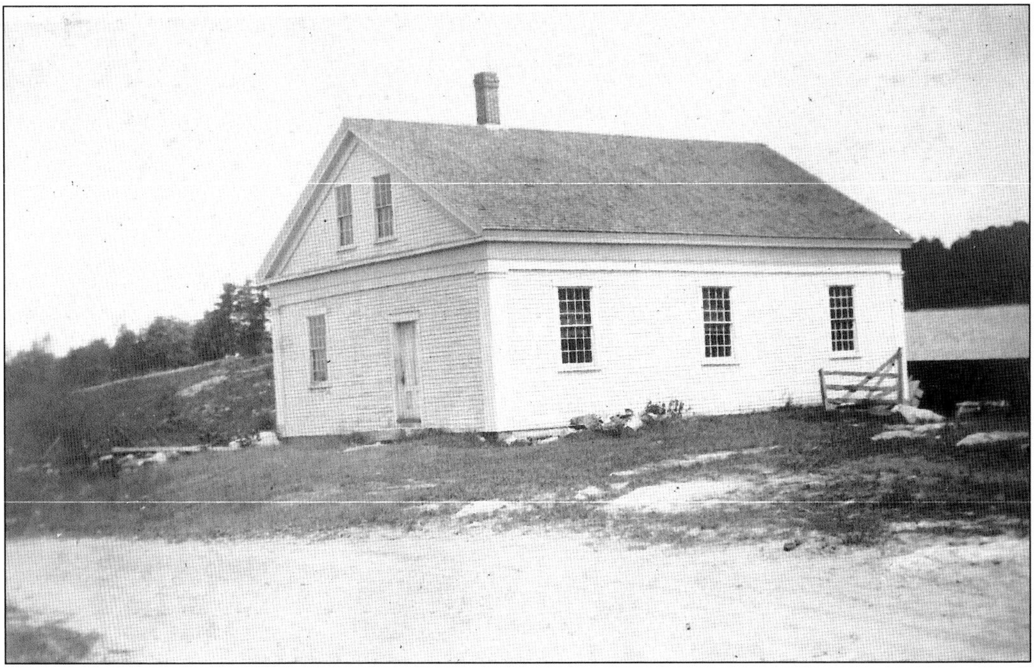

This structure was the Shapleigh Town Hall until those offices moved to the old Lindsey High School about 1955. For several years thereafter, it was known as the Community House. In 1980, the Shapleigh Community Library officially took over the facility, and it is still in operation today.

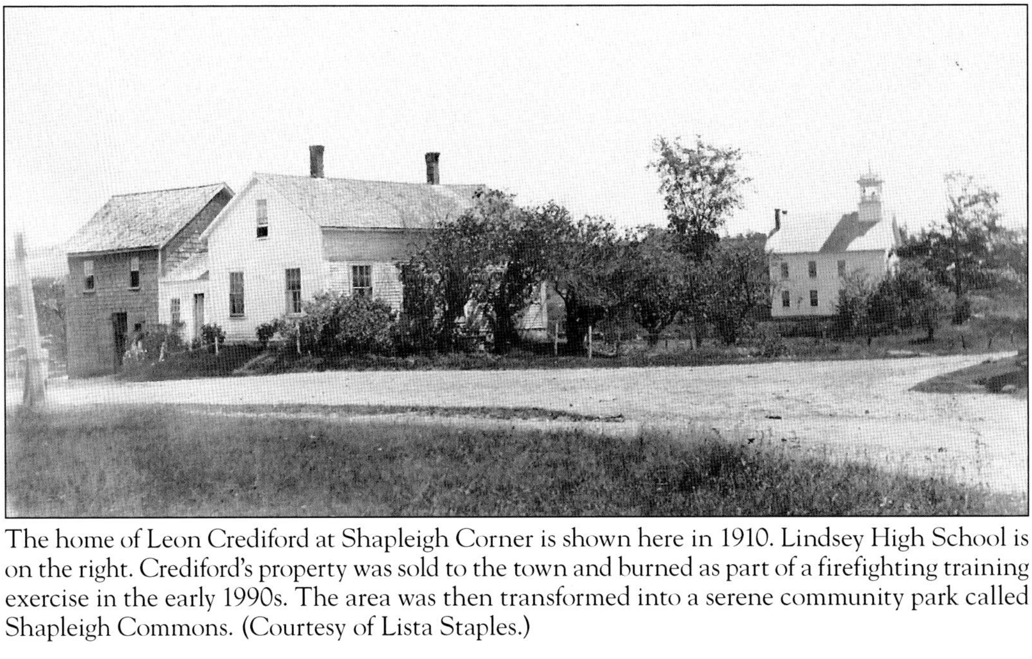

The home of Leon Crediford at Shapleigh Corner is shown here in 1910. Lindsey High School is on the right. Crediford's property was sold to the town and burned as part of a firefighting training exercise in the early 1990s. The area was then transformed into a serene community park called Shapleigh Commons. (Courtesy of Lista Staples.)

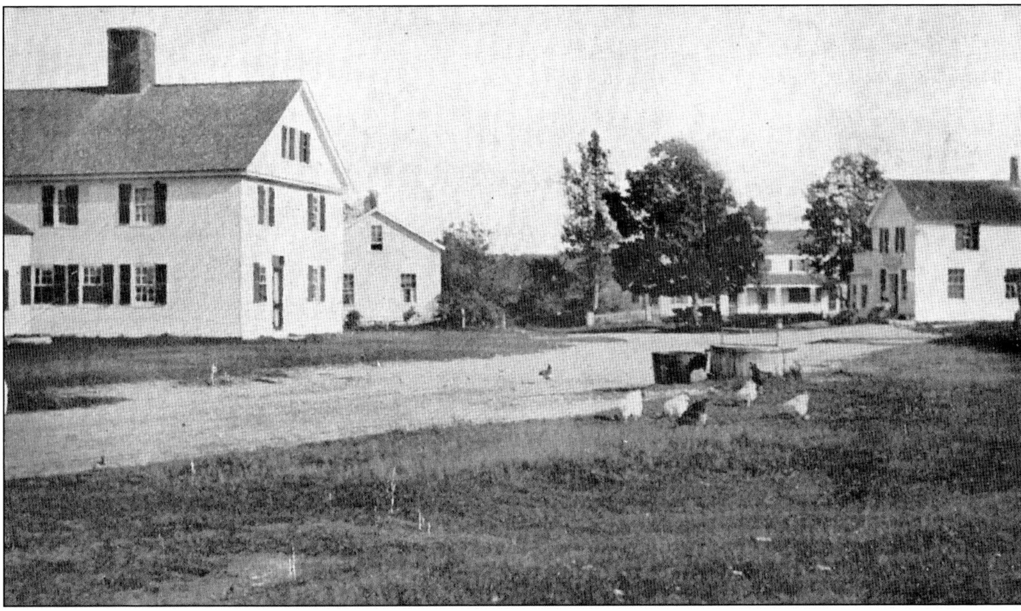

This view of Shapleigh Corner heading south from North Shapleigh was taken in the early 1900s. Patch's General Store is on the right.

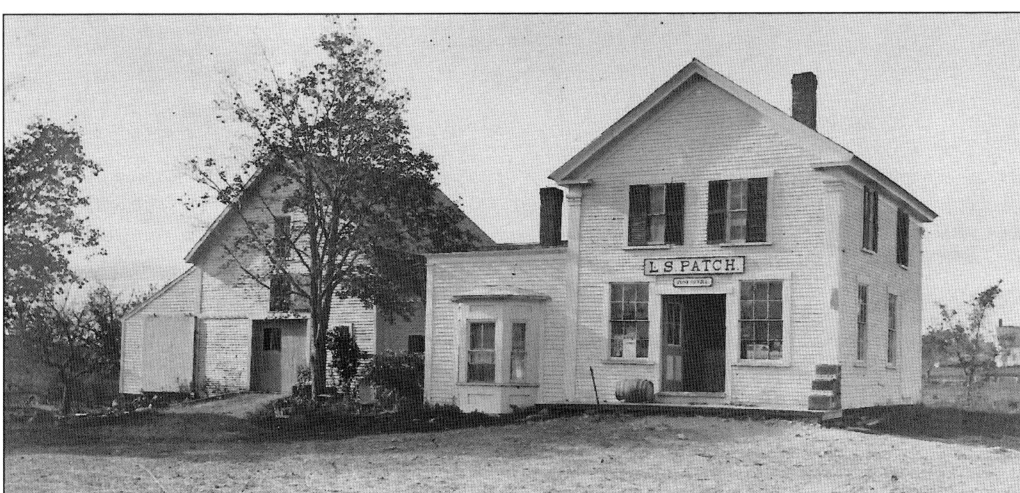

This building has been home to a general store at Shapleigh Corner since 1823. Leroy Patch was its proprietor and postmaster for 44 years, from 1896 until 1940, retiring at age 77. He prided himself on the long hours both the store and the post office were kept open. Every morning at 4:00, he opened up, and he stayed open until 10:00 at night, including Sundays. At one time, Patch held five public offices in Shapleigh at the same time.

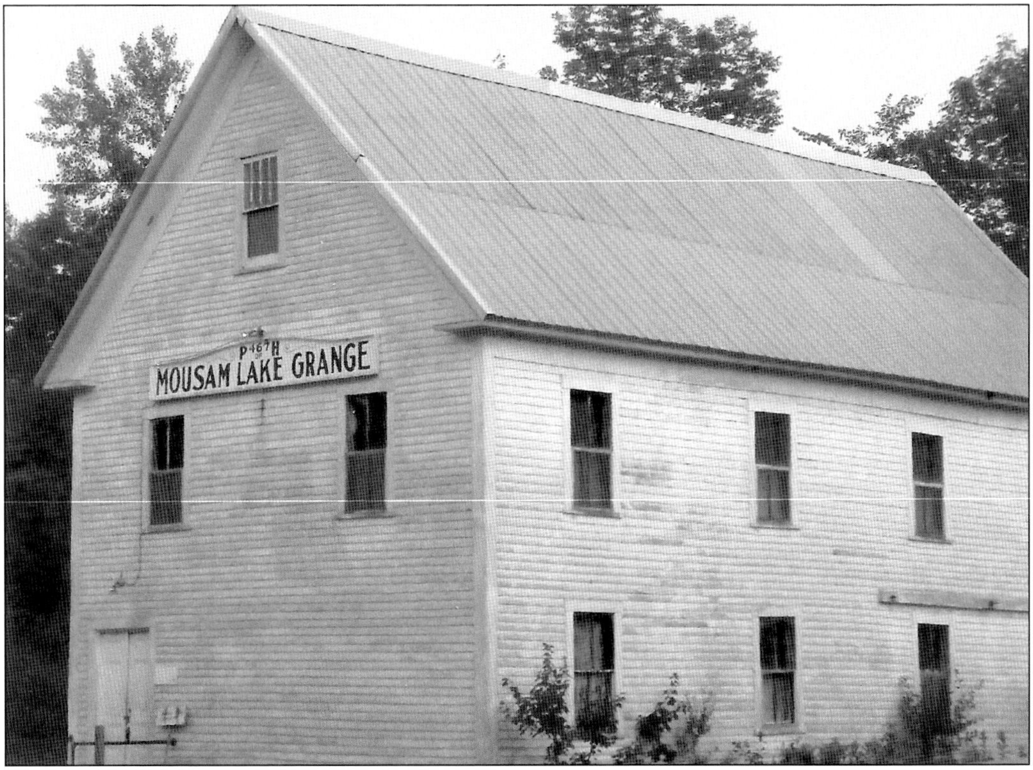

Originally located in Alfred, this building was purchased by the Mousam Lake Grange in 1921. The building was taken down and moved to its present location on the Back Road in Shapleigh. Reconstruction was completed and dedicated in 1922. The grange is still active and conducts regular meetings.

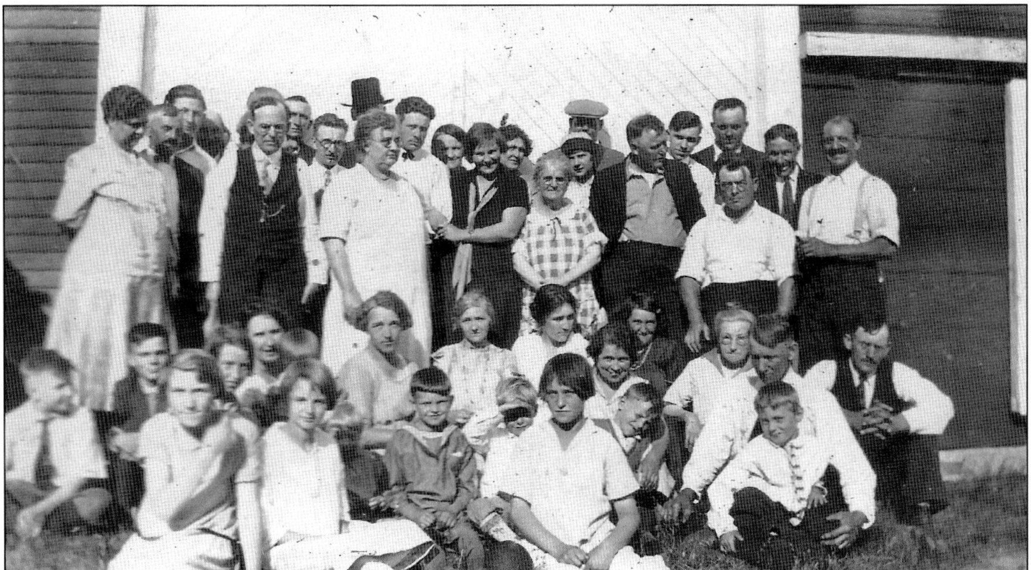

Members of the Mousam Lake Grange in the late 1920s gather with their families for a picture during a summer picnic.

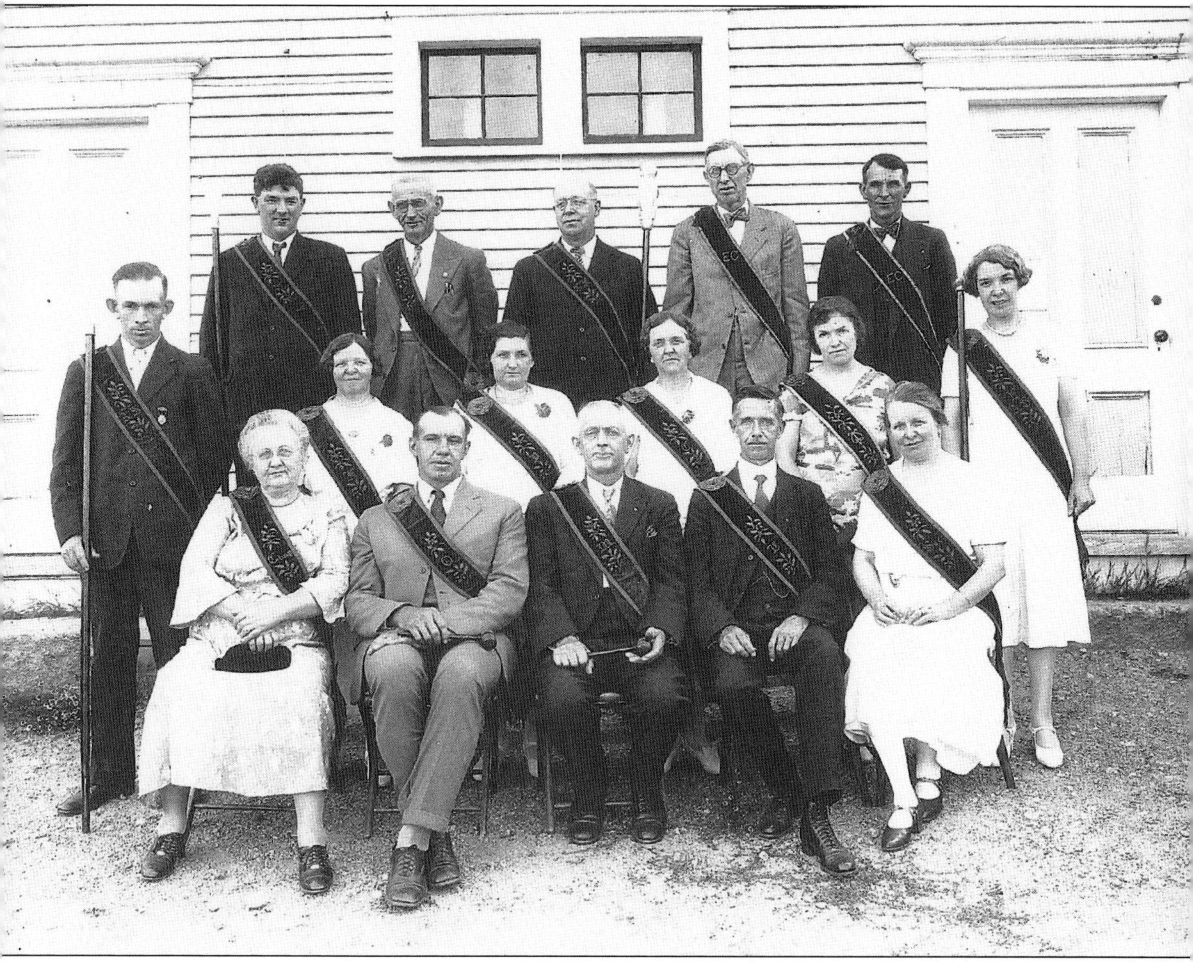

Newly elected officers of the York County Pomona Grange are shown here around 1955. For over half a century, beginning in the 1870s, the Grange in Maine numbered some 50,000 members in more than 400 locations throughout the state. Active on behalf of Maine's rural populace, the Grange lobbied the Maine Legislature to improve the quality of education in the state's public and vocational schools and to reform the taxation system to make it more equitable. In addition, as the first major organization in the United States to grant women equal rights, the Grange provided an opportunity for rural females to escape the drudgery of the farm home so they could take advantage of the educational and social aspects of the order. Seated, second from the left, is Leon Crediford of Shapleigh. (Courtesy of Melissa Conner.)

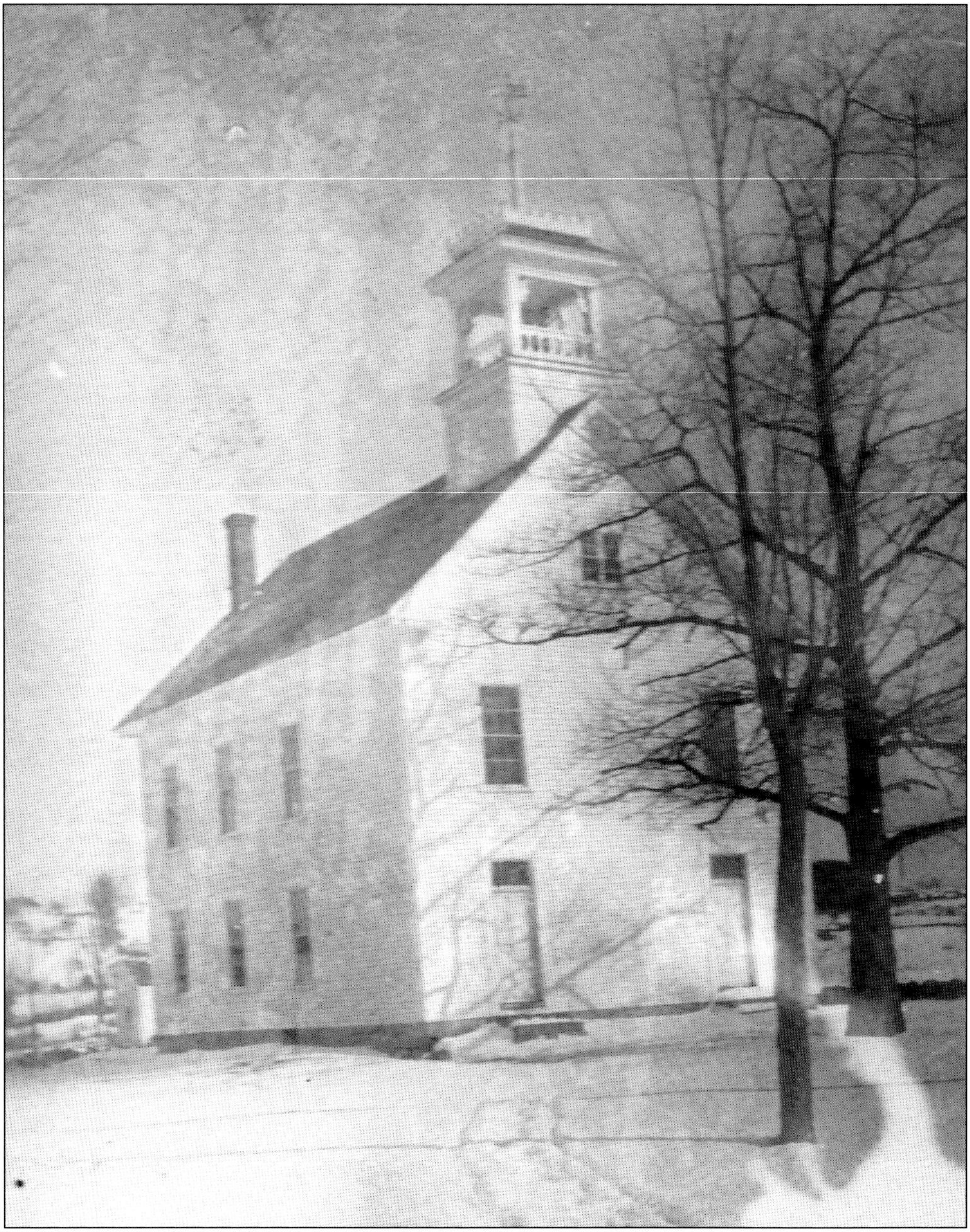

Built in 1877, the Lindsey High School building still stands proudly and now houses the Shapleigh town offices. In his will, George Lindsey bequeathed to the town of Shapleigh the sum of $5,000 for a public high school, provided the town would raise half as much and erect a suitable building at Shapleigh Corner. Among those who donated were Frank Hargraves of North Shapleigh, who gave a bell, and Thomas Goodall of Sanford, who provided a bookcase plus $100 towards a library. The completed school was neatly furnished with patent seats and desks of ash and black walnut. The first floor of the building included grades one through eight, and the high school was on the second floor. Students at the elementary level numbered between 30 and 40, all of whom were instructed by one teacher. The school operated until 1942. The building then remained vacant until about 1955, when the town offices took over.

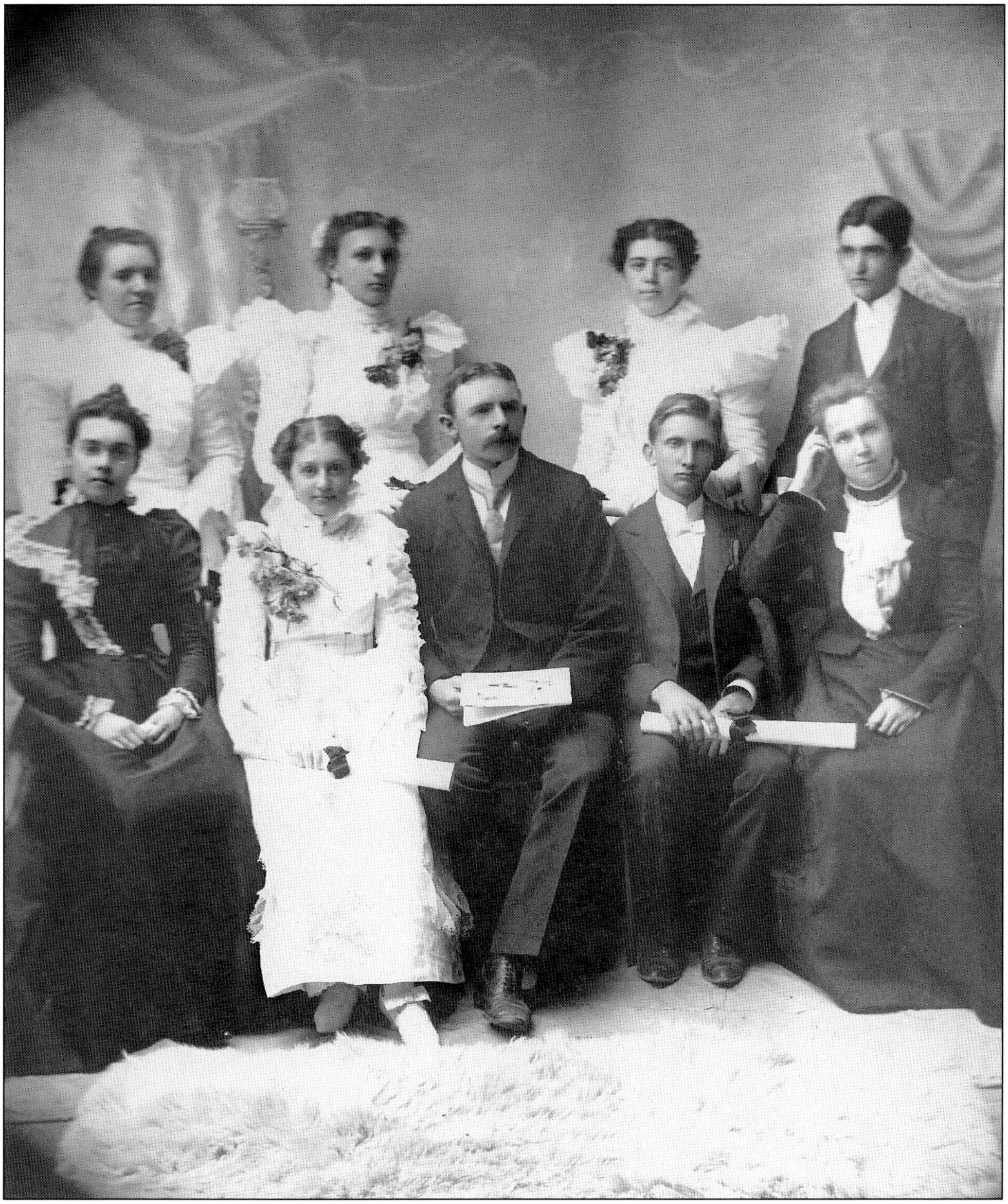

The Lindsey High School graduating class of 1899 is pictured here. From left to right are (first row) Myrtie Abbott (teacher), Gertrude Thyng, Frank Thompson (principal), Elmer Trafton, and Leora Hanson (teacher); (second row) Annie Ham, Augusta Newbegin, Fannie Abbott, and Ambrose Thing. Fannie Abbott became a teacher and taught in district schools until her marriage to Reuben Lowe. She had two children and made North Shapleigh her home for the next 72 years. A loving wife and doting mother, she was a member of several civic organizations as well as the Mousam Lake Grange and the Acton-Shapleigh Historical Society. At the age of 91, she was the recipient of the Boston Post Cane award. Longevity seems to run in the Lowe family, as her daughter Mildred was also the recipient of the Boston Post Cane award at the age of 97. (Courtesy of Elwyn Lowe.)

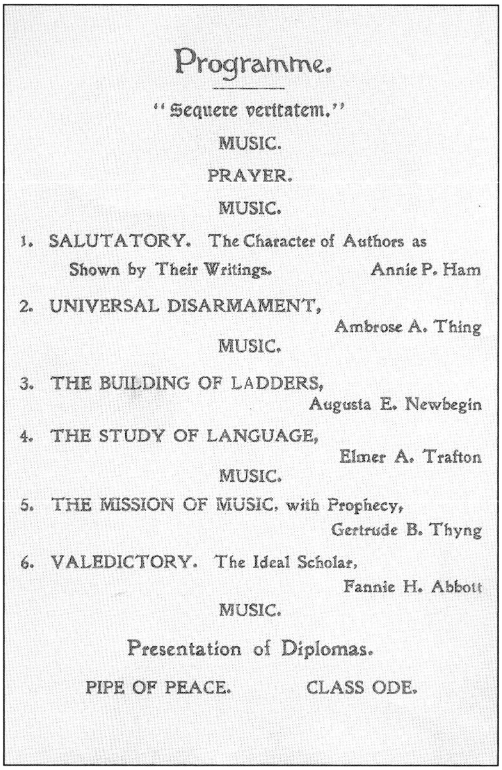

Programme.

"Sequere veritatem."

MUSIC.

PRAYER.

MUSIC.

1. SALUTATORY. The Character of Authors as Shown by Their Writings. Annie P. Ham

2. UNIVERSAL DISARMAMENT, Ambrose A. Thing

MUSIC.

3. THE BUILDING OF LADDERS, Augusta E. Newbegin

4. THE STUDY OF LANGUAGE, Elmer A. Trafton

MUSIC.

5. THE MISSION OF MUSIC, with Prophecy, Gertrude B. Thyng

6. VALEDICTORY. The Ideal Scholar, Fannie H. Abbott

MUSIC.

Presentation of Diplomas.

PIPE OF PEACE. CLASS ODE.

This is a graduation program from Lindsey High School for the class of 1899. Exercises were held at the Baptist church on Friday, April 21, 1899, at 8:00 p.m. Lindsey High School held its first public graduation in 1886. (Courtesy of Elwyn Lowe.)

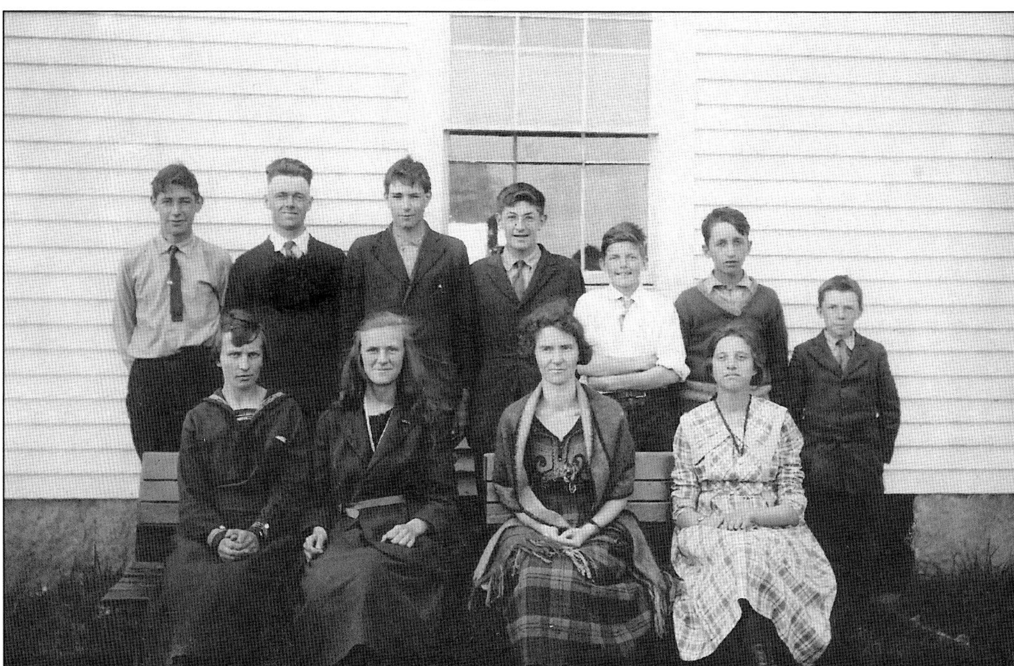

Pictured here are Lindsey High School students in 1918. From left to right are (first row) Era Ross, Ella Beale, Miss Callahan (teacher), and Inez Bickford; (second row) Waldo Meader, Carl Pike, Wil Thyng, Kenneth Meader, Homer Wright, Mule Hooper, and Russell Smith.

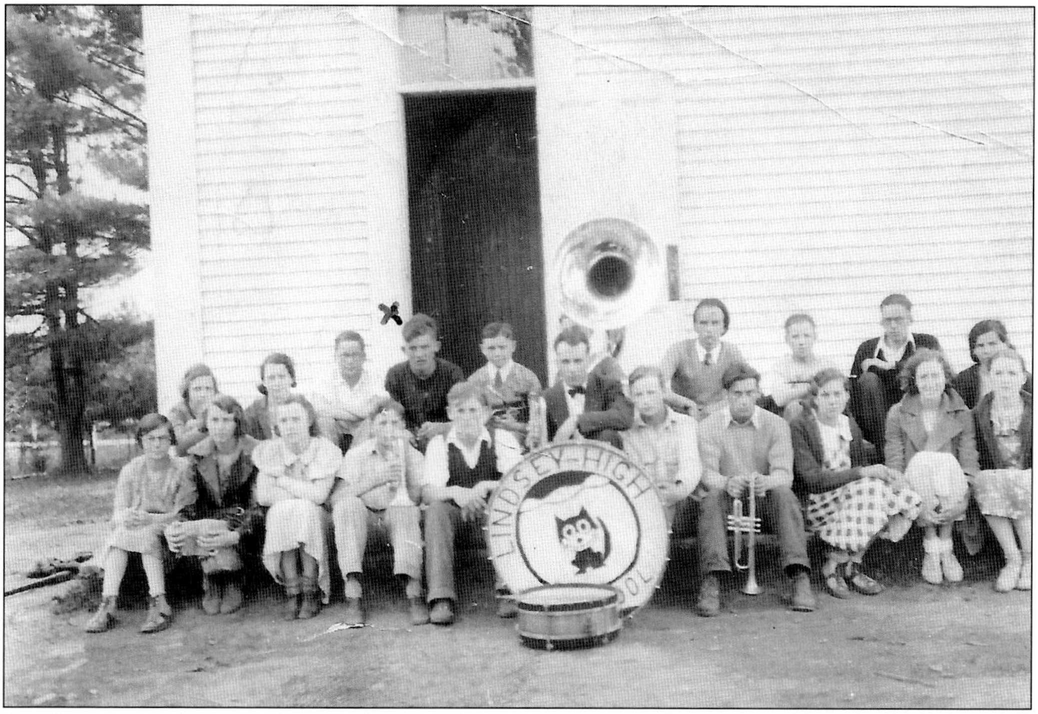

Band members from Lindsey High School around 1931 are, from left to right, (first row) three unidentified, Karl Robinson, Ralph Blanchard, Dennis Long (teacher), Leonard Sprague, Fred Mansur, Mary Rankin, Marion Stanley, and Arlene Blanchard; (second row) Bertha Hunt, Ruby Stanley, unidentified, George Rankin, two unidentified, ? Long, unidentified, Lester Abbott, and unidentified.

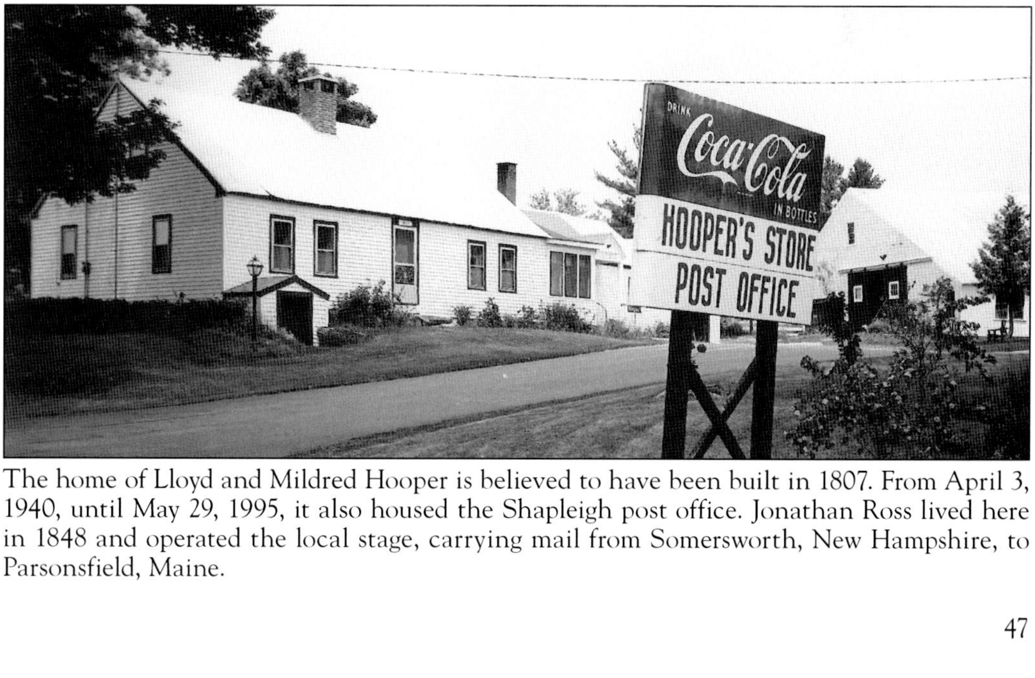

The home of Lloyd and Mildred Hooper is believed to have been built in 1807. From April 3, 1940, until May 29, 1995, it also housed the Shapleigh post office. Jonathan Ross lived here in 1848 and operated the local stage, carrying mail from Somersworth, New Hampshire, to Parsonsfield, Maine.

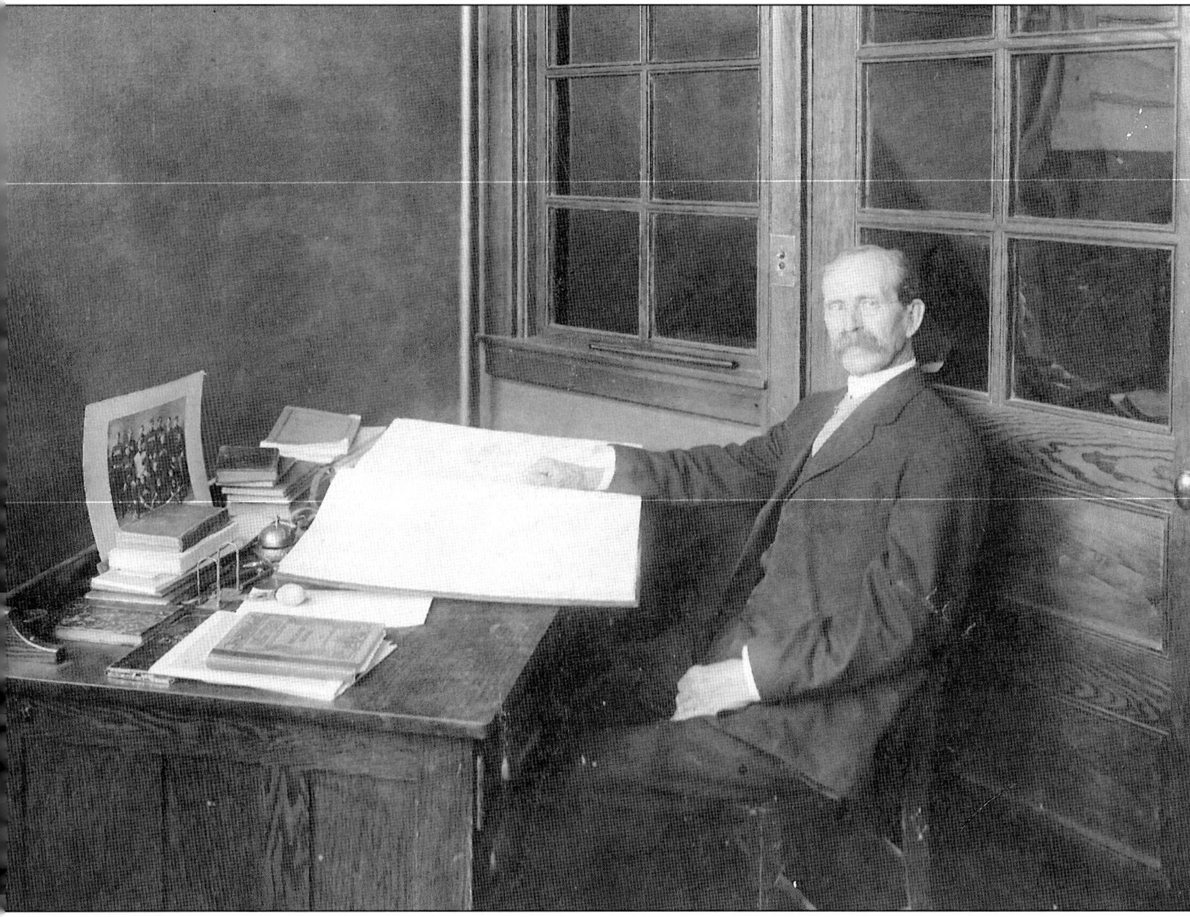

George Crediford graduated from Lindsey High School in 1886 and took up the teaching profession, which he followed for more than 20 years. Crediford was a civic-minded citizen and held many different positions during his lifetime, including Shapleigh town treasurer, superintendant of Shapleigh schools, Union Park Association treasurer, Maine state representative, master of the Mousam Lake Grange, master of the York Pomona Grange, and member of the Maine State Grange. Crediford married Mary Emery of North Shapleigh, and together they had one son, Leon. Like his father, Leon was very active in the community and was general secretary of the Acton fair for 33 years. The Crediford family lived on Owls Nest Road in Shapleigh for over 100 years. (Courtesy of Melissa Conner.)

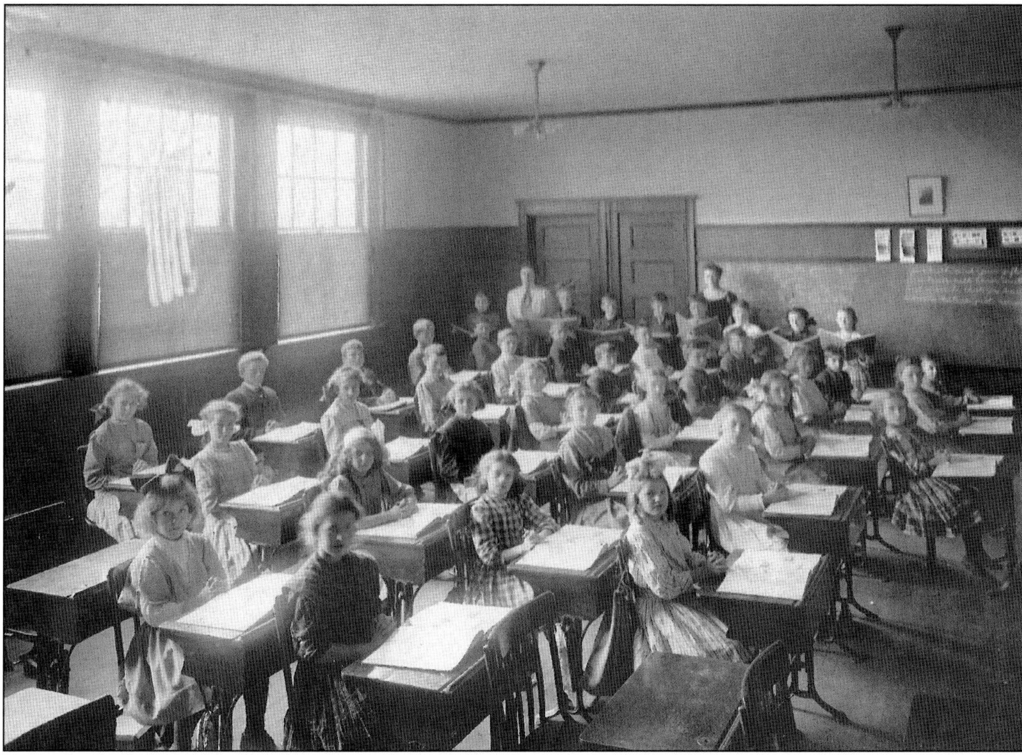

Although the name of this school and its pupils are unknown, this picture depicts a typical classroom of the early 1900s. The schoolhouses were usually built where the land was as nearly useless as possible. Any spot was good enough if it were in the geographic center of the district and, ideally, the children were to walk no more than 2 miles to school. (Courtesy of Melissa Conner.)

A quilting bee is pictured here on the lawn of the Crediford farm. From left to right are Nellie Merrow, Mary Emery Crediford, Nettie Hussey Staples, Lizzy Emery, Leon Crediford, Nida Hassen, Jennifer Merrow, and Louise Merrow. The idea of piecing together bits of valuable fabric as a way of saving money and putting to good use what would otherwise be wasted is a long tradition that immigrated with the first American settlers. (Courtesy of Lista Staples.)

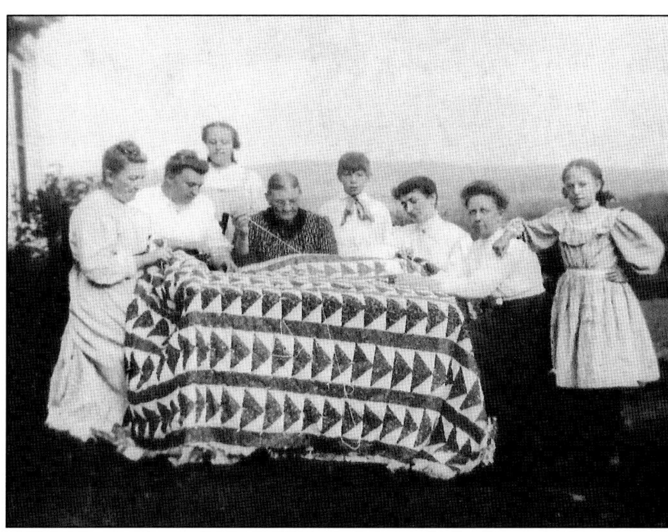

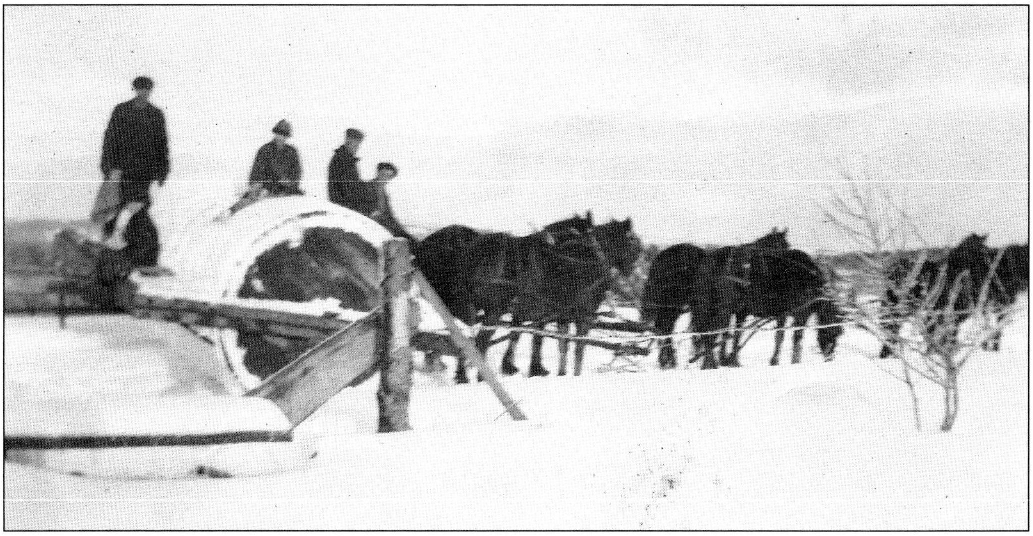

A team of horses takes a break from pulling a snow roller. Snow was packed down on the roads to make a wide, hard, smooth surface. Rolling was an improvement over plowing because it kept the roads wide and did not confine automobiles, carriages, wagons or sleighs. (Courtesy of Herman Abbott.)

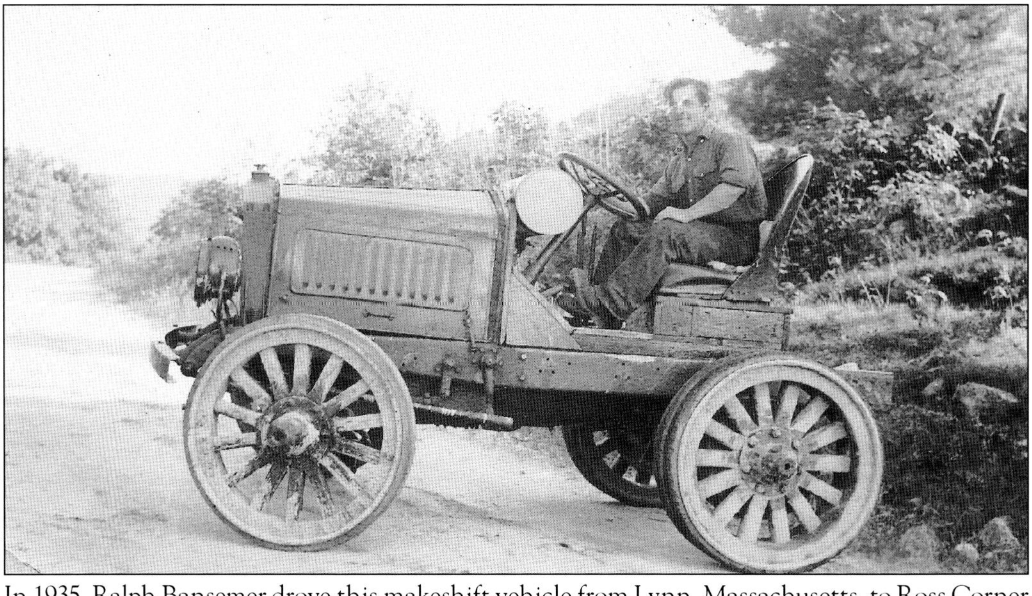

In 1935, Ralph Bansemer drove this makeshift vehicle from Lynn, Massachusetts, to Ross Corner for his friend Carl Pike. The trip took Bansemer three days to complete because the vehicle's top speed was only 4 miles per hour! (Courtesy of Robert Pike.)

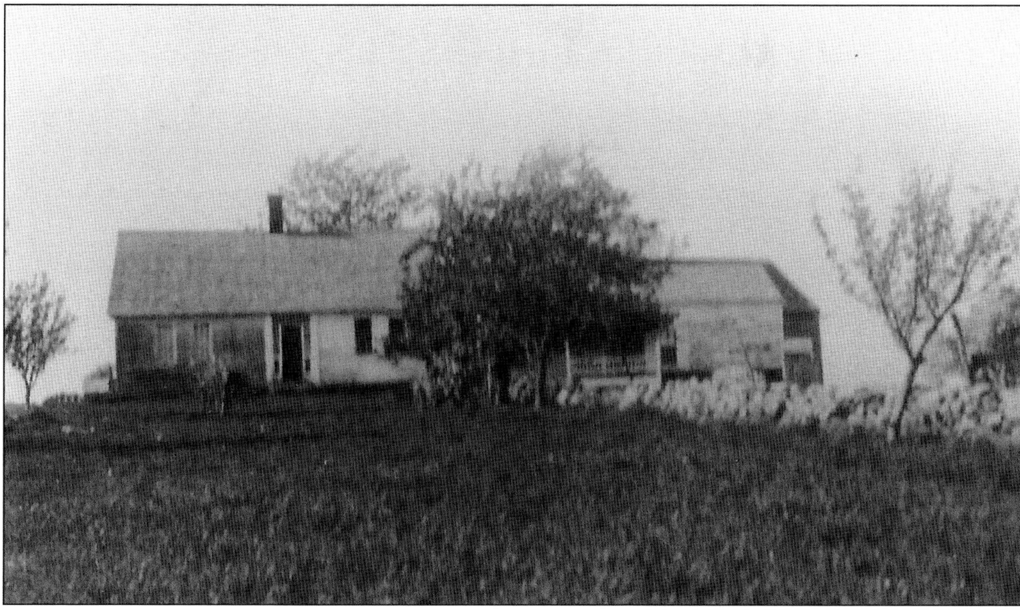

Noah Staples and his brothers came to Massachusetts from England in 1670. Some of this family then moved to southern York County and walked to Shapleigh, where they built their first home in 1797. Staples's son, James, built the present-day home on a tract of land that was formerly an old Native American cornfield, across from the original home on Staples Lane. The early settlers believed there was a large rock on the land where the natives scalped the white men. The family was supported by their dairy farm, where they sold milk, eggs, and many vegetables. The farmstead has been continuously owned by descendants of Noah Staples for over eight generations. Pictured are Noah's great-grandson William Staples and his wife, Cora, in front of their home in the late 1880s. (Both, courtesy of Melissa Conner.)

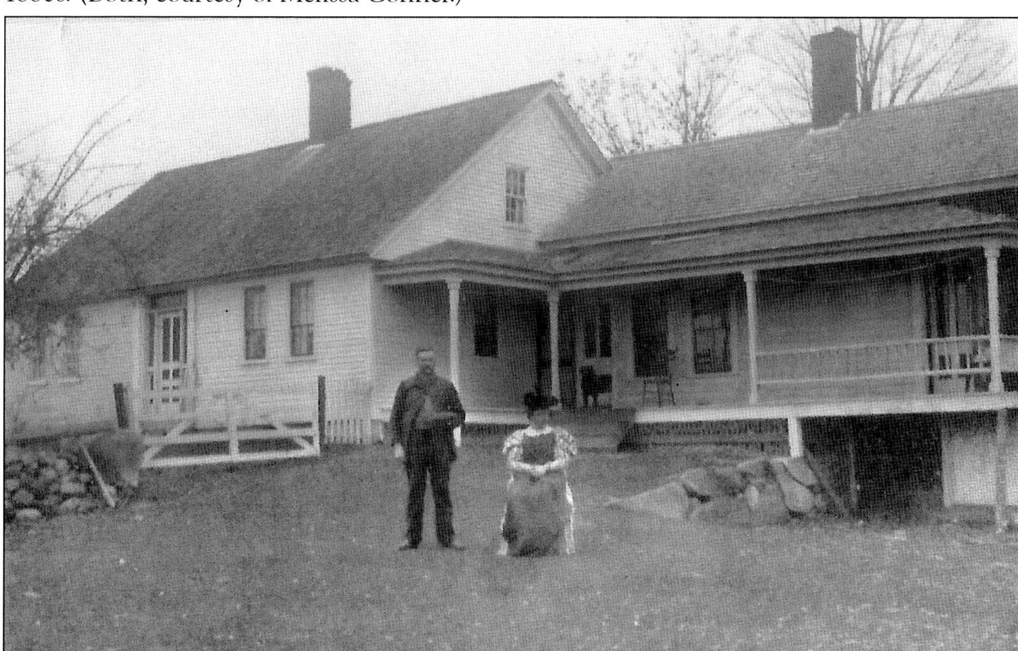

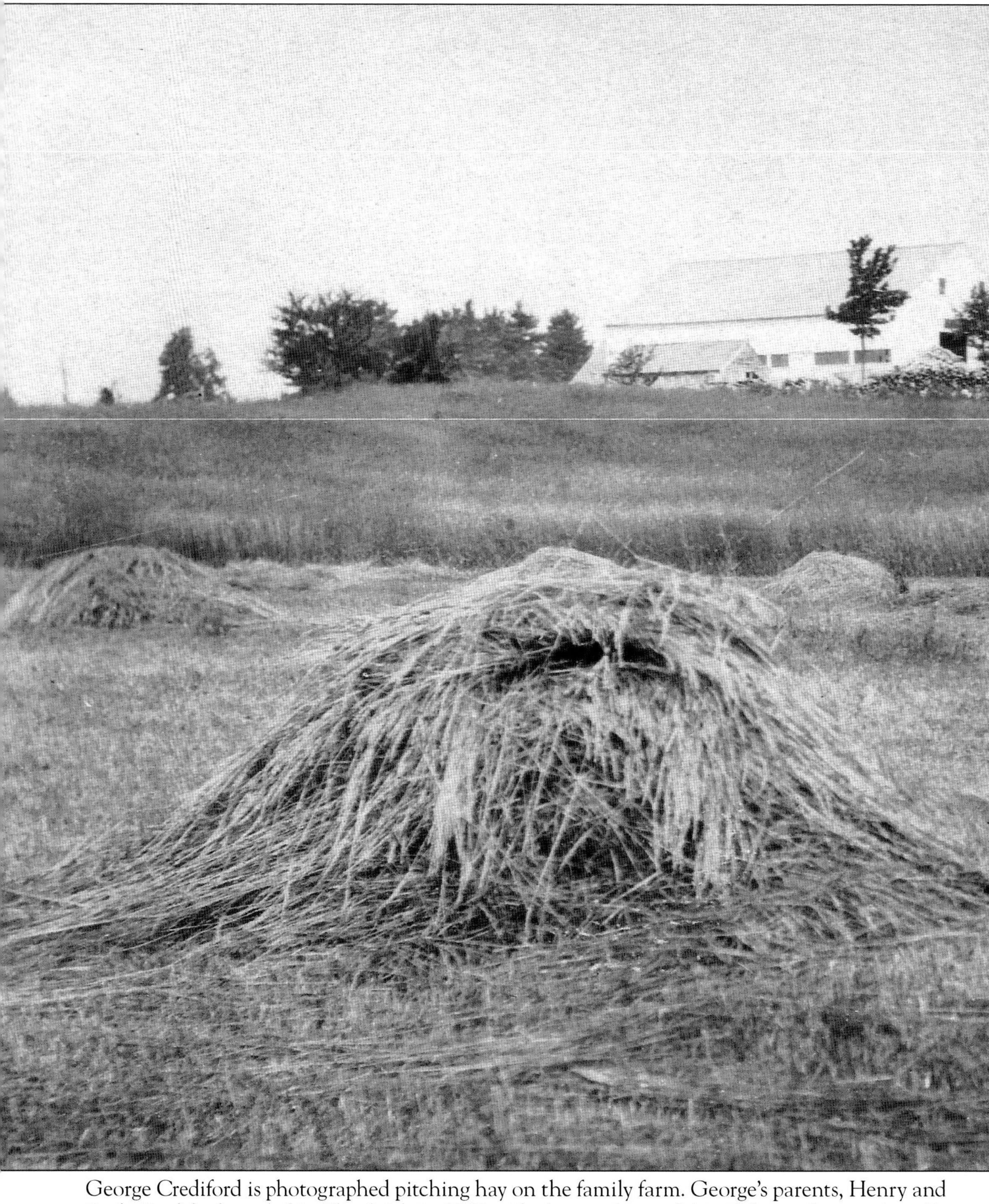

George Crediford is photographed pitching hay on the family farm. George's parents, Henry and Ruth Crediford, settled in Shapleigh in 1867 with the purchase of this 325-acre farm, originally known as the Major Huntress farm. Located on top of the hill on Owls Nest Road, it has beautiful views in all directions. The two-and-a-half-story house with an ell had a large wooden shed connected to a piggery, a large barn with a silo, and a small attached shed with two brooders and

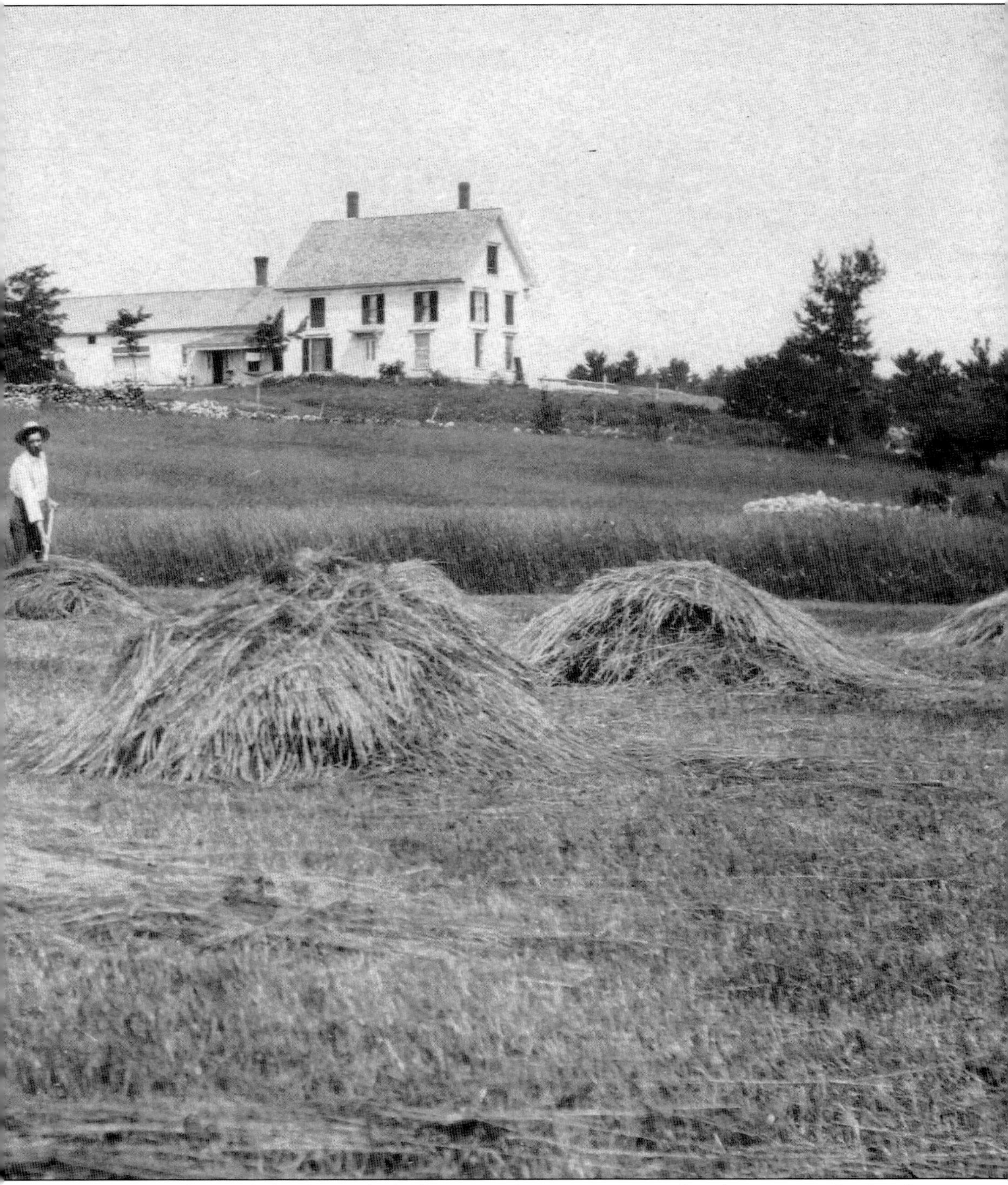

a hen house. The fertile lands supplied tillage, meadow, pasturage, and timber to assist the family with its thriving dairy business. The farm also contained 250 fruit trees. Due to the loving hands of its owners, the buildings survived the 1947 fire with no damage and remained in the Crediford family for over 100 years. (Courtesy of Melissa Conner.)

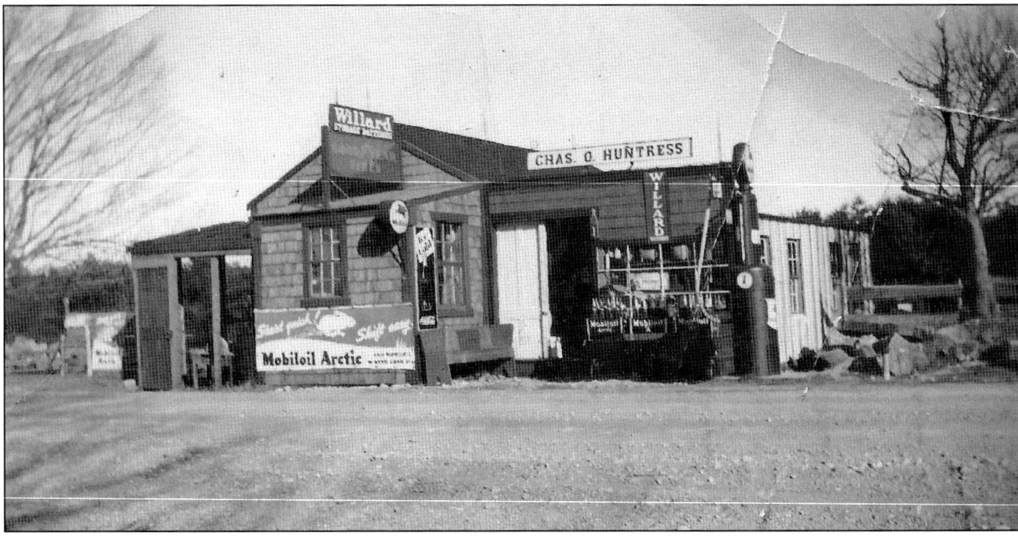

Charles O. Huntress's store across from his home on the Back Road in Shapleigh is pictured here. Huntress sold gas, automotive parts, and antiques at this location from the 1930s until he moved his business to Shapleigh Corner in the early 1940s. The building burned in the 1947 fire. (Courtesy of Joan Huntress.)

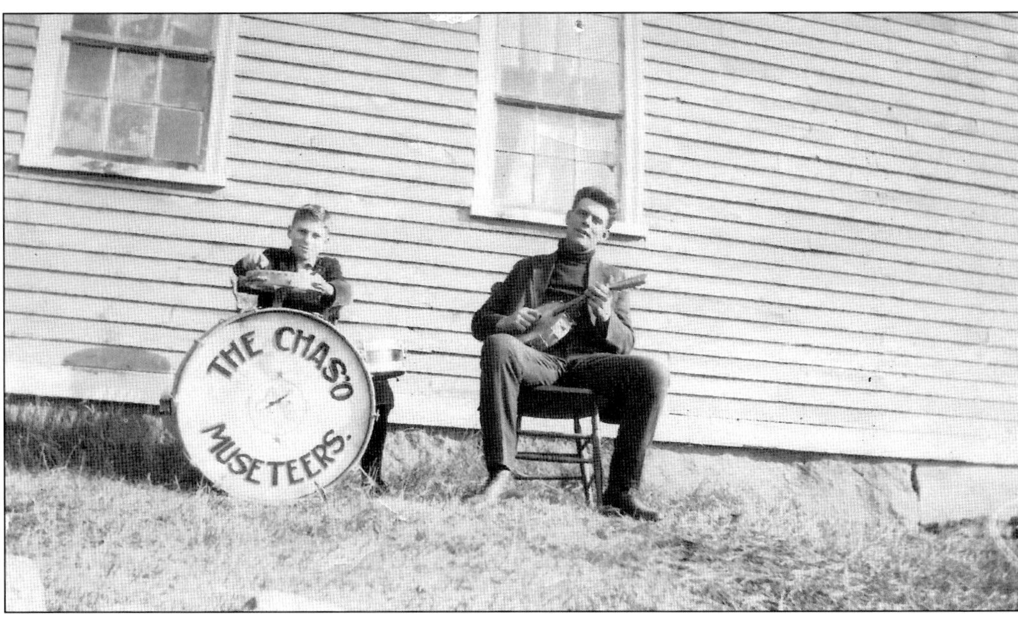

It is rehearsal time for the Chaso Museteers. They practiced as often as time permitted in order to keep up with the latest in dance tunes. Carl Huntress and his father, Charles O., formed the band and performed on a regular basis at area dance halls. (Courtesy of Charles Huntress.)

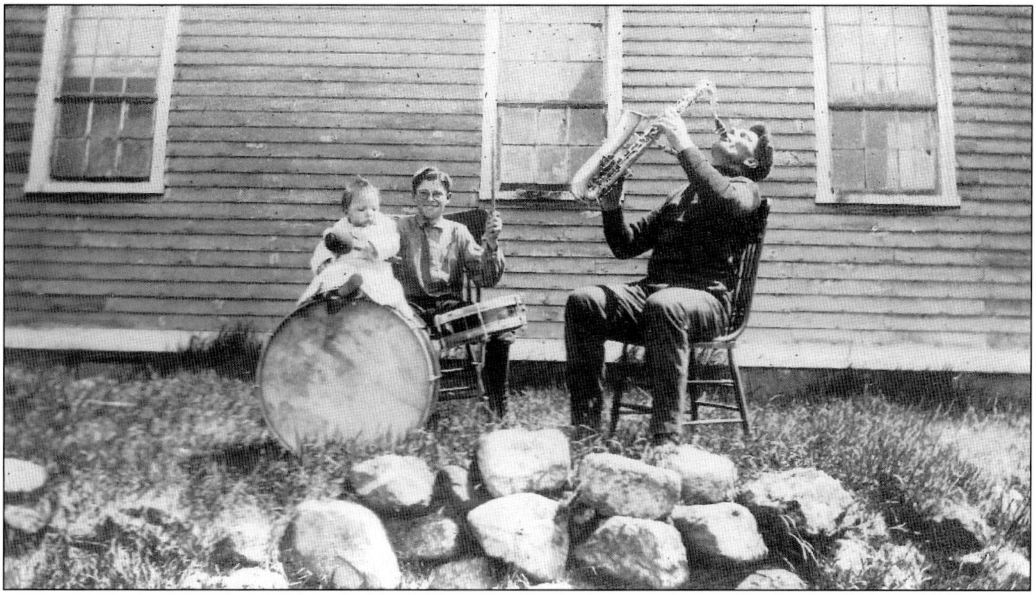

Saxophone, drum, banjo, guitar, violin, and tambourine were just a few of the instruments played by the Chaso Museteers. From left to right are Fred Huntress, Carl Huntress, and Charles Huntress. (Courtesy of Charles Huntress.)

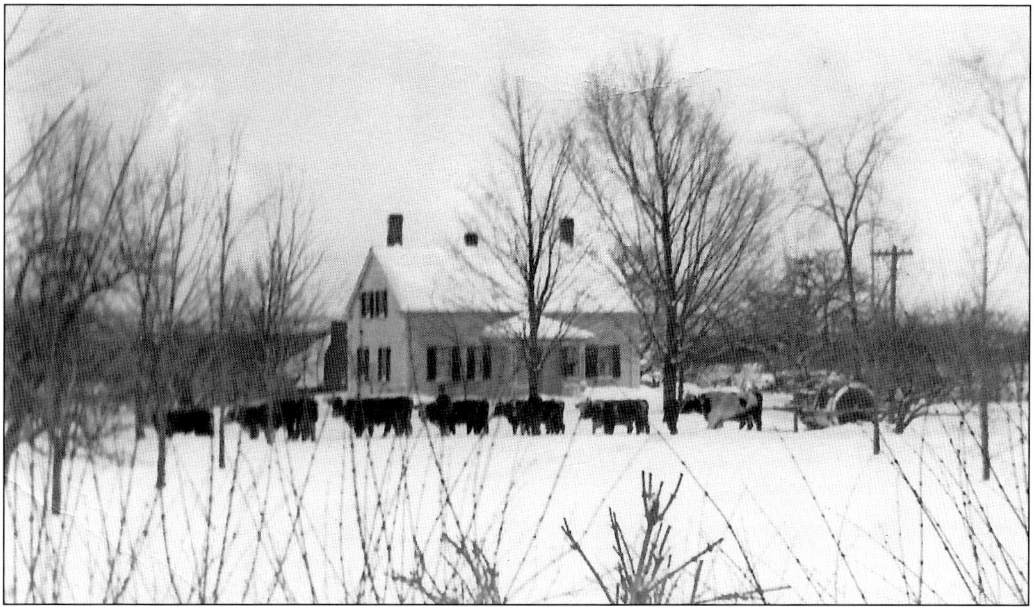

A team of eight oxen is rolling snow on February 21, 1920, in Shapleigh. The snow roller would turn on an axle and was hitched to a team of horses or oxen with a brace that was also used to clean snow from the roller. (Courtesy of Lista Staples.)

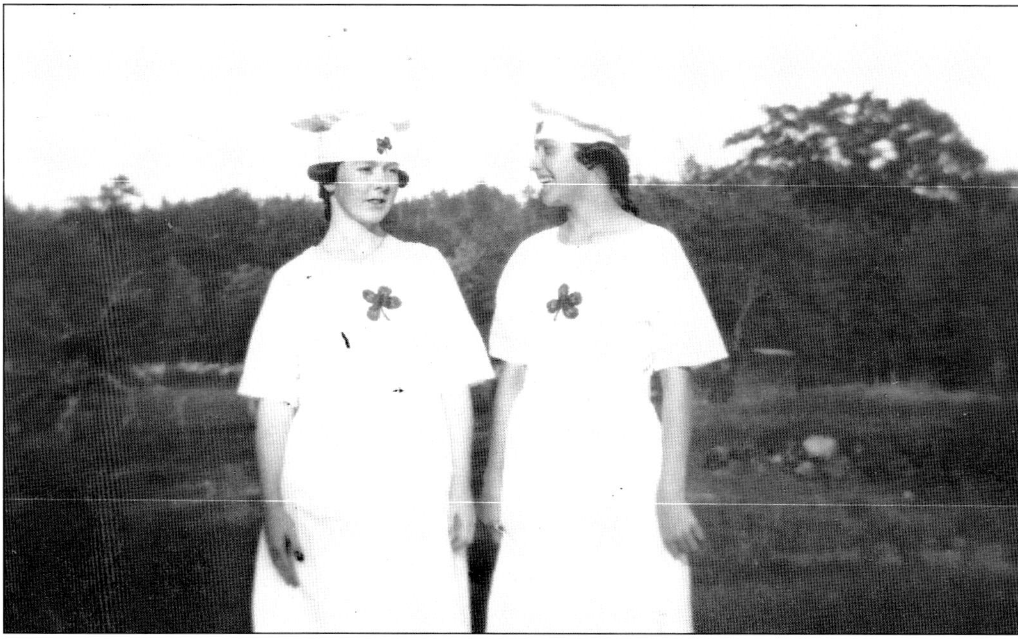

Jessie Hobbs and Eleanor Murray are in their 4-H uniforms. The first 4-H club in the state of Maine was started in York County in 1913 and called Agricultural Boys Club. In 1914, the Homemakers Club for girls was formed in Shapleigh. In 1918, the two combined to make the Four-leaf Clover Club. In 1956, the boys and girls were once again separated and the boys club was then called the Mountaineers.

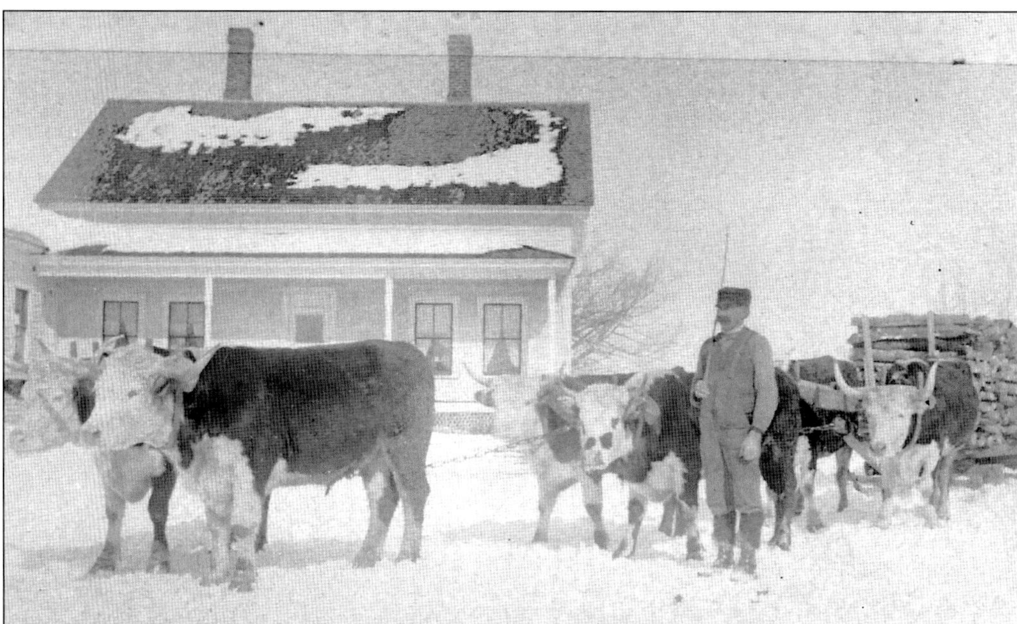

Hauling logs, moving houses, plowing fields, and pulling carts were just a few of the ways a typical farmer would use his team of oxen. One house in North Shapleigh was cut in two by handsaw, and with the aide of 10 yoke of oxen, both halves were moved approximately 4 miles to Ross Corner, where they were reassembled.

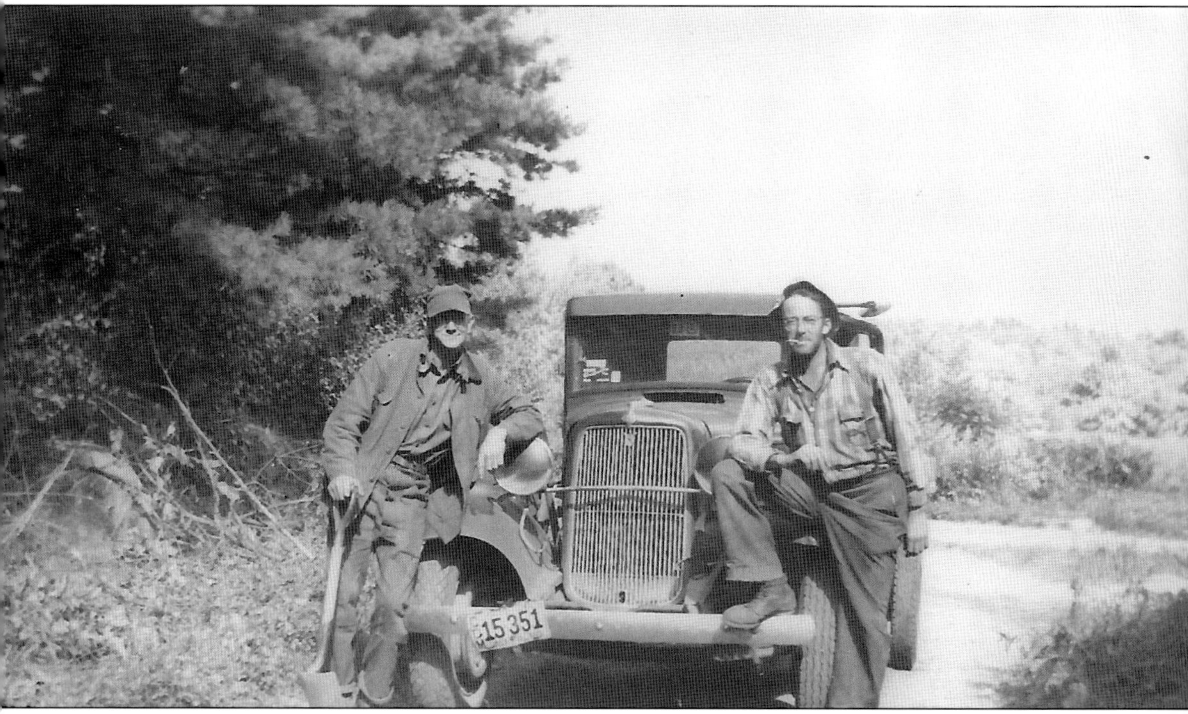

Ross Corner locals Harley Cook (left) and Lester Abbott take a break from working on the roads. This picture was taken during World War II, as is evidenced by the top halves of the automobile headlights being painted black. The idea was that automobiles could be driven during air raids with this stipulation, so as not to be visible from the air. During this time, homeowners were mandated to have darkening shades and citizens were at the ready to extinguish all lighting if the air raid alarm were activated. Some families also took it upon themselves to build fallout shelters in their basements and to stockpile canned goods. This was all for naught, as there were no actual air raids in the continental United States. In the early 1960s, many of these shelters were reestablished with the threat of a nuclear air raid. (Courtesy of Herman Abbott.)

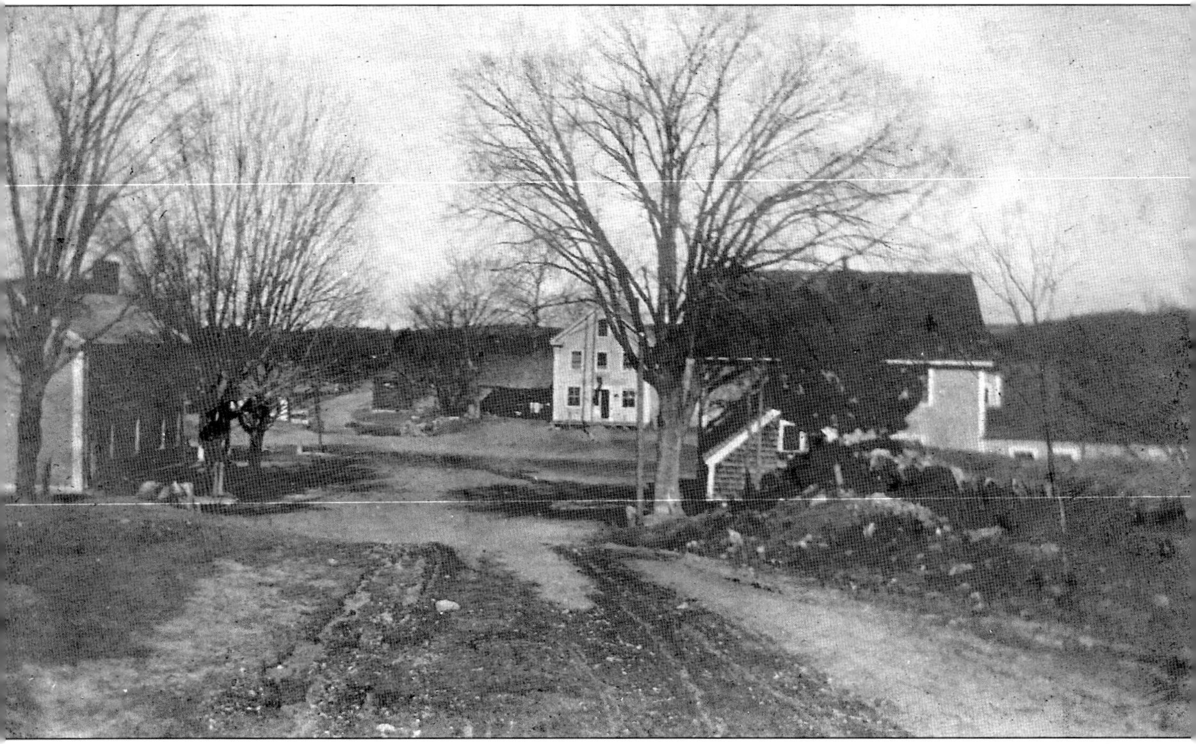

In October 1947, high winds and extremely dry conditions fueled a raging wildfire that swept the state from Bar Harbor to Kennebunkport. On October 22, 1947, Ross Corner was among those areas suffering enormous loss. A majority of Maine communities did not have fire departments, and volunteer firefighters had little or no training and only a few Indian-brand firefighting tanks and shovels to fight the blaze. Setting backfires (deliberately set in the path of oncoming flames to consume tinder and deprive the targeted fire of fuel) was the only way they believed they could control the wildfire. This picturesque village was once a vibrant community with two general stores, a post office, a church, a one-room schoolhouse, two blacksmith shops, a butcher shop, and a stagecoach inn. Every building in this scene was destroyed by the inferno. (Courtesy of Herman Abbott.)

At the beginning of the 20th century, Ross Corner was a busy little community. The large eight-bedroom house on the left was originally a stagecoach inn built by Andrew Ross, for whom Ross Corner is named. The inn had 13 rooms, all furnished with fine antiques and decorated in different colors. The stagecoach would arrive daily from Newfield with passengers, supplies, and mail. Due to the relatively primitive modes of transportation of the day, many passengers would spend the night at the inn, allowing for a home cooked meal and a good night's rest before continuing on with their travel plans. Ross Corner was also home to a famous basket maker named Gene Swinerton. Swinerton ran a one-man operation, crafting thousands of baskets. Some of the more popular varieties were clam, fruit, and sewing and clothes hampers, some of which are still in existence. (Courtesy of Herman Abbott.)

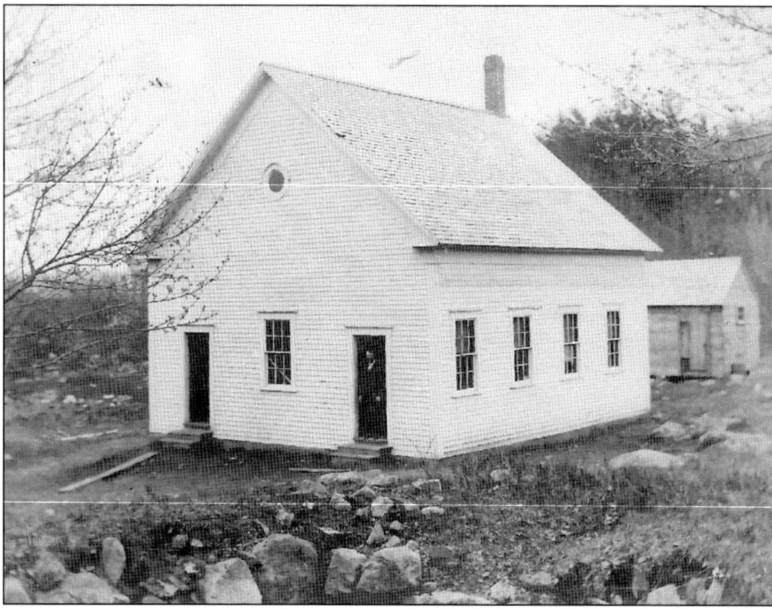

The Lincoln School in Ross Corner is pictured here. In 1907, twenty-six pupils attended the fall term at this one-room schoolhouse. No matter how many scholars, there was never any thought to providing more than one teacher. Lincoln School was just another one of the many casualties of the 1947 fire. (Courtesy of Herman Abbott.)

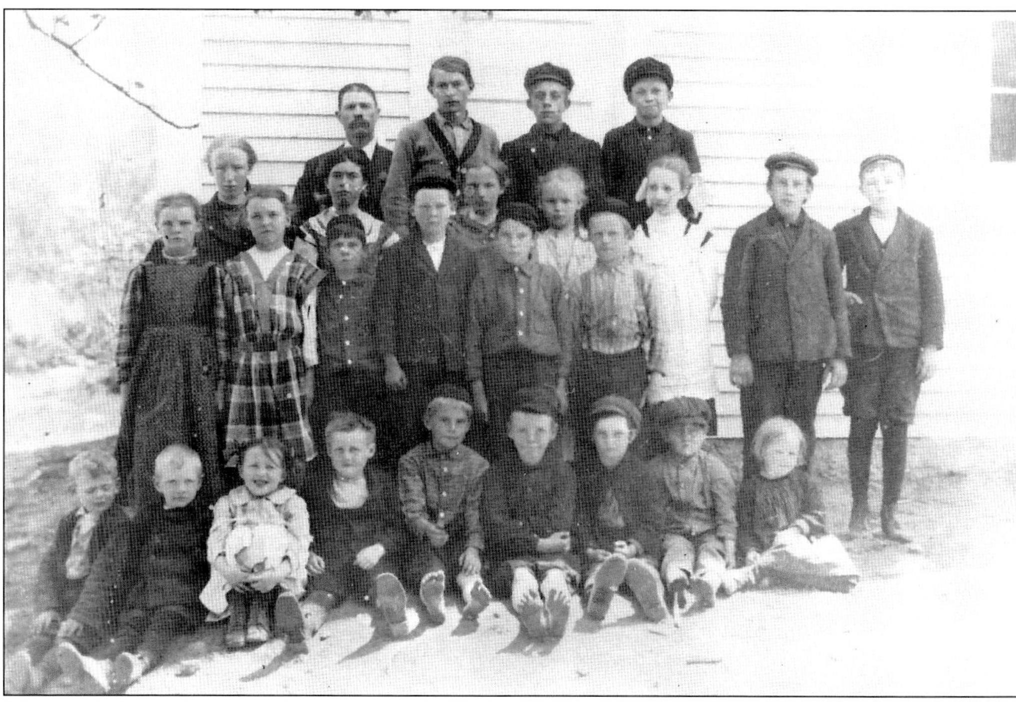

This is the Lincoln School class of 1908. Students from left to right are (first row) unidentified, John Thyng, Martha Thyng, Cyrus Thyng, Leon Beal, Carl Pike, Howard Nason, Delbert Brown, and Mary Scott; (second row) Carrie Andrews, Ruth Pike, Sidney Beal, Walter Quimby, Roscoe Beal, and Perley Scott; (third row) Elsa Scott, Beatrice Hamilton, Edna Scott, Effie Scott, Marie Thyng, Harry Hussey, and Chester Giles; (third row) William Thyng (teacher), Arthur Sprague, Isaac Hussey, and Linwood Haines.

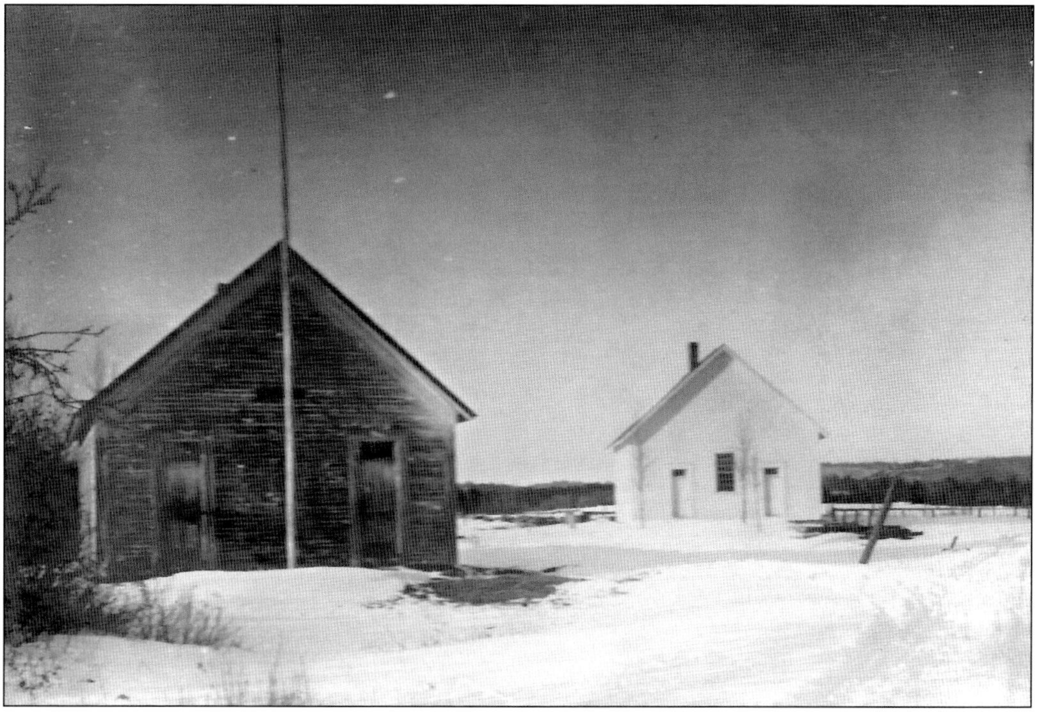

The Methodist school and church on Owl's Nest Road near Ross Corner is shown here. The 1891–1892 school year was cancelled due to diphtheria. Few pictures remain of these two buildings, as both were lost in the 1947 fire. (Courtesy of Melissa Conner.)

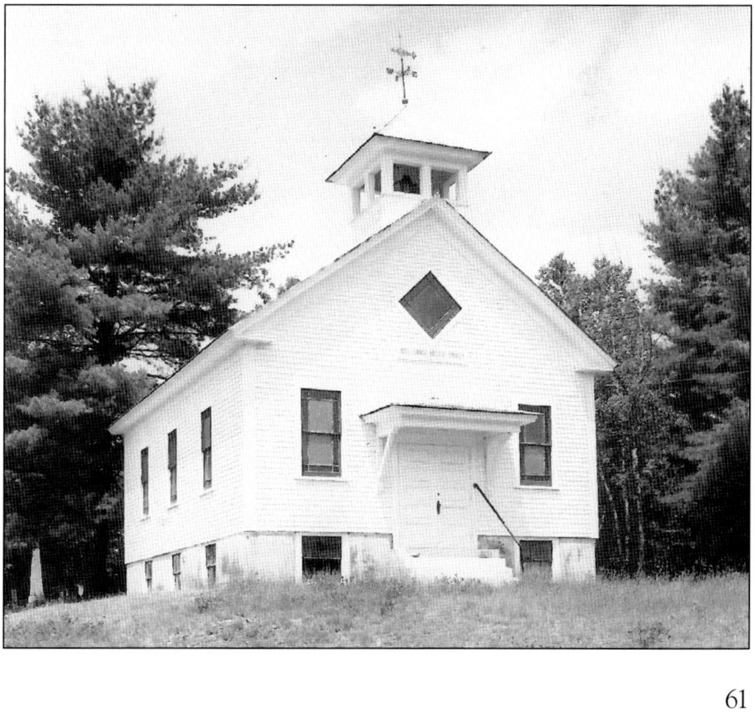

In 1834, a Baptist church was erected in Ross Corner. After a fire burned it to the ground in 1910, the present church was built in 1913. After years of intermittent use, regular services were reestablished in the summer of 2008. It is one of the few buildings that did not succumb to the forest fire of 1947.

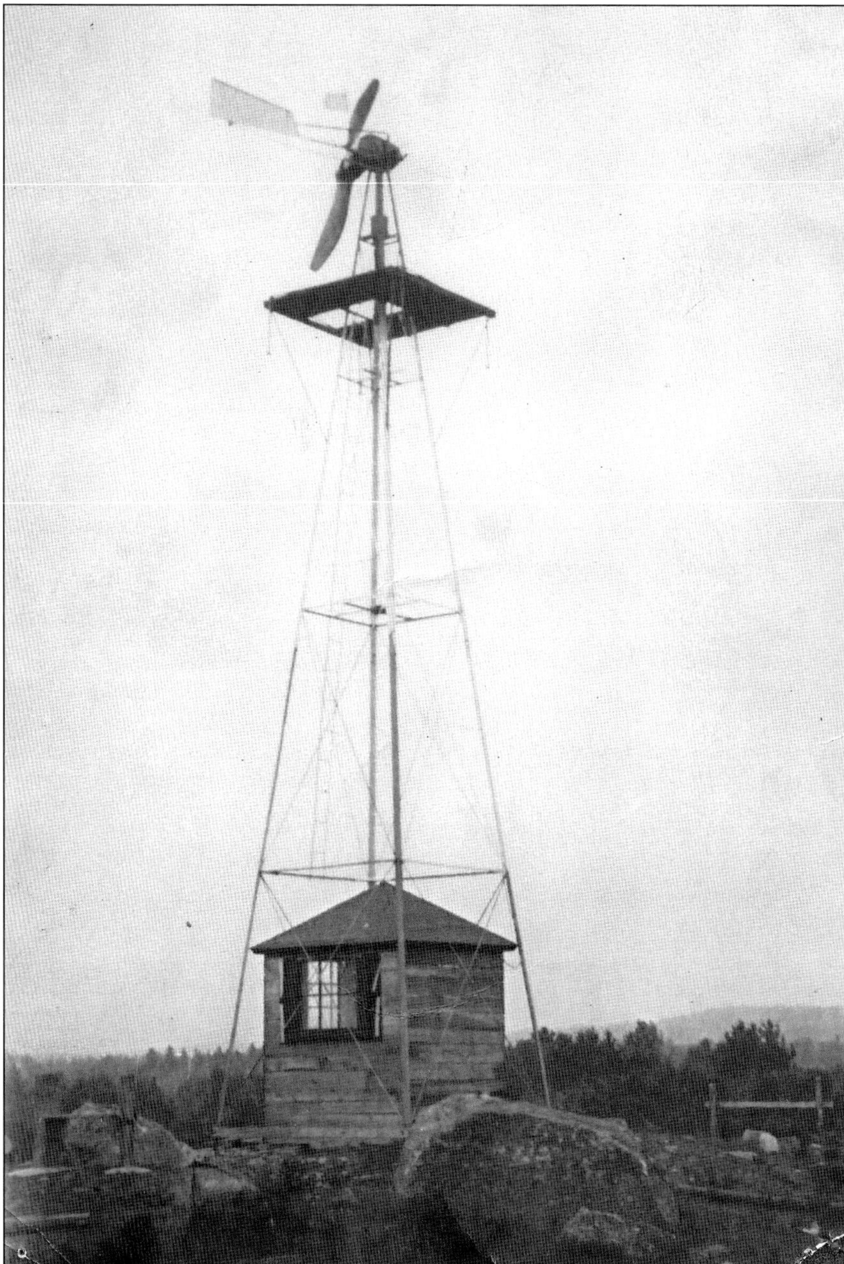

Carl Pike built this 40-foot windmill in 1925 on his father's property on Gore Road in Ross Corner. This windmill generated the first electricity in the area, which brought electric lights, a water pump, a corn sheller, a grindstone, and a compressor to the Pike household. Pike was a visionary for his time and a mechanical tinkerer throughout his life. Many farmers used windmills to pull water from the ground, but Pike expanded upon this principle. The windmill survived the fire of 1947, but the house was ravaged. Pike was clearly ahead of his time, as wind is now becoming popular as an effective means of power. In fact, Pike's son, Robert, who shares his father's passion for mechanics, has recently located this windmill and has plans to reconstruct it and utilize its power. (Courtesy of Robert Pike.)

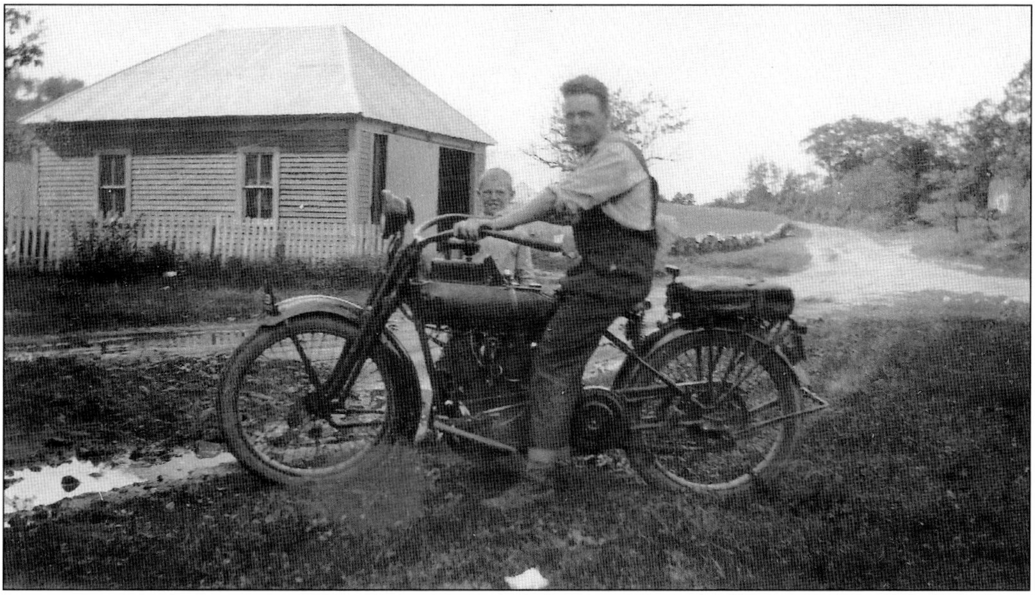

Carl Pike drove his 1925 Indian motorcycle to and from Lynn, Massachusetts, where he attended the General Electric apprentice course. Pike worked as a mechanical specialist at General Electric's Aircraft Instrument Design Engineering Research and Development Lab for 40 years and held several government patents. (Courtesy of Robert Pike.)

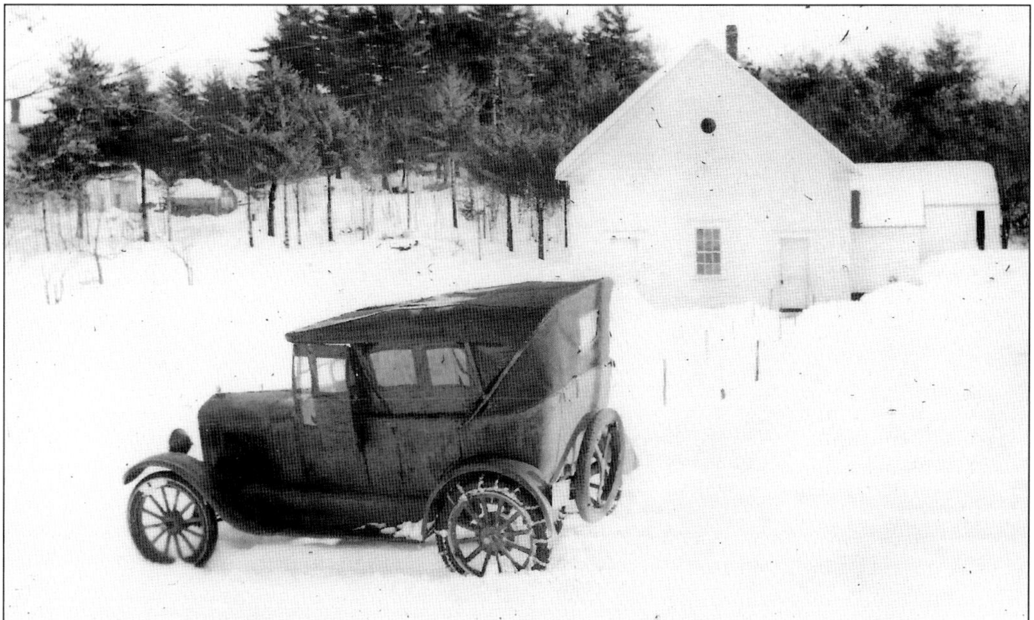

Mail delivery during the winter in Ross Corner is shown here. Benjamin Franklin was appointed the first U.S. postmaster in 1795. The first post office in Shapleigh was established on August 24, 1797. The U.S. Post Office issued its first postage stamps in July 1847. The Lincoln School is in the background. (Courtesy of Herman Abbott.)

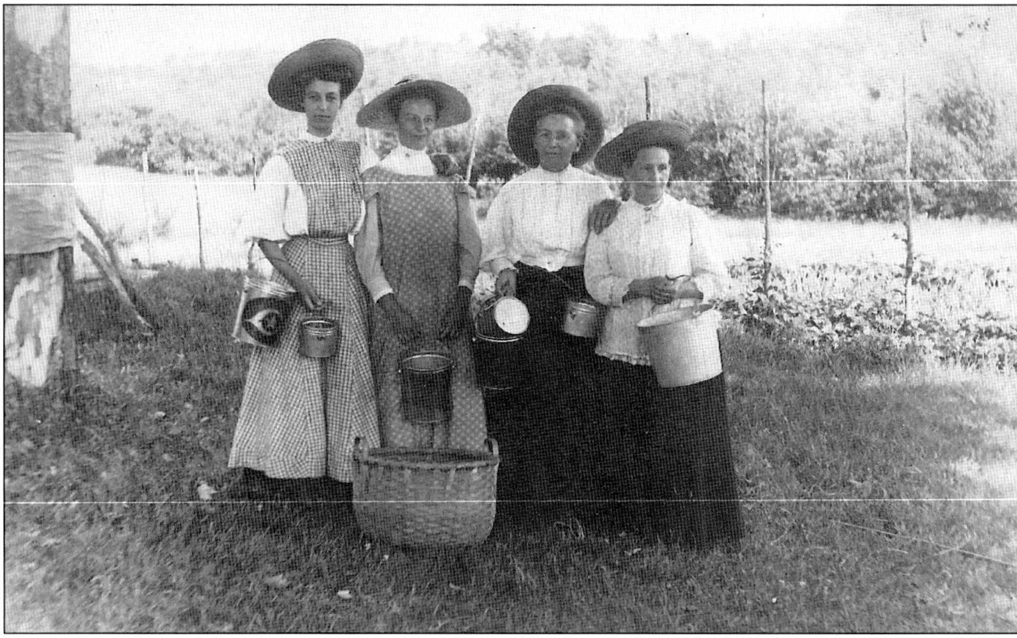

Picking wild blueberries along the road to North Shapleigh provided income for locals. At the beginning of the 20th century, the price of blueberries was 10¢ per quart and an entire family could make $100 per season and be financially set for the winter. The blueberries were shipped via rail to Faneuil Hall market in Boston. Harvesting was done by hand until 1822, when a native Mainer invented the blueberry rake (a close-tined special rake). Traditionally, Native Americans used the berries, leaves, and roots for medicinal purposes. The fruit was also used as a fabric dye and combined with meat into a nutritious jerky. (Both, courtesy of Herman Abbott.)

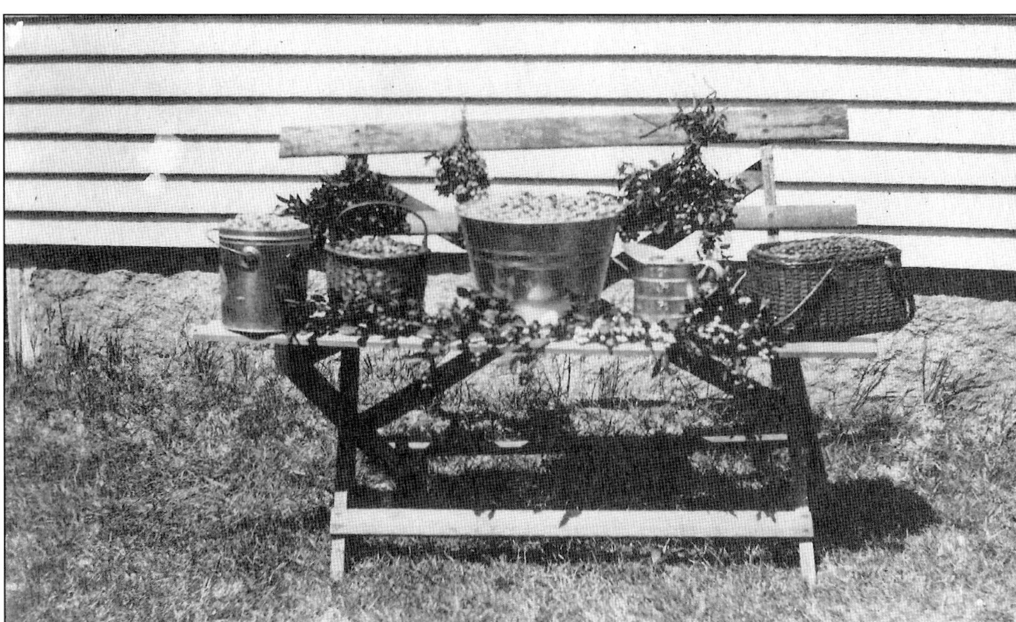

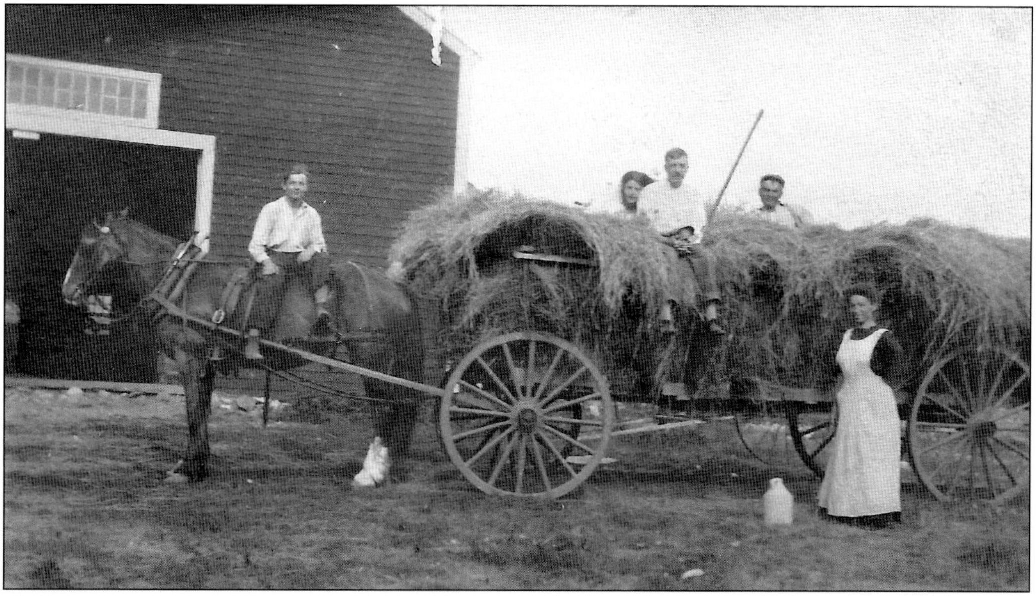

Haying time at Dieschbourg Farm in Shapleigh, like all farms, was a necessary but time-consuming chore. Hay was first cut and dried in the field, then raked into piles. It was pitched from the field onto a hay wagon, then pitched again from the wagon to the hayloft, all by hand.

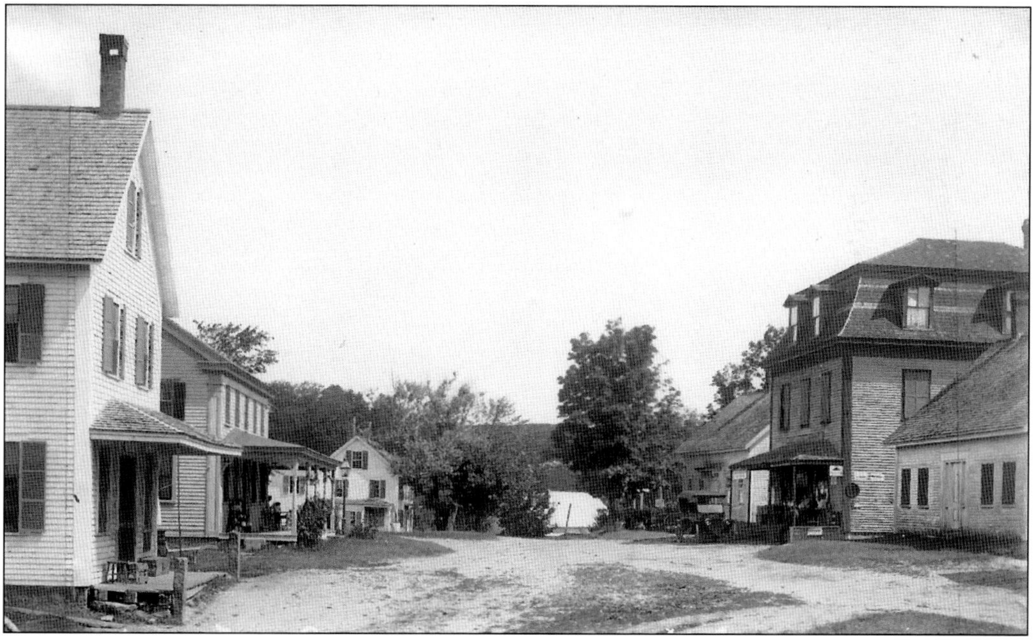

This is a northerly view of the center of North Shapleigh village during the early 1900s. At one time, this village was the business center of Shapleigh. The closing of Hargraves Woolen Mill in 1904 greatly affected the people and businesses of this village. The first building on the left is Coffin's Store, and the three-story building on the right was a general store built in the 1870s that burned to the ground in 1972.

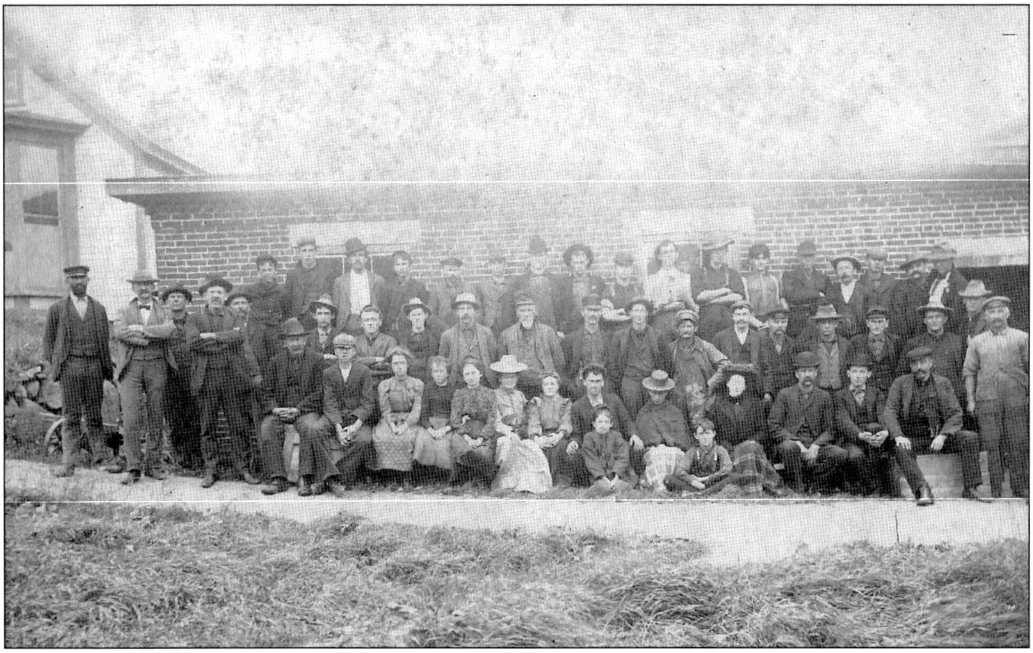

Employees of Hargraves Woolen Mill worked long, hard days earning a respectable living. Originally a custom carding and woolen mill, the facility later produced blue blouse flannels, cashmere, blankets, waterproof material for overshoes, and fabrics for ladies' wear. The mill operated on two 10-hour shifts and grew to acquire four sets of 1,600 spindles; at its peak, employees numbered between 60 and 75. Men and women came from surrounding towns for the opportunity to work. With the influx of these workers, the need for a boardinghouse was great. Hargraves Boarding House was built to house and feed workers that lived outside of town. Hargraves Woolen Mill closed in 1904, and both the mill (1928) and boardinghouse (1940s) were torn down. During the years after the mill closed, the boardinghouse was vacant for several years before being renovated as a dance hall.

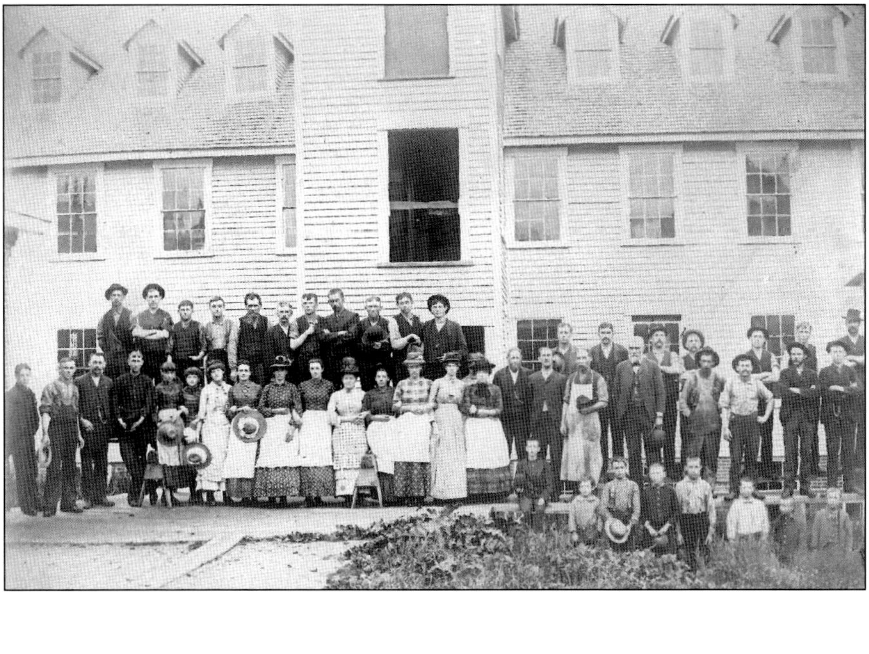

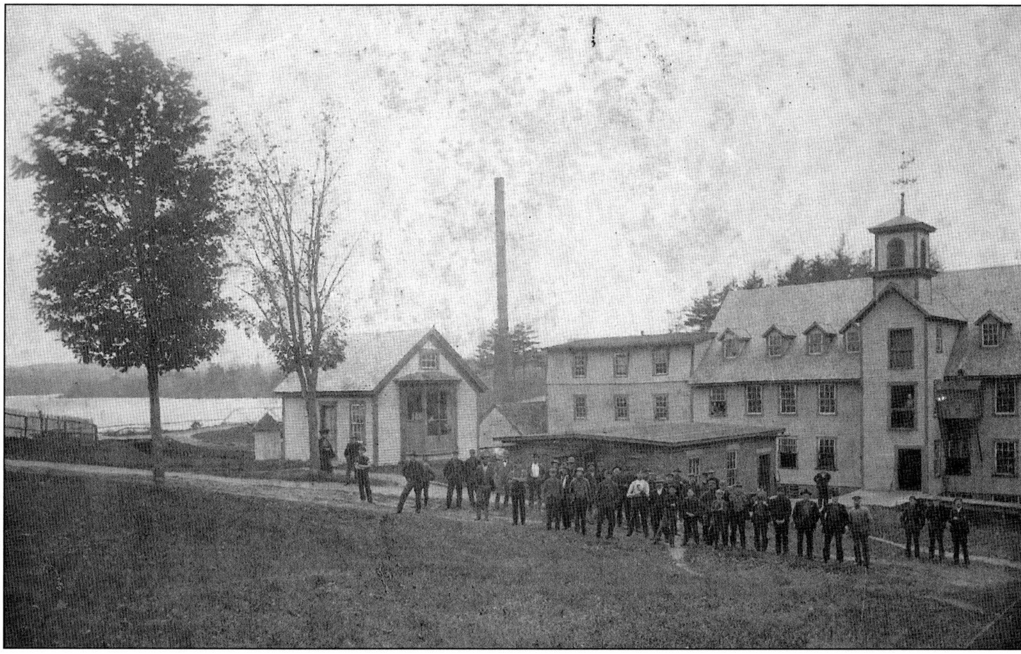

Hargraves Woolen Mill was erected by John Hargraves in 1844 on the banks of Little Ossipee River in North Shapleigh. This picture was taken in 1893, when the mill was thriving.

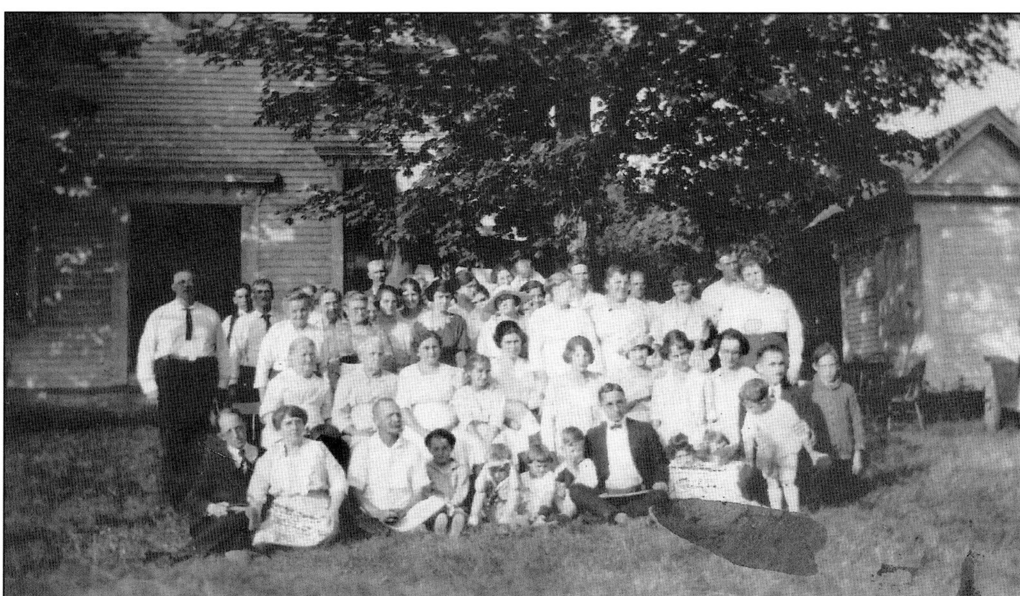

The congregation at North Shapleigh Freewill Baptist Church is photographed in the early 1900s. Year-round services were held until 1903, shortly before the closing of the Hargraves Woolen Mill in 1904. Summer services commenced until 1956, when attendance had increased enough to warrant services on a year-round basis again. An automatic gas heater and electric lights were also installed in 1956.

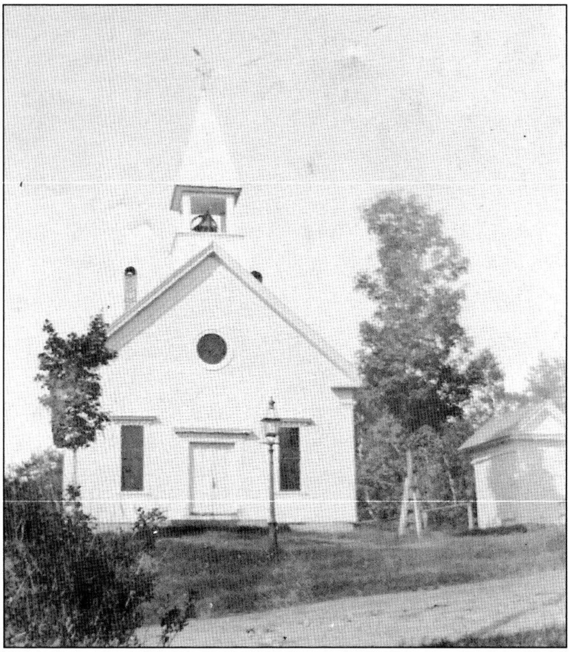

Built in 1866, the North Shapleigh Freewill Baptist Church was originally known as the North Shapleigh Meetinghouse. The church was officially organized on March 22, 1876, with 38 members. Local residents John Lowe and his wife, Hannah, were the first two people to receive baptism here.

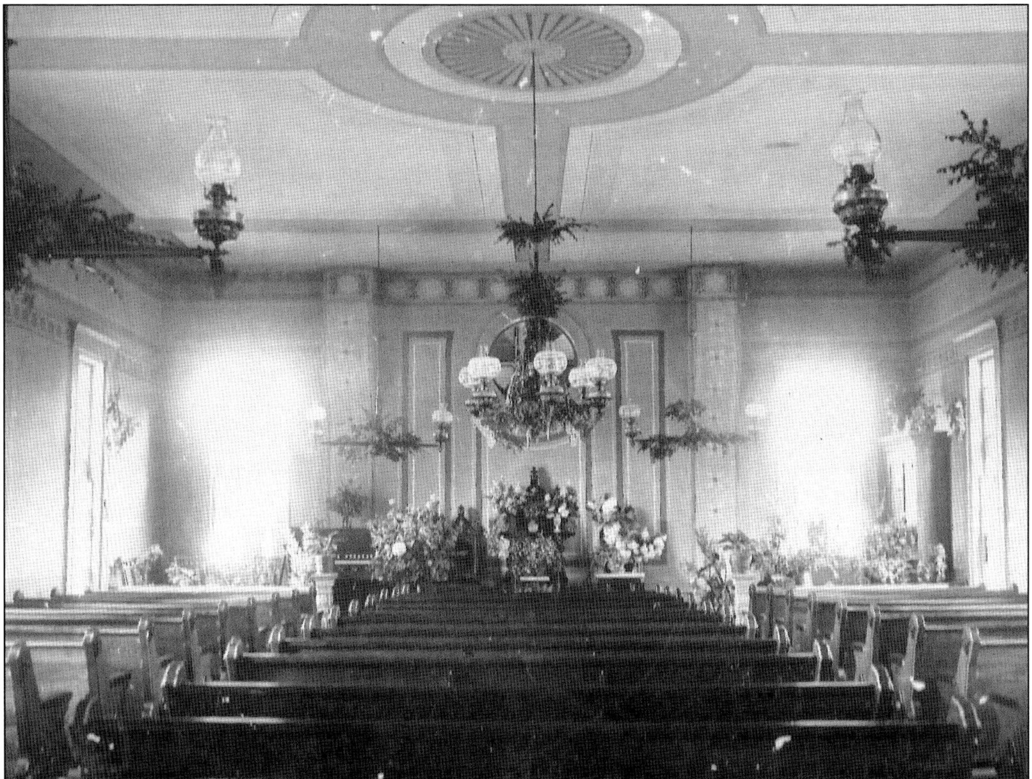

The inside of the North Shapleigh Freewill Baptist Church is beautiful as the sun shines in the windows on Christmas Day, 1888. Church services are currently held only once a year during the summer.

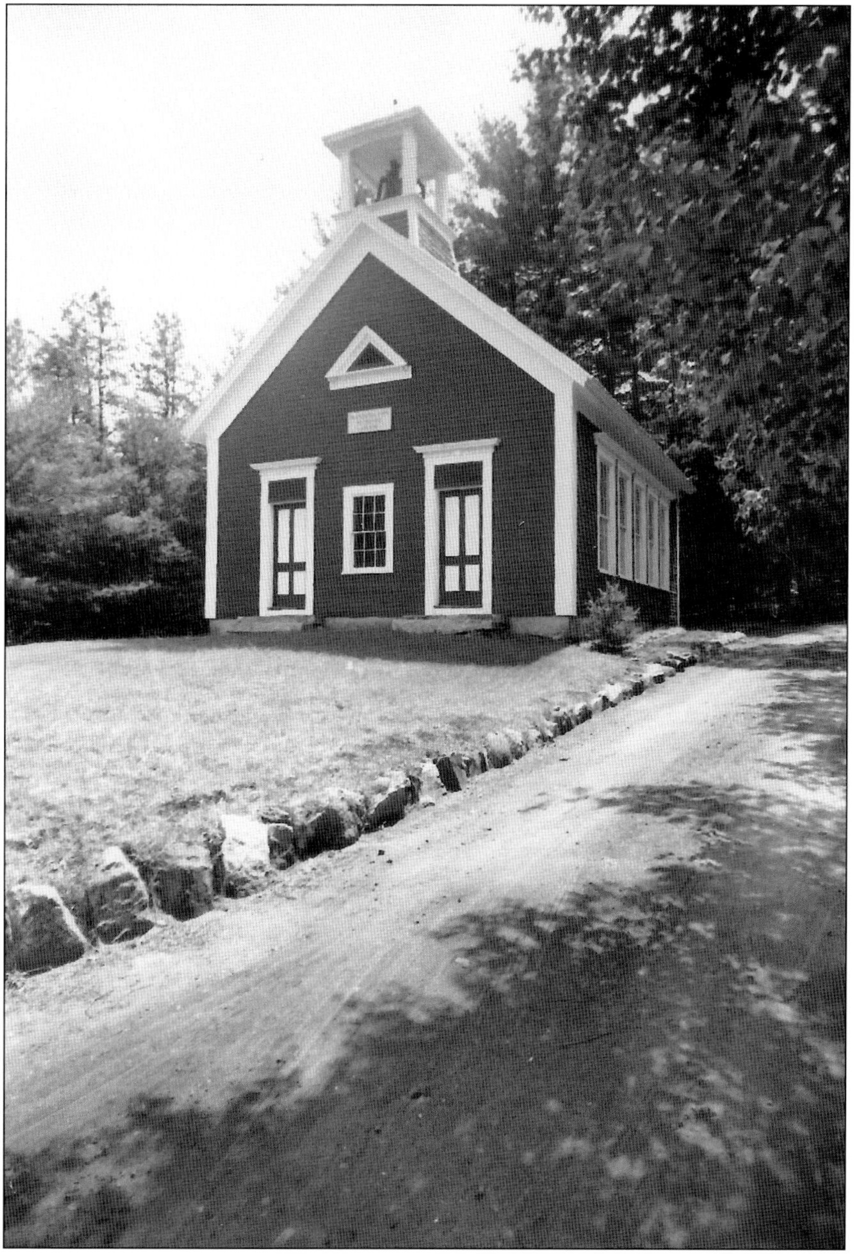

The Washington School in North Shapleigh was built in 1866 and closed in 1942. Children sat at individual desks that were bolted to the floor, with boys on one side of the room and girls on the other. Students rarely faced each other and focused their attention entirely on the teacher, who was the sole source of instruction and discipline in the classroom. The switch—a narrow branch of green wood often cut by the student in trouble—was introduced in the mid-1800s. By the 1890s, a paddle was sometimes kept within sight behind the teacher's desk. The threat of these devices was used as a motivator for students to behave in school. This building was later sold to John Shevenell, who owned the land it sits upon. Believing this way of life would soon disappear forever, Shevenell lovingly and painstakingly restored it in the early 1970s. The school is still privately owned.

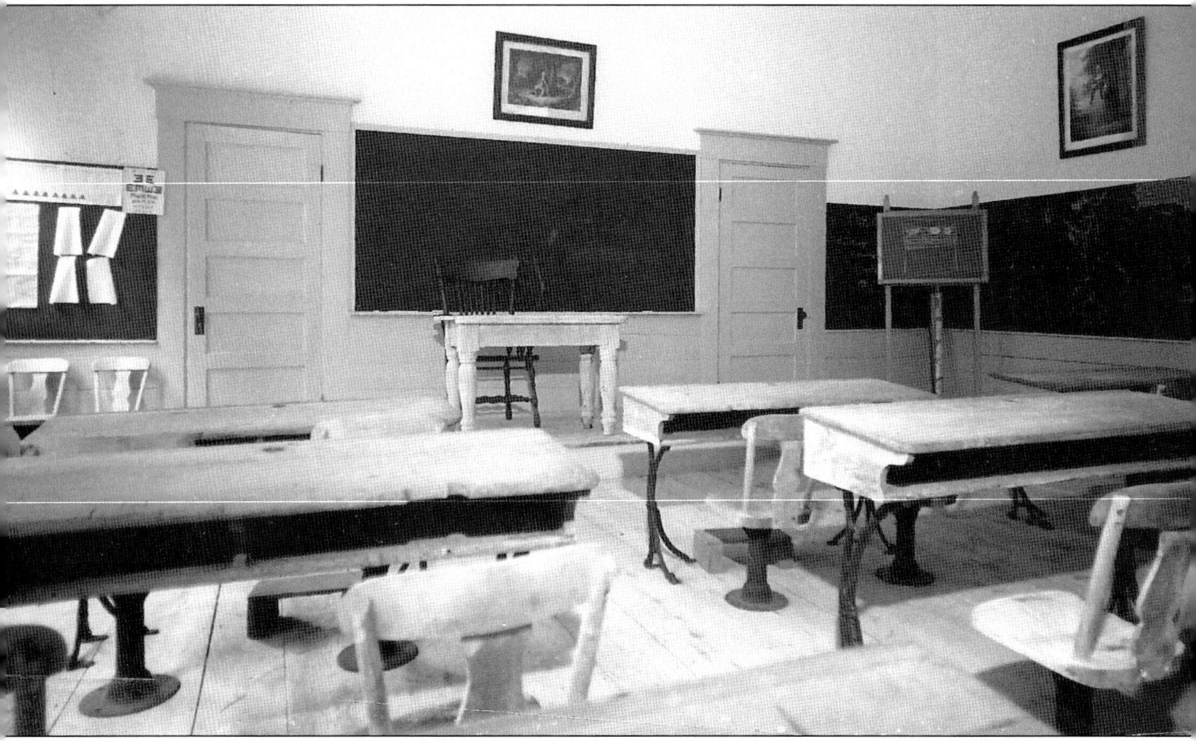

This is a view of the inside of the Washington School in North Shapleigh. Younger children sat at the front of the room, closest to the teacher. This arrangement enhanced the teacher-centered learning environment so popular in schools throughout American history at that time. The first blackboard was introduced in 1809. Early blackboards were made from pine lumber and covered with a mixture of egg white and carbon from charred potatoes. Teachers and students wrote with chunks of chalk and erased with cloth rags. When slate boards became available, teachers used cylinders of white, soft chalk and a felt eraser. These blackboards and slate boards were laborious apparatuses, and the accompanying chalk dust was the bane of all teachers. The blackboard was an important instructional device, allowing the teacher to illustrate lessons by directing the attention of the entire class. Blackboards have given way to white dry-erase boards, and even those are becoming more obsolete with the advent of online lessons and laptop computers.

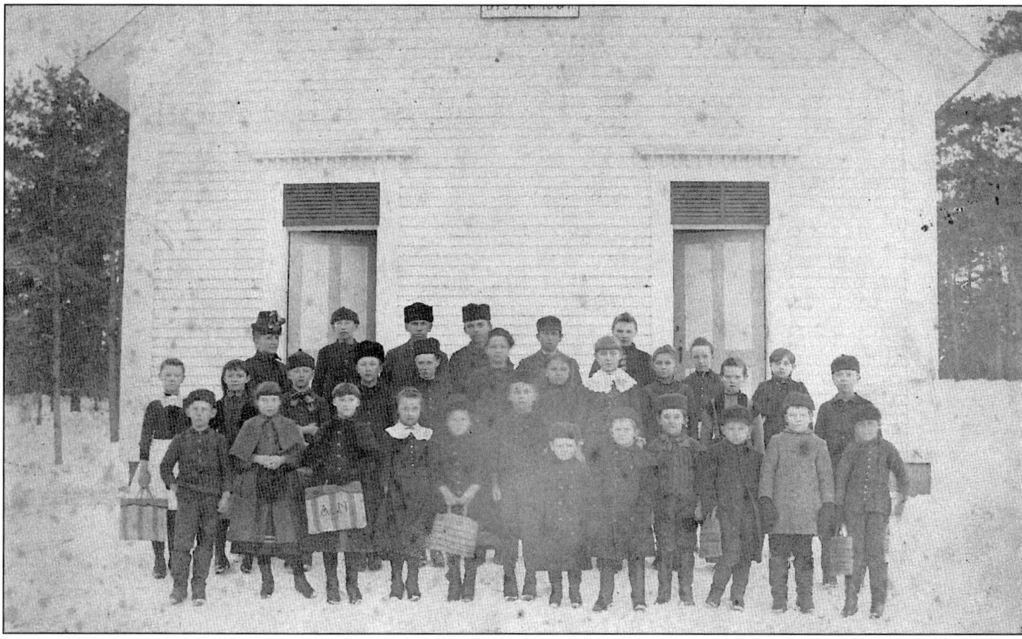

Washington School, North Shapleigh, is shown here on Christmas Day, 1889. With more and more mill workers moving into North Shapleigh, the village quickly became the new business center of Shapleigh.

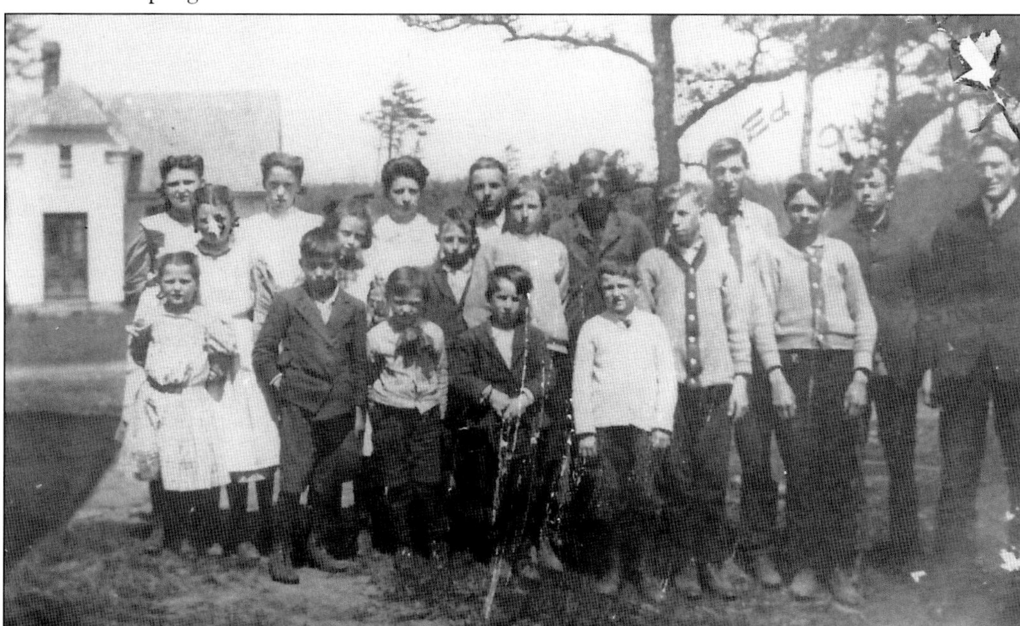

Students from the Washington School in North Shapleigh are photographed around 1912. From left to right are (first row) Elizabeth Whitten, Fred Hammond, Roland Gerrish, Lester Hammond, and Harold Whitten; (second row) Marion Whitten, Mildred Lowe, Sidney Hammond, Allie Gordon, Charles Hammond, and Harold Curtis; (third row) Ethel Whitten, Hazel Sylvester, Mariam Hammond, Raymond Dunnells, Charles Sylvester, Edgar Dunnells, John Sylvester, and teacher Clarence Pike. (Courtesy of Elwyn Lowe.)

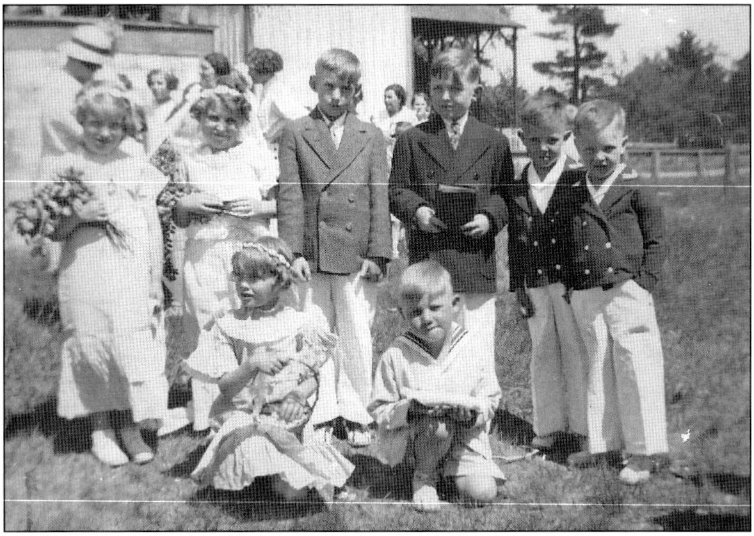

In Shapleigh, the last day of school was often a field trip to the fairgrounds. Washington School of North Shapleigh students are, from left to right, (first row) ? Van Horn and Ernest Houston; (second row) ? Van Horn, Jeannette Houston, Earl Reed, Shepley Ross, Raymond Bean, and Reginald Bean. (Courtesy of Elwyn Lowe.)

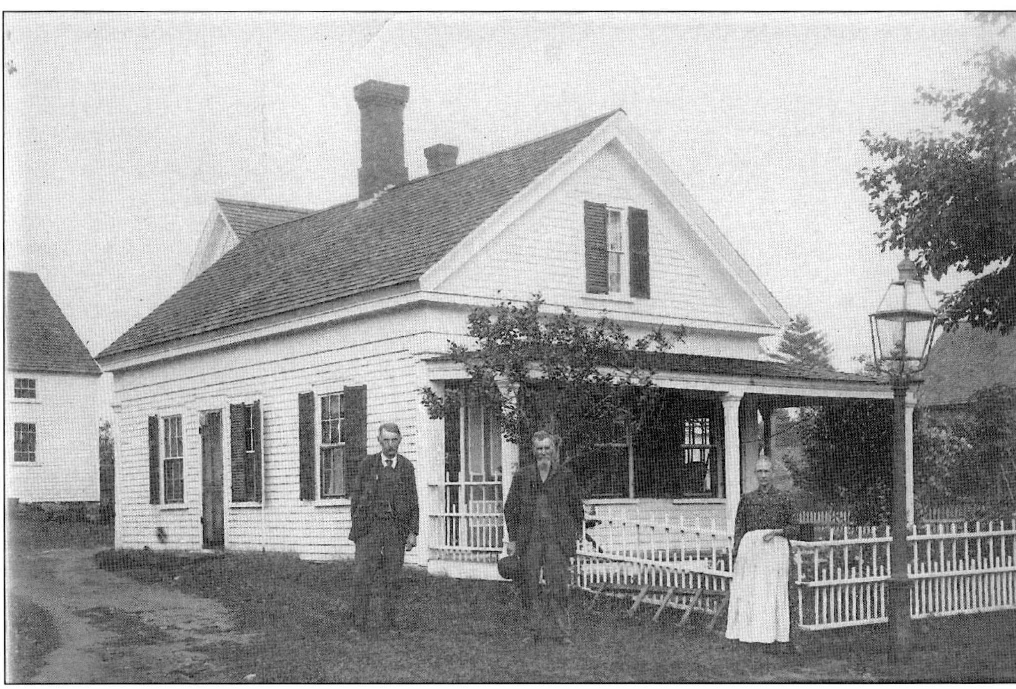

John Lowe (center) is in front of his home on Main Street in North Shapleigh. North Shapleigh's main street was lined with gas lamps, a testament to the village's affluence. John Hargraves, owner of Hargraves Woolen Mill, purchased the lamps and had them installed in several areas of town, including in front of the Freewill Baptist Church.

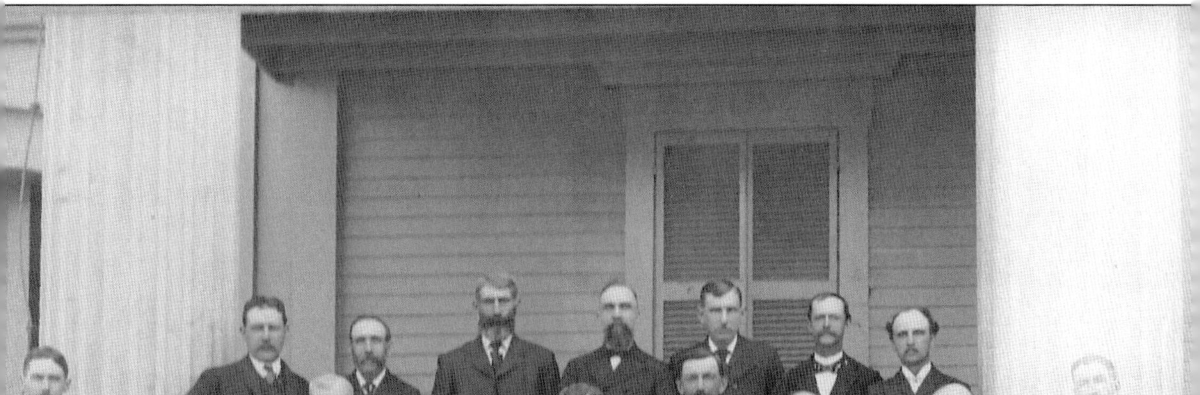

In all criminal cases and in those civil cases where monetary compensation is sought, the parties have a constitutional right to a jury trial. Trial juries were once also called traverse juries. Members of a traverse jury in Alfred, Maine, around 1900 are, from left to right, (first row) William S. Mathews, J. Byron Campbell (foreman, Biddeford), L. A. Smith (clerk, Saco), Jared Whitman (Old Orchard), James W. Smith (Kennebunkport), Eben Blaisdell (South Berwick), and John Lowe (North Shapleigh); (second row) Newell T. Fogg (sheriff, Sanford), J. S. P. Jones, (deputy sheriff, Lebanon), George C. Hayes (North Berwick), Ira T. Smith (North Waterboro), Daniel B. Andrews (Berwick), Simerc N. Ricker (Alfred), T. V. Smith (Buxton), George F. Piper (Biddeford), and Daniel Weare (York); (third row) John Moulton (Newfield), John R. Wentworth (Kittery), E. W. Moulton (East Parsonsfield), Munroe Goodwin (Saco), Charles P. Dutch (Kennebunkport), James N. Waterhouse (Dayton), and Lewis B. Libby (Sanford). (Courtesy of Elwyn Lowe.)

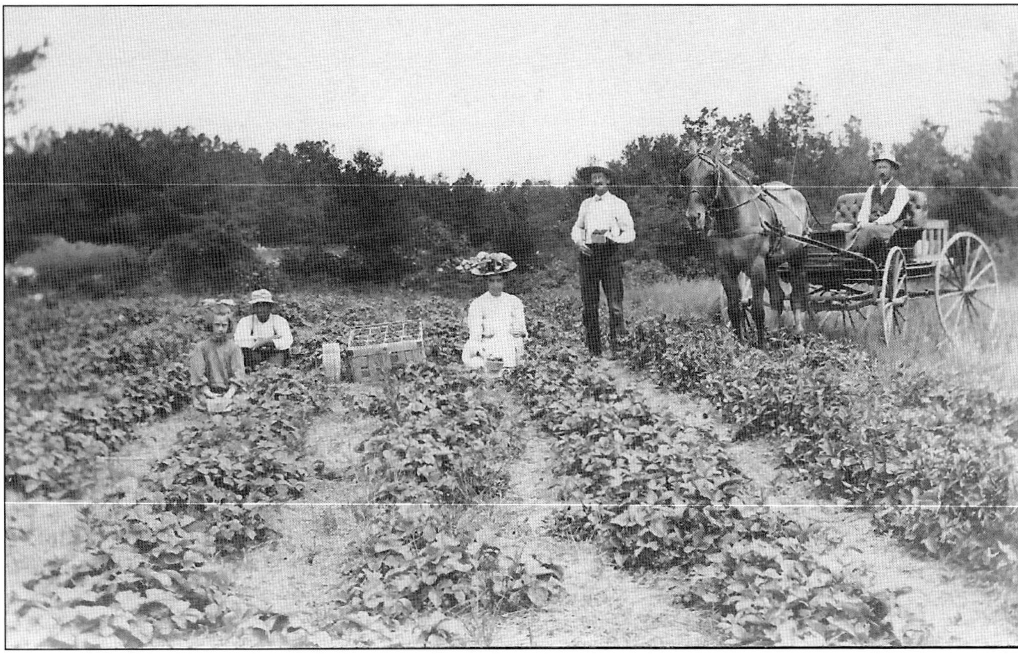

The Lowe strawberry farm in North Shapleigh is pictured around 1910. From left to right are Mildred Lowe, Ernest Lowe, Fannie Lowe, Herbert Lowe, and Reuben Lowe sitting in the horse-drawn carriage. (Courtesy of Elwyn Lowe.)

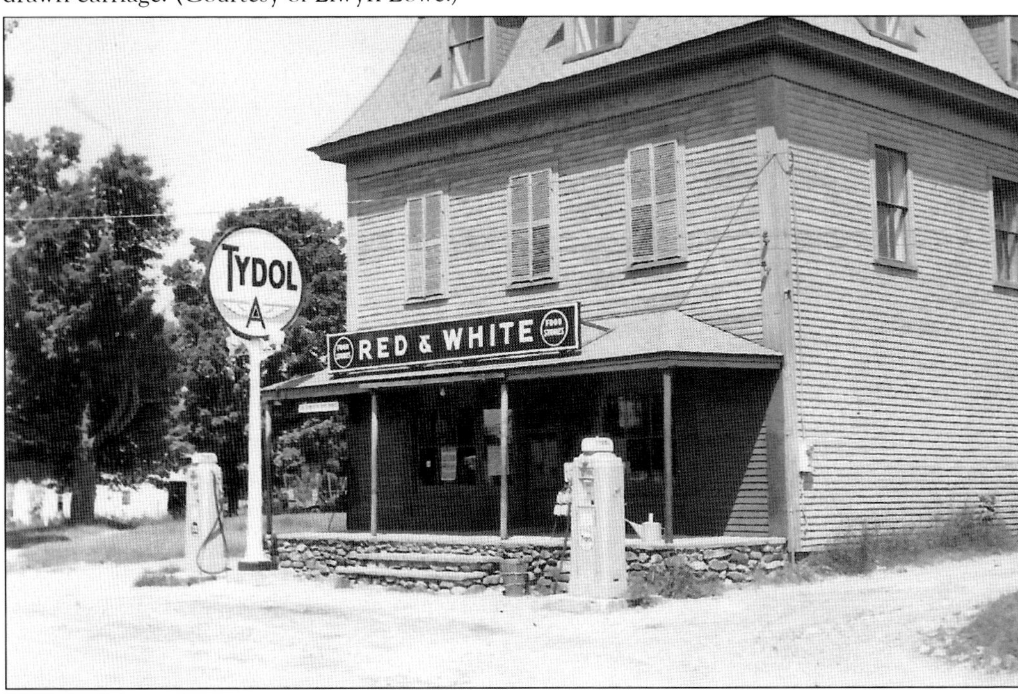

Owen Ross ran the Red and White General Store and post office in North Shapleigh from 1926 until 1956. The second floor was living quarters, and the Oswego Tribe, Independent Order of Red Men, held meetings on the third floor for many years. Unfortunately, this building burned to the ground in 1972. (Courtesy of Myrtle Howard.)

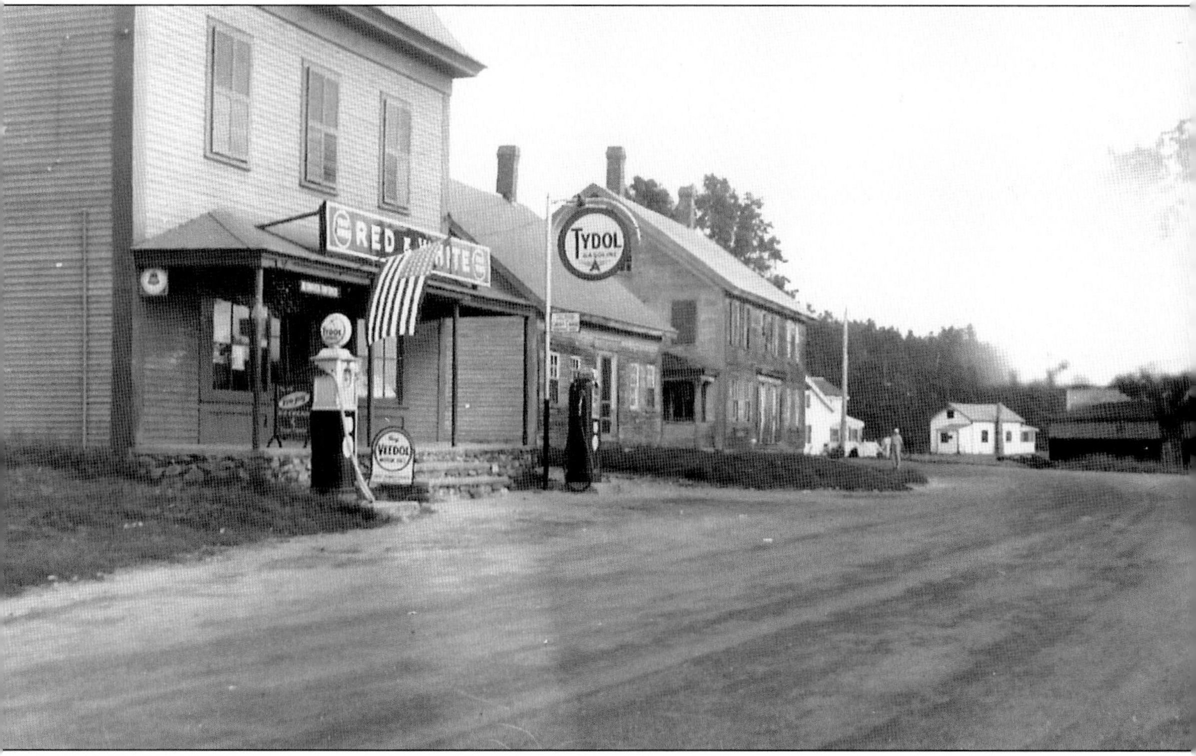

This is a view of Main Street in North Shapleigh looking south. Pictured here is the general store, and to the extreme right is the dance hall, originally the Hargraves Boarding House. In North Shapleigh's heyday, there were two general stores, an active church, a post office, a one-room schoolhouse, a woolen mill, sawmill, blacksmith shop, a forge and foundry, a box shop, and a leatherboard factory. The leatherboard factory manufactured artificial leather using leather scraps and other materials. Despite North Shapleigh's potential to become the business center of Shapleigh, the closing of Hargraves Woolen Mill marked the end of its economic growth, and there are presently no businesses within North Shapleigh. Over time, it has reverted back to its original status as a rural community that many descendants of the original settlers call home. (Courtesy of Donna Applebee.)

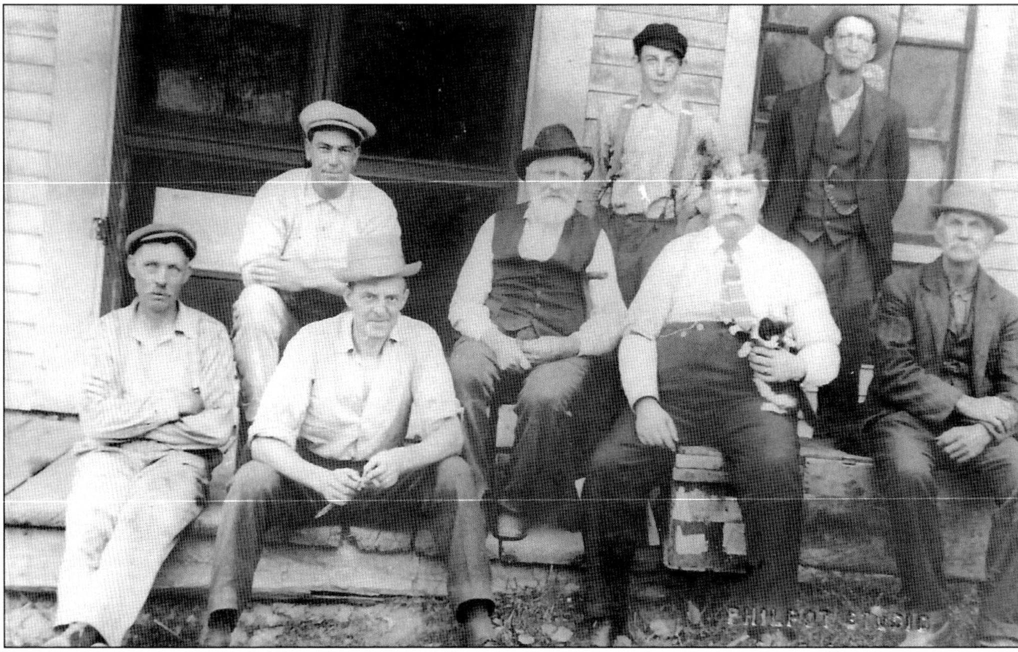

Locals sit outside James Coffin's General Store in North Shapleigh. From left to right are (first row) Everett Webber, ? Foster, Frank Furlong (holding cat), and Albert Davis; (second row) Charles Ham, James Coffin, Sidney Hammond, and Phineas Ham. Coffin was also the first postmaster in North Shapleigh. The North Shapleigh post office (zip code 04060) was closed in 1997.

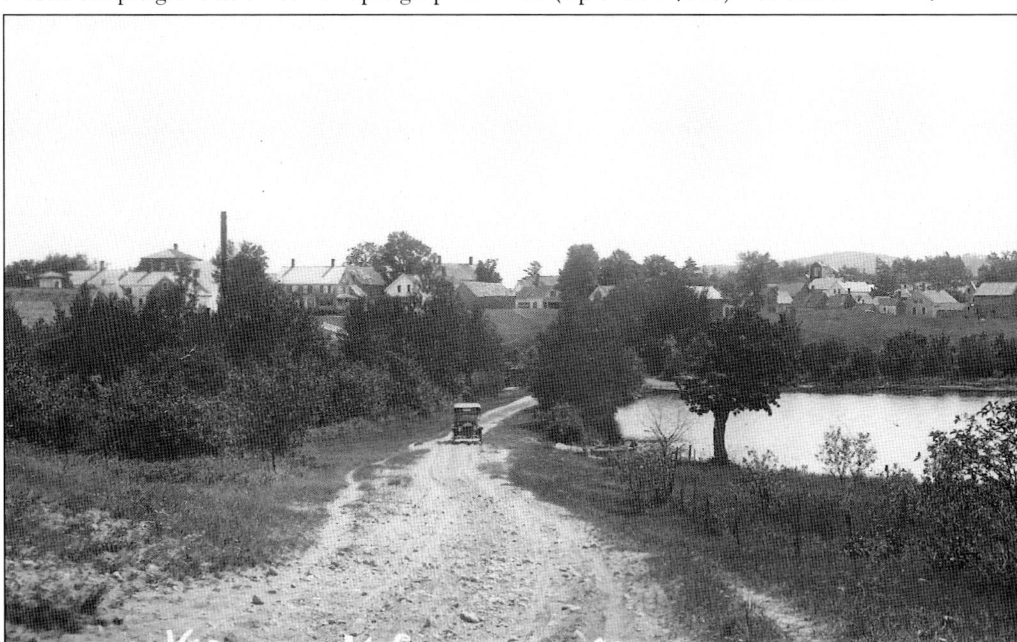

This view from the bridge looks towards the center of the village of North Shapleigh. Formerly known as Shapleigh Iron Works or Twombly's Mills, North Shapleigh is located in the northern part of town and borders Newfield. The tall chimney of the Hargraves Woolen Mill can be seen on the left.

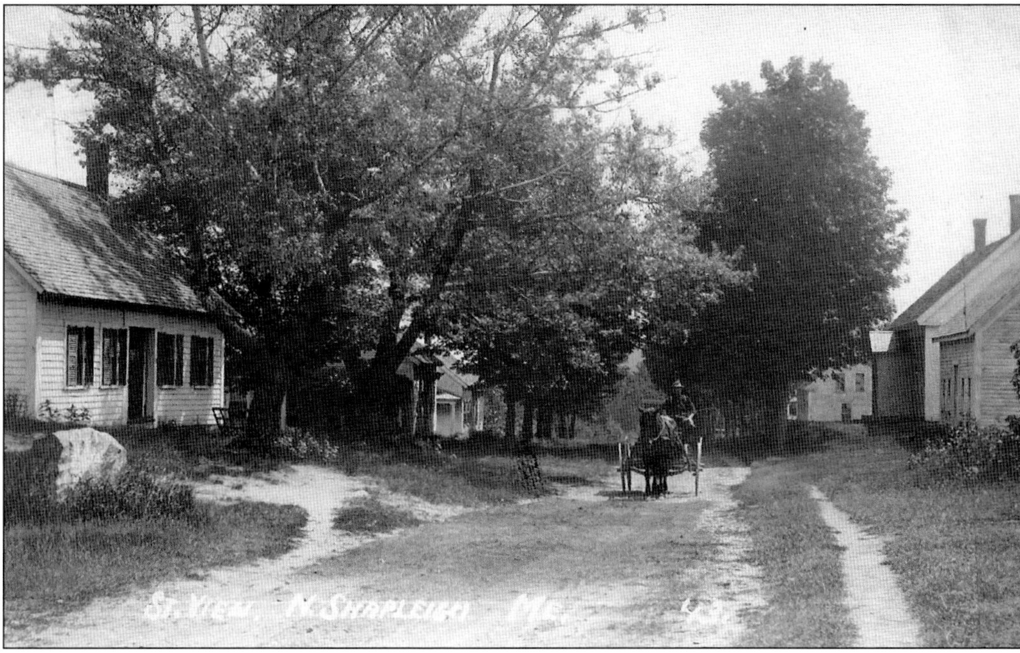

A horse and buggy travel along the beautiful, tree-lined streets of North Shapleigh as it looked at the turn of the century. The white house on the left was moved to this location by oxen from the corner of Mann Road and Main Street. Although paved now, many of the rural roads of Shapleigh are still canopied by mature trees.

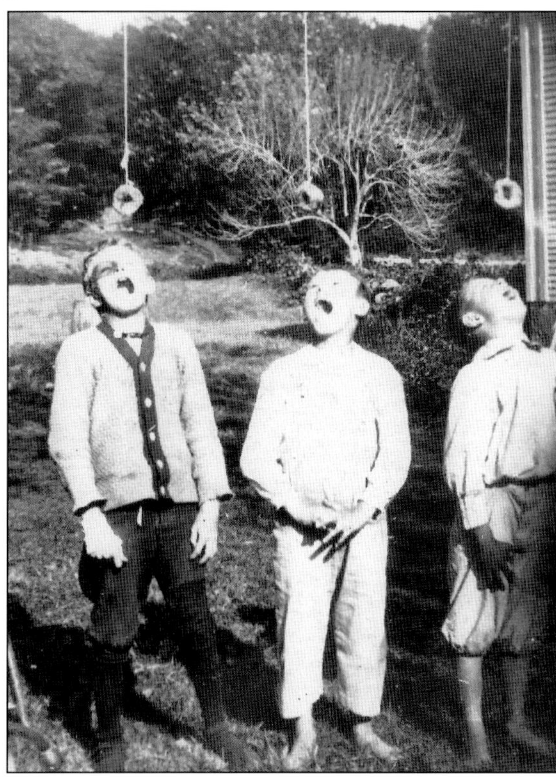

Although life in the country was full of hard work, there was always time for a little fun and games. Young boys play a round of "bite the doughnut" that provides lots of amusement for everyone, as adults control the height.

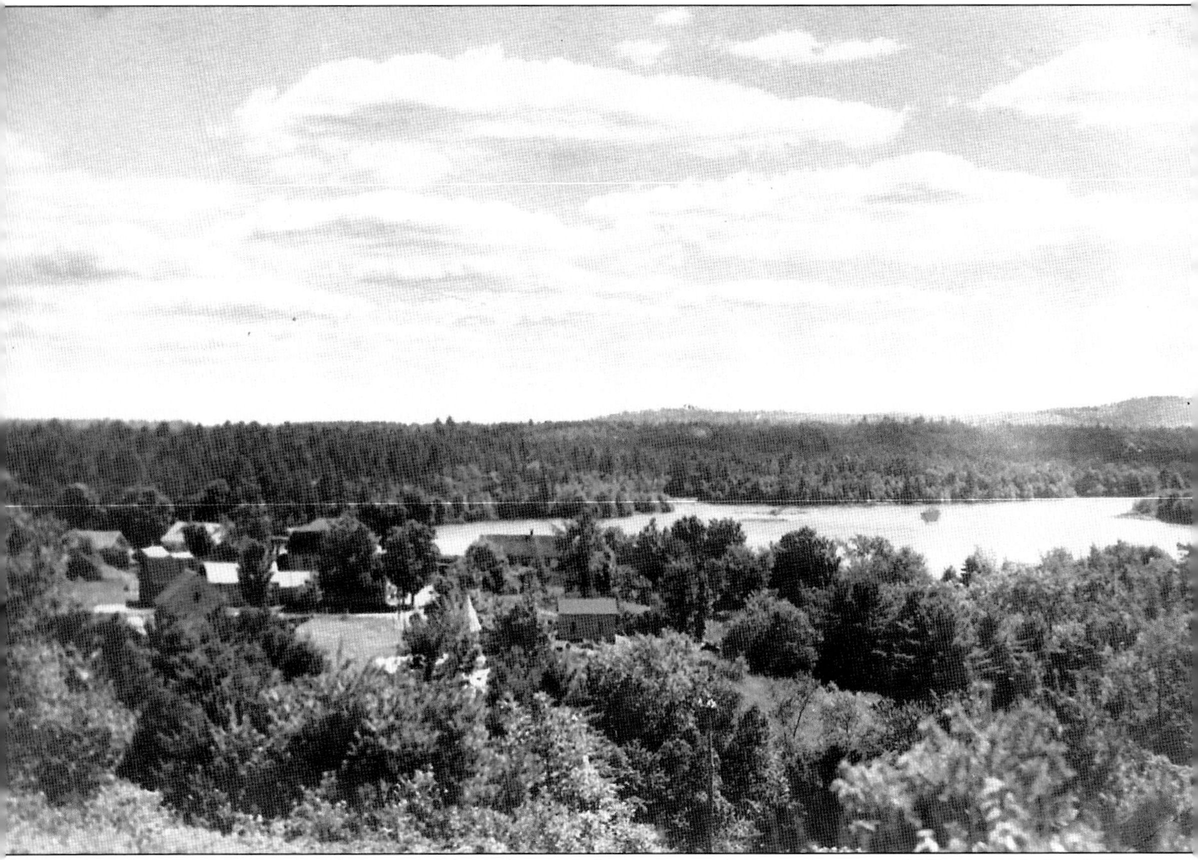

This is a view of North Shapleigh and Little Ossipee Pond from Whitten Hill in 1935. In 1799, Joseph and William Linscott chose this area to build a sawmill and a blacksmith shop. This photograph represents the typical landscape of Shapleigh as it showcases the dense forests, rolling hills, lakes, and villages. These geographic features are what drew many of the early settlers. Despite the economic hardships of Shapleigh and its villages over the years, the town and its people still maintain a public school system, an independent government and its offices, several churches, fire and rescue departments, civic organizations, a post office, and many private businesses. Since the time of this picture, Shapleigh's population has increased to over 2,500 permanent residents. As is evident of the continued growth of this area, it is safe to say that many of these same features continue to attract new residents and businesses.

Two

The Lakes Region

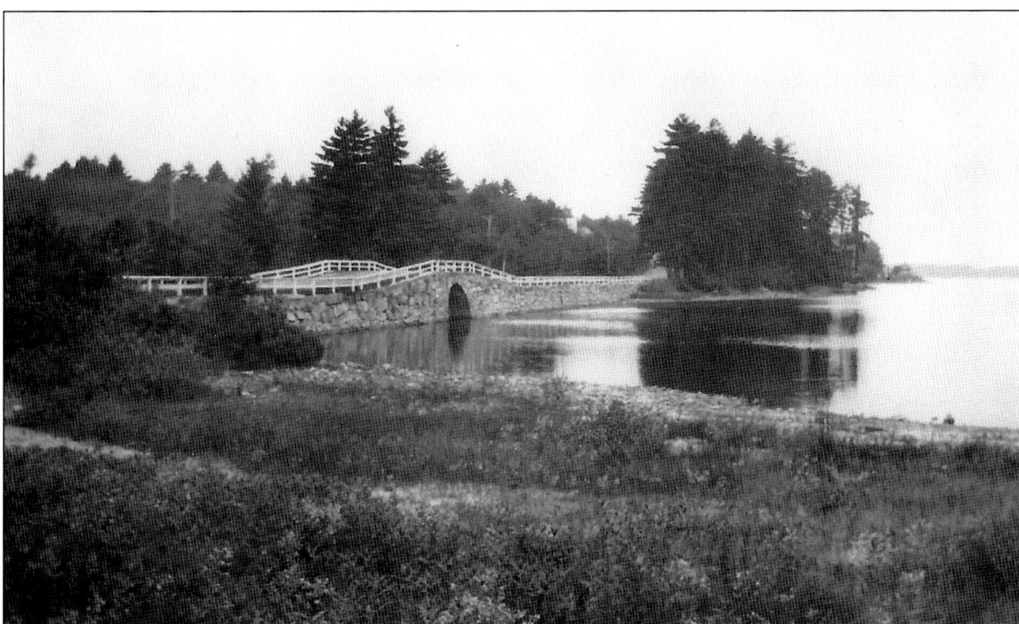

This stone bridge separates Acton and Shapleigh and is considered the "Gateway to the Lakes Region." There are 16 freshwater lakes and ponds within its borders, namely Mousam Lake, Square Pond, Great East Lake, Wilson Lake, Horn Pond, Balch Lake, Loon Pond, Hansen Pond, Moose Pond, Swan Pond, Pine Springs Lake, Silver Lake, Granny Kent Pond, Little Poverty Pond, Goose Pond, and Little Ossipee Pond.

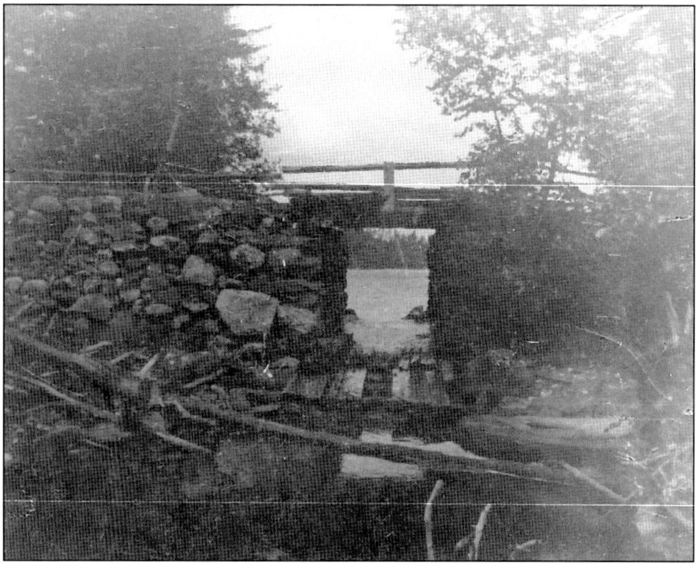

Capt. William Rogers came to Emery Mills and built what would be the first bridge across the Mousam Lake narrows shortly before 1776. Rogers also built what is believed to be the first house in the West Parish, later known as Acton. This crude wooden bridge was built for foot traffic and the occasional horse and buggy. In 1903, the bridge and the Emery Mills Dam were reconstructed. The bridge was reengineered to accommodate increased traffic to Acton and neighboring towns.

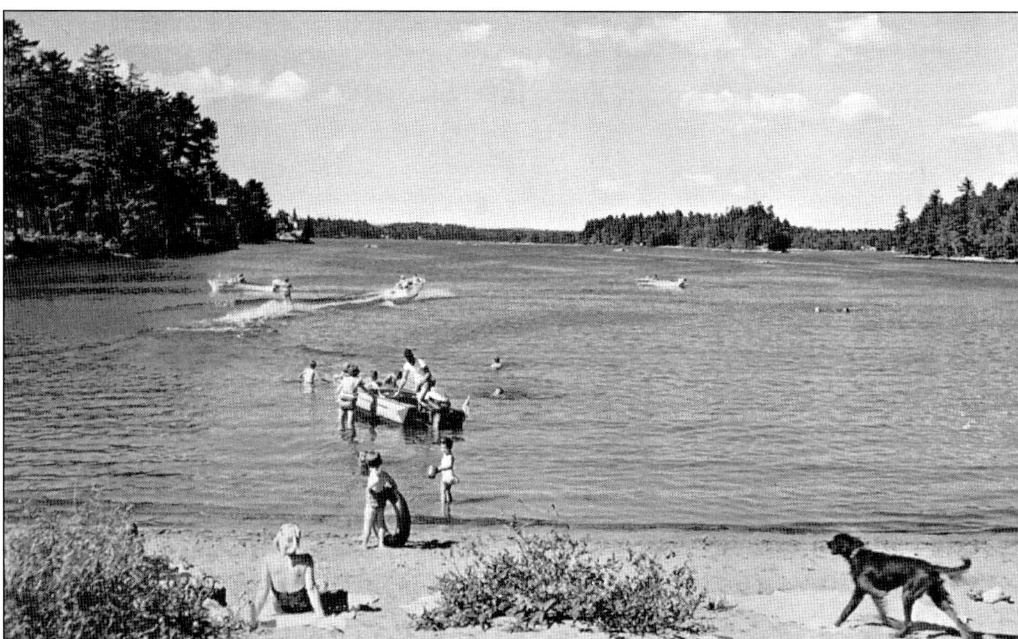

The public beach at lower Mousam Lake is pictured in 1976. Swimming, boating, sunbathing, and playing in the sand are always a favorite pastime for summers in Maine. This beach is located at the junction of Route 11 and 109. The times may have changed, but the activities at this beach are still the same today. (Courtesy of Melissa Conner.)

This aerial view of Mousam Lake was taken in 1955. Originally named Long Pond, this narrow, 5-mile-long lake is stocked with brook, brown, and lake trout. At almost 100 feet deep, it is ideal for summer and winter fishing. Mousam Lake has many coves and inlets that makes it perfect for kayaking, canoeing and motorboating. In the past 50-plus years, the shoreline has become dotted with camps, cottages, and year-round homes. (Courtesy of Marguerite Stanley.)

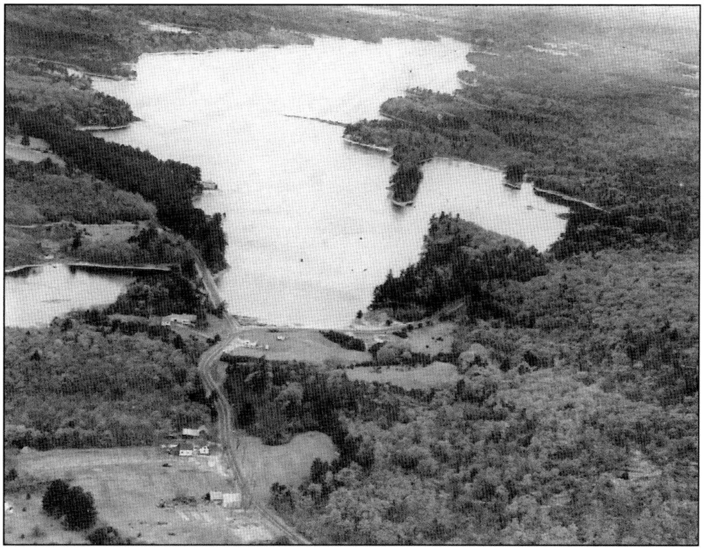

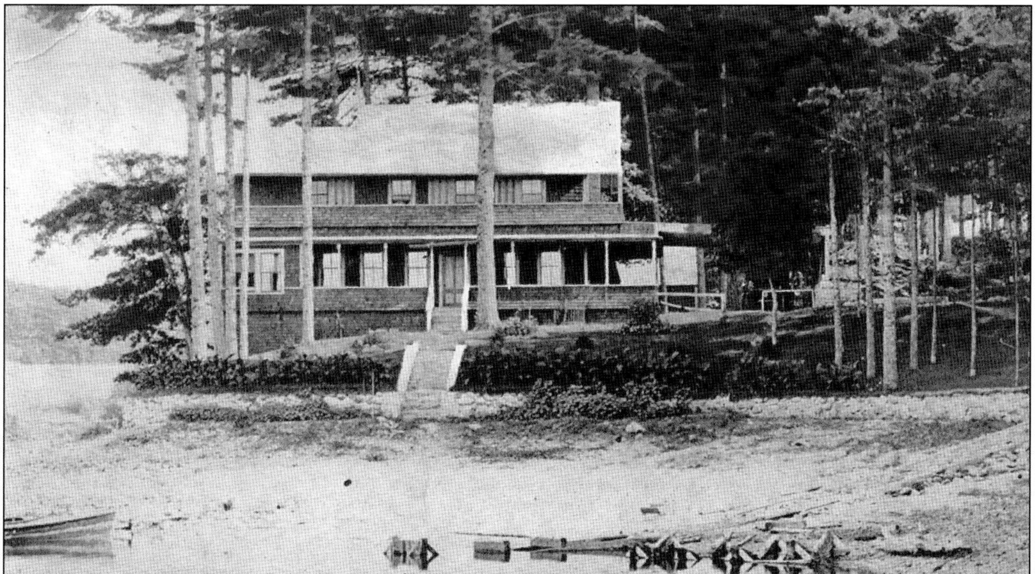

Ernest Goodall was an avid hunter/fisherman and loved to entertain. In the late 1800s, he built what he called "The Long Pond Club House" on the western shore of Mousam Lake. The second floor housed guest bedrooms, each with its own lockable entry. Goodall, a prominent businessman from Sanford, used his clubhouse as a retreat for many of his friends and professional associates.

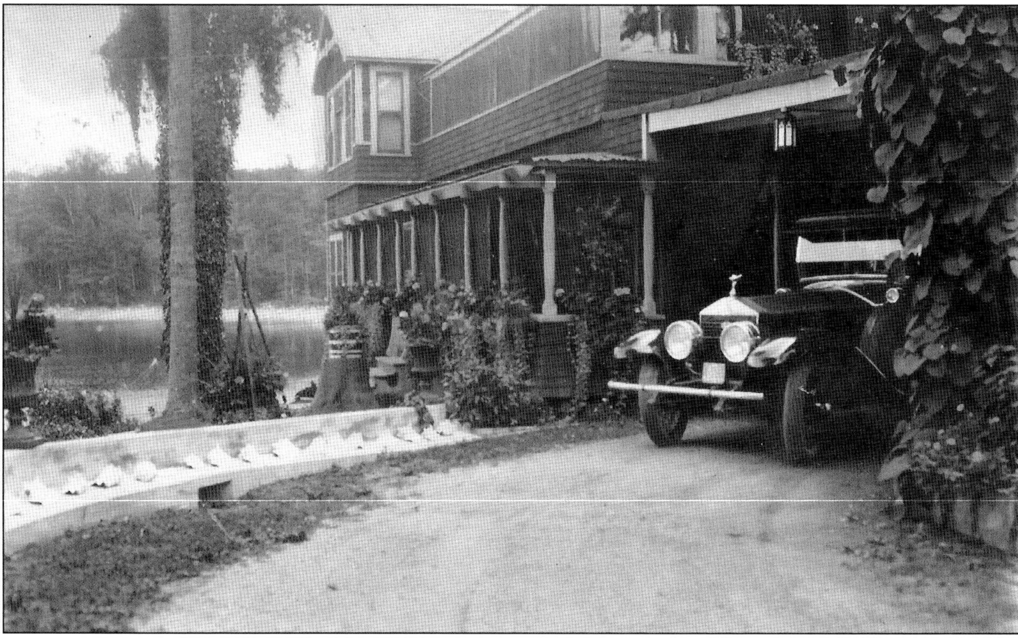

Ernest Goodall's Rolls Royce is parked under the portico at the Long Pond Club House around 1920. Incidentally, in 1899, Goodall purchased the first automobile in Sanford, a Marlboro Steamer, which with a full head of steam could reach a speed of 45 miles per hour.

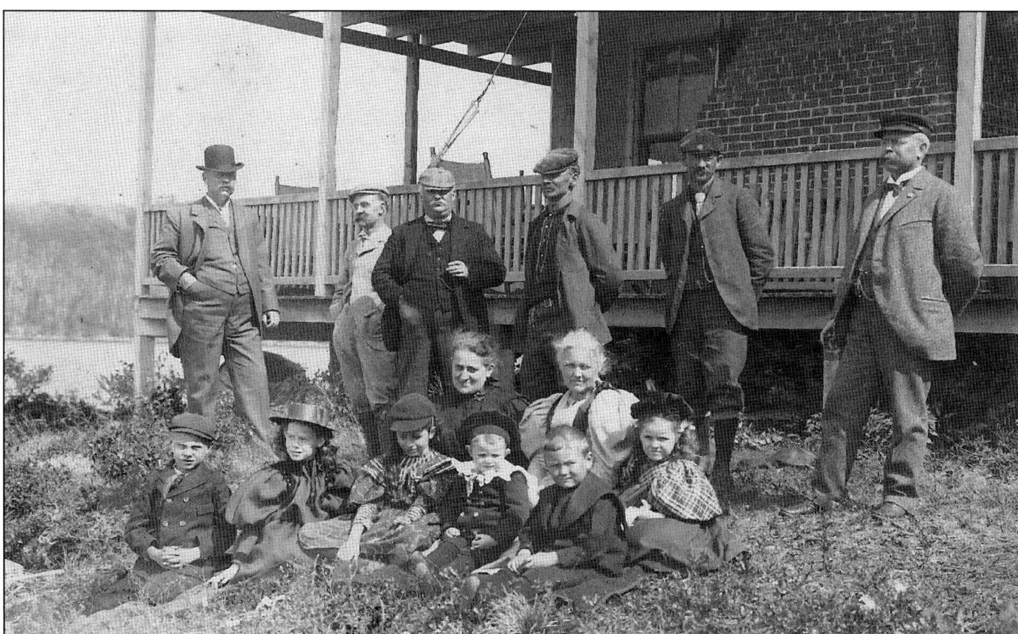

Members of the Goodall family are at one of their camps on Mousam Lake. The Goodall families were prominent summer residents of Mousam Lake who also owned properties on Square Pond and Great East Lake.

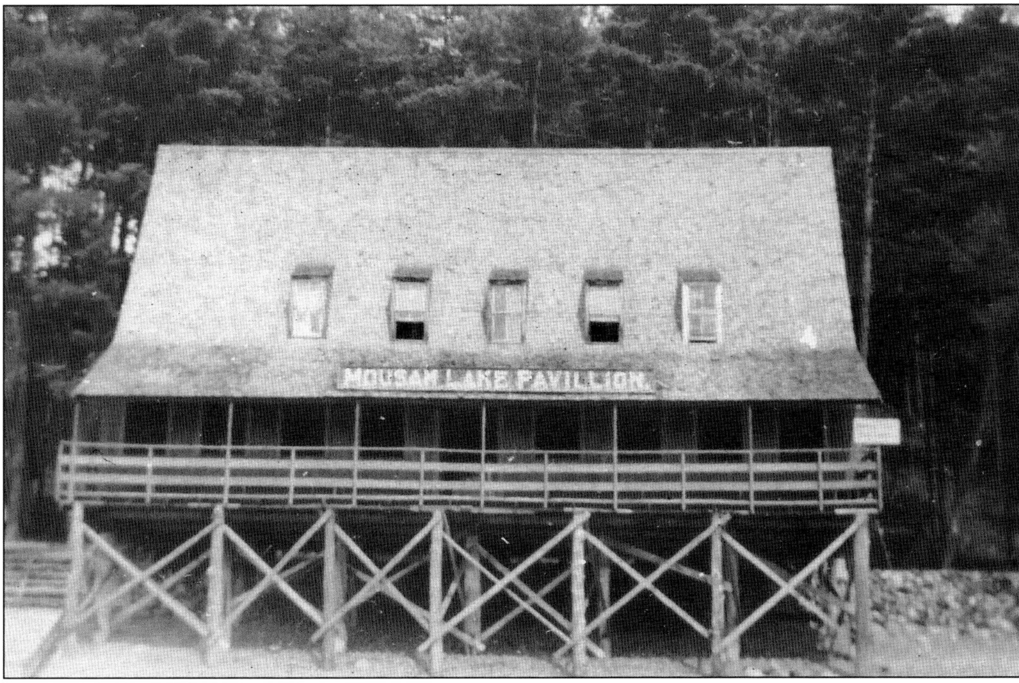

The Mousam Lake Pavilion, part of the G.A.R. (Grand American Republic) camps, is pictured in 1914. As the water level of the lake increased, the pavilion eventually sat over the water. In 1917, the entire complex was purchased by Charles and Alice Meader. Meader tore down the original pavilion and built a new dance hall he called "Meader's Casino."

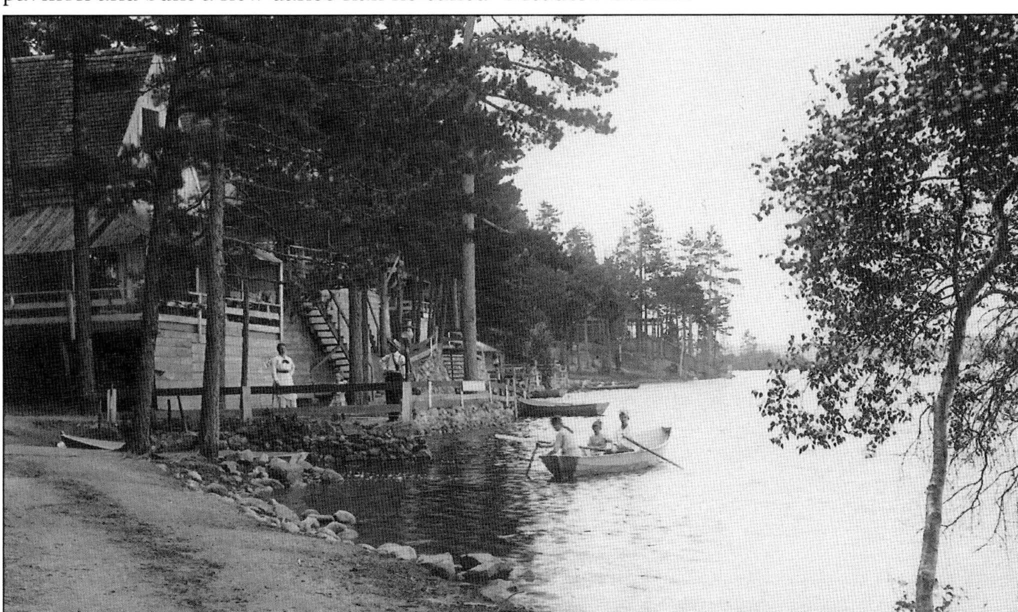

Each of the nine G.A.R. camps was named after a Civil War general except for the first one, Admiral Dewey. The others were Generals Miles, Sheridan, Needham, Grant, Hooker, Anderson, Banks, and Butler. Individual portraits were displayed inside the respective cottages. The complex also contained a store, an icehouse, a boathouse, stables, and a bandstand.

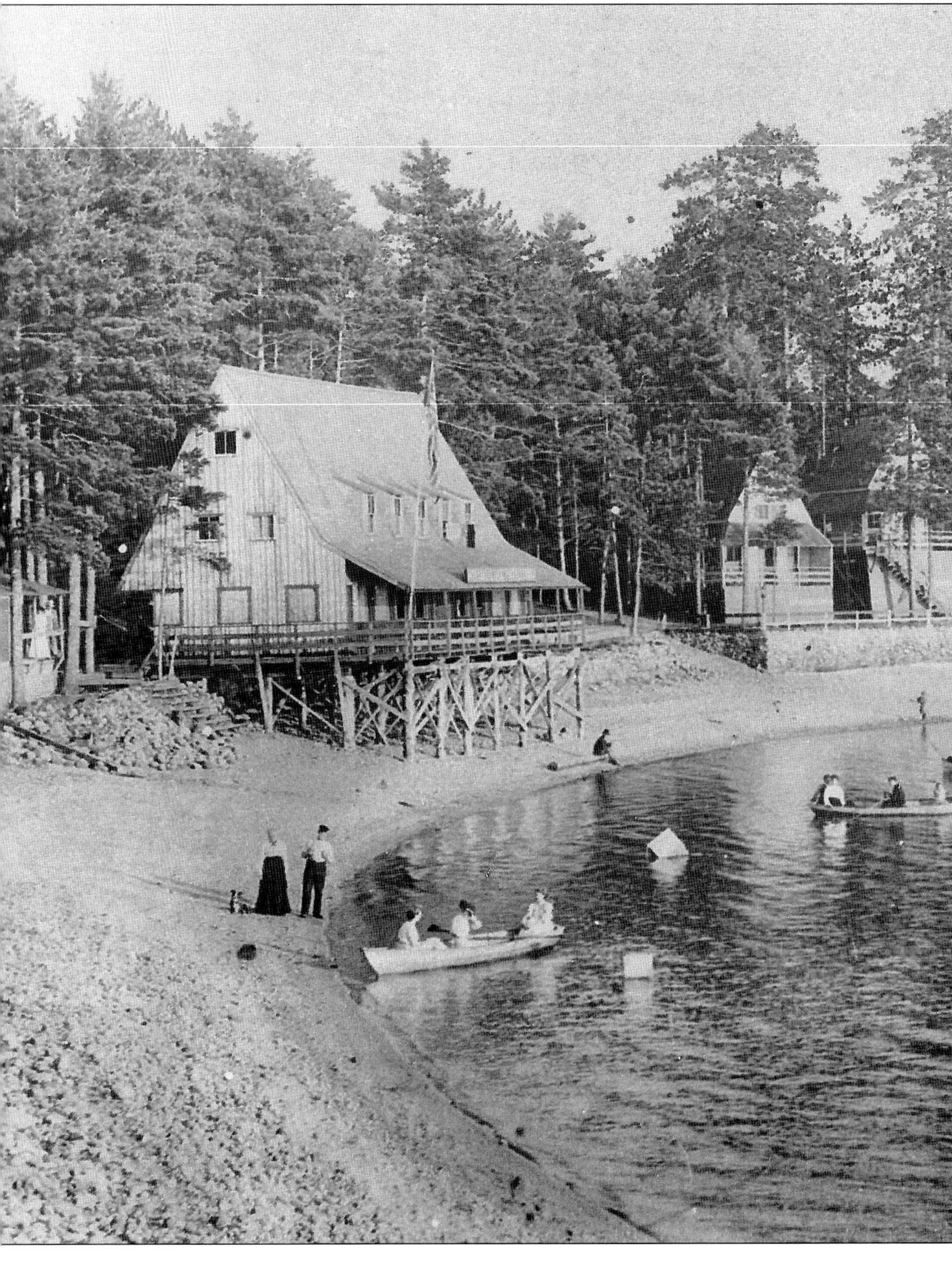

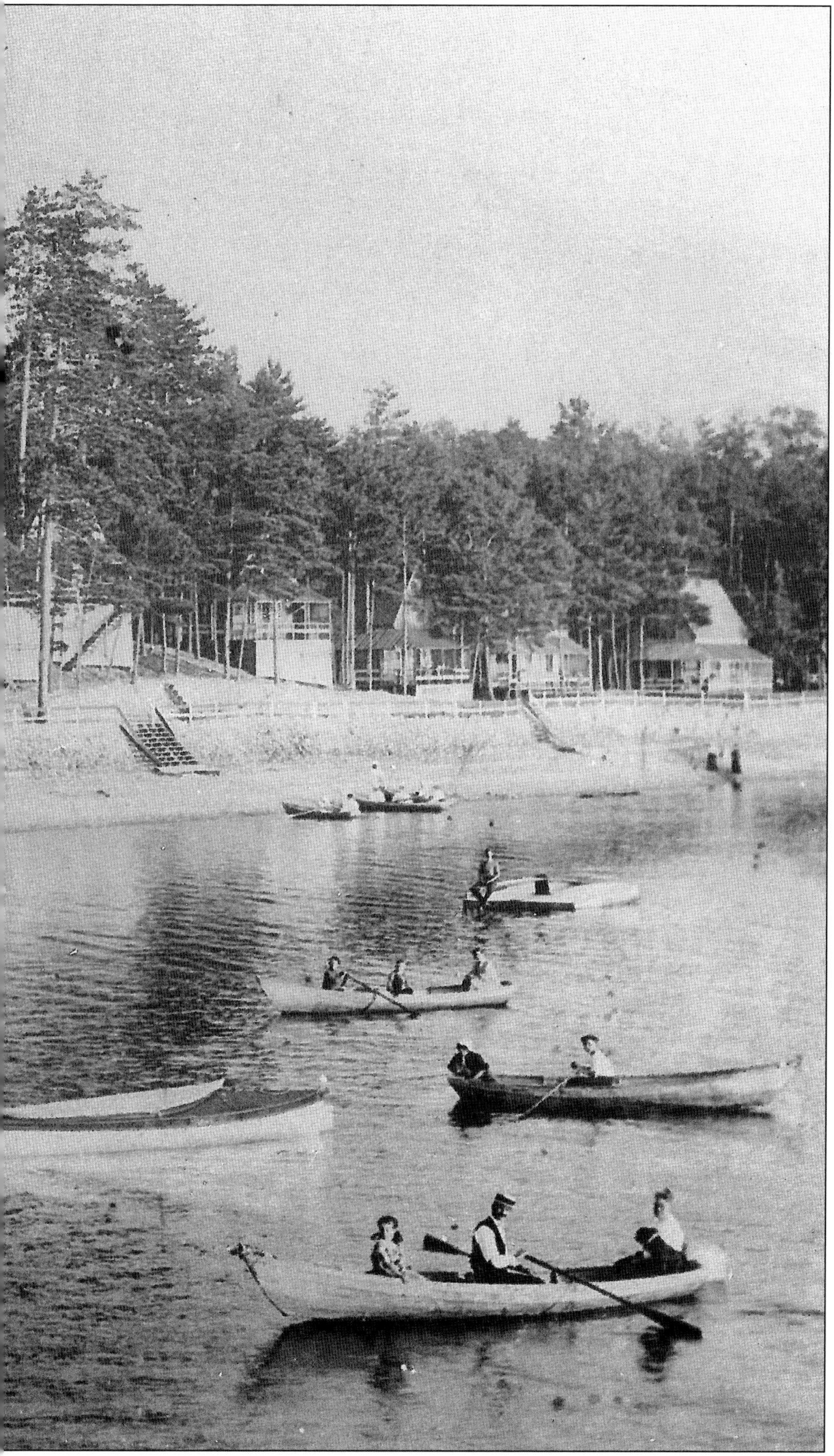

In 1896, Asa Lerned had nine camps built on Mousam Lake in Shapleigh. Lerned called this complex the G.A.R. camps. The cottages were furnished with four spring beds, cook stove, dishes, silver knives and forks, spoons, and lamps. Fuel and lights were also supplied. Renters had to furnish sheets, pillow slips, towels, and napkins. Milk and ice were free. The complete cost was $1.25 per day. Many affluent families, some traveling from out of state, would rent these cottages annually. Many a child learned how to swim, row a boat, and fish off these shores.

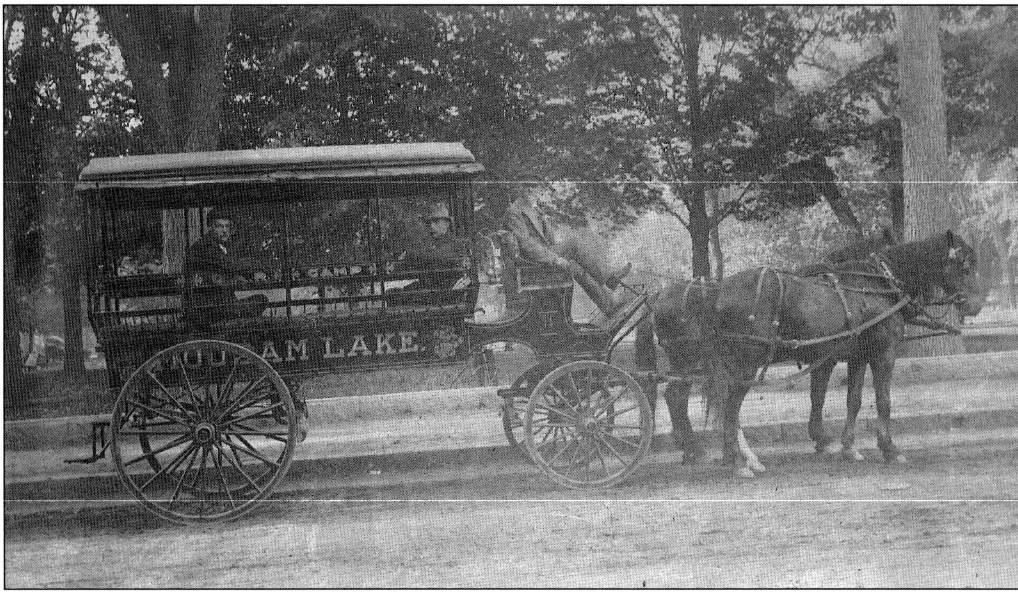

Asa Lerned transported his summer guests to and from the G.A.R. camps in this carryall for 50¢ each way, with children riding for half price. Passengers were picked up and dropped off at the Springvale train depot 5 miles away.

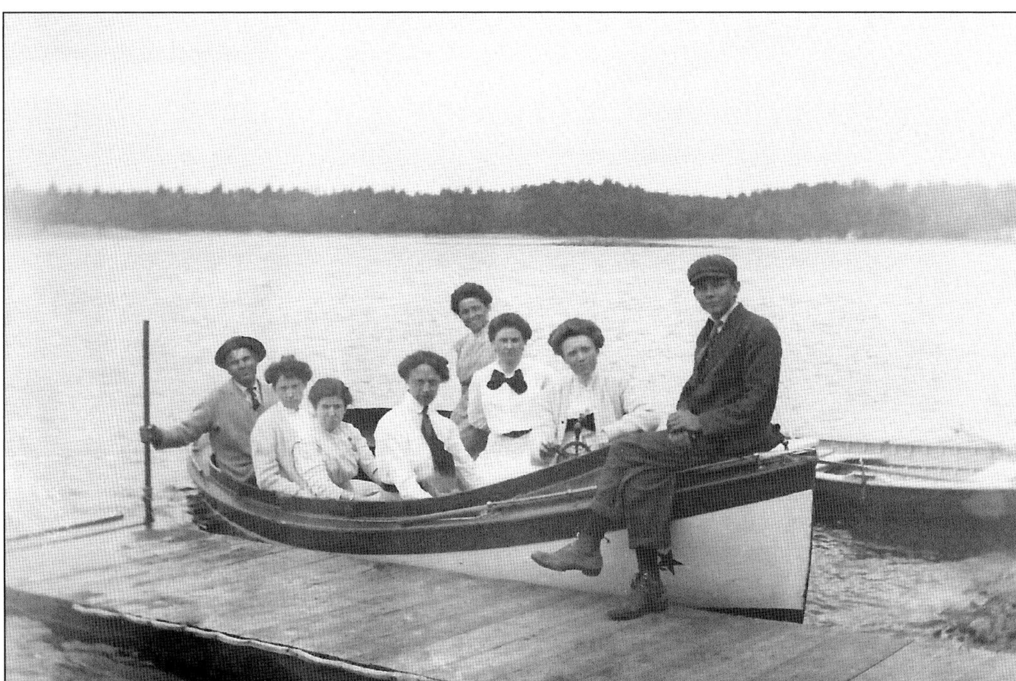

A beautiful day for a leisurely boat ride on Mousam Lake is photographed here. Each G.A.R. cottage also had its own rowboat for the renters to enjoy. Mousam Lake is surrounded by splendid scenery and mountains and is 5 miles long and 1 mile wide. It is interesting to note that even boating was an event that one dressed up for.

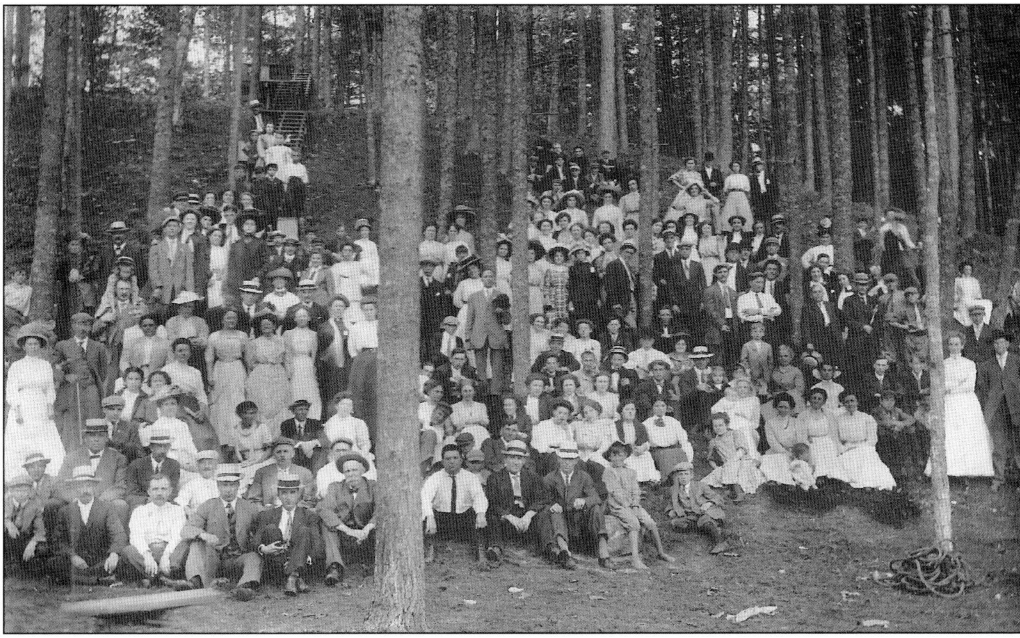

In August 1913, approximately 1,300 Springvale shoe shop workers and their families enjoyed a summer outing at the G.A.R. camps on Mousam Lake. Dancing, boating, and competitive games were among the list of activities for all to enjoy. In the bottom picture, women have their hammers and nails in hand, ready to compete against one another to see who can pound the most nails into a stump in a limited amount of time.

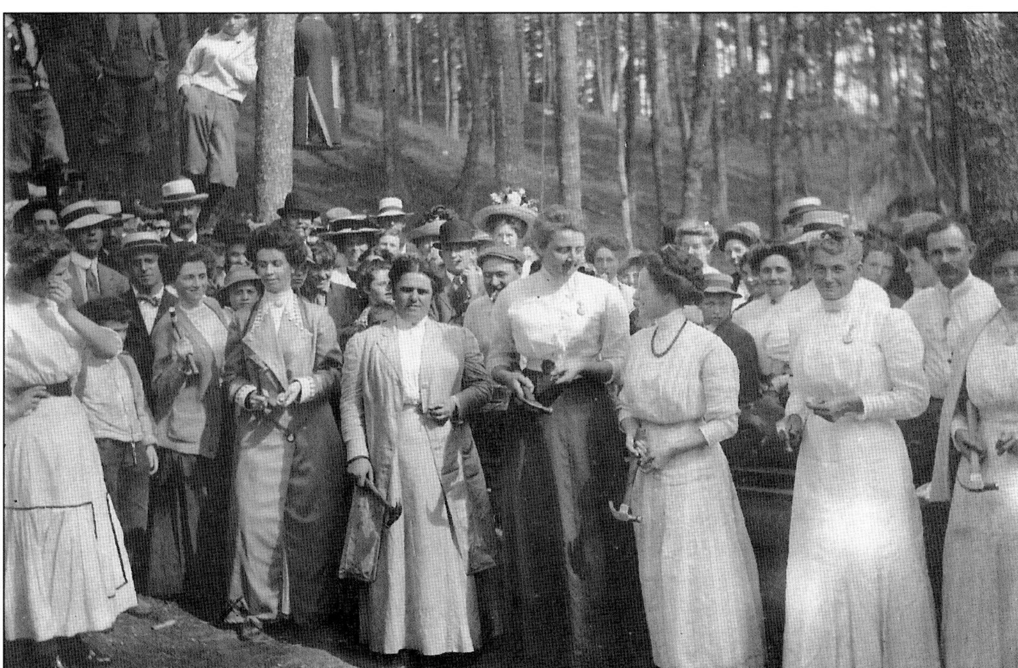

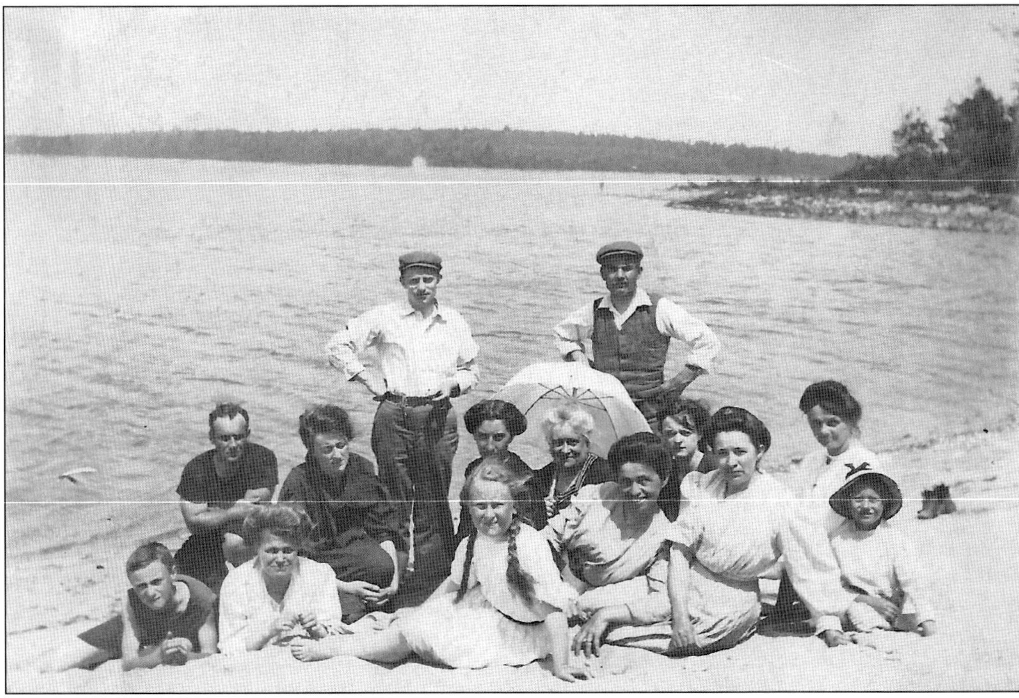

Spending summers at the lake is a way of life for many New Englanders and a time for families and friends to reunite and make memories that will last a lifetime. If one were fortunate enough to own a camp on a lake, chances were that the house was always full of visiting friends and relatives. This is true even in today's society—everybody loves going to camp!

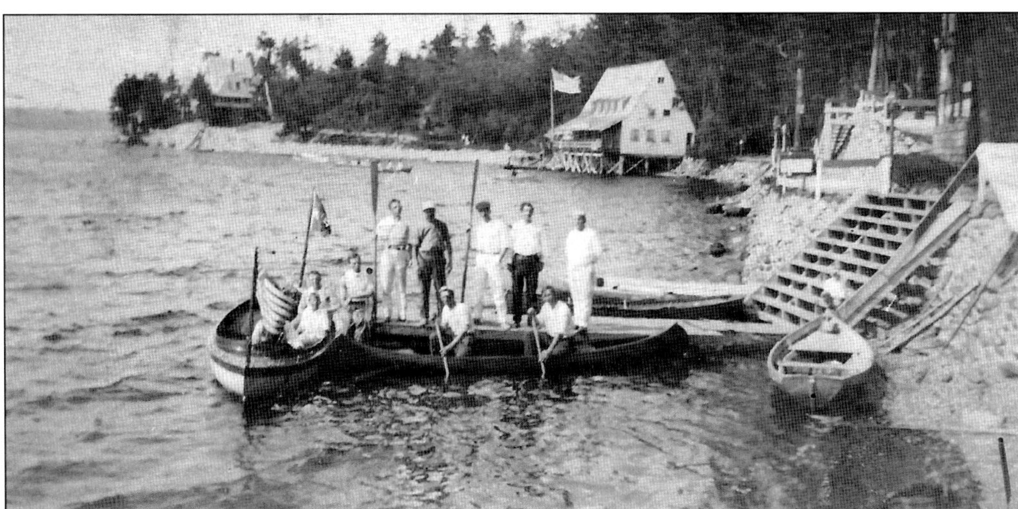

Families enjoyed the lazy days of summer on Mousam Lake. It was not uncommon for women and children to move to the camp for the entire summer, with the men folk joining them on the weekends, after their workweek was finished. Many families continue this summer strategy today.

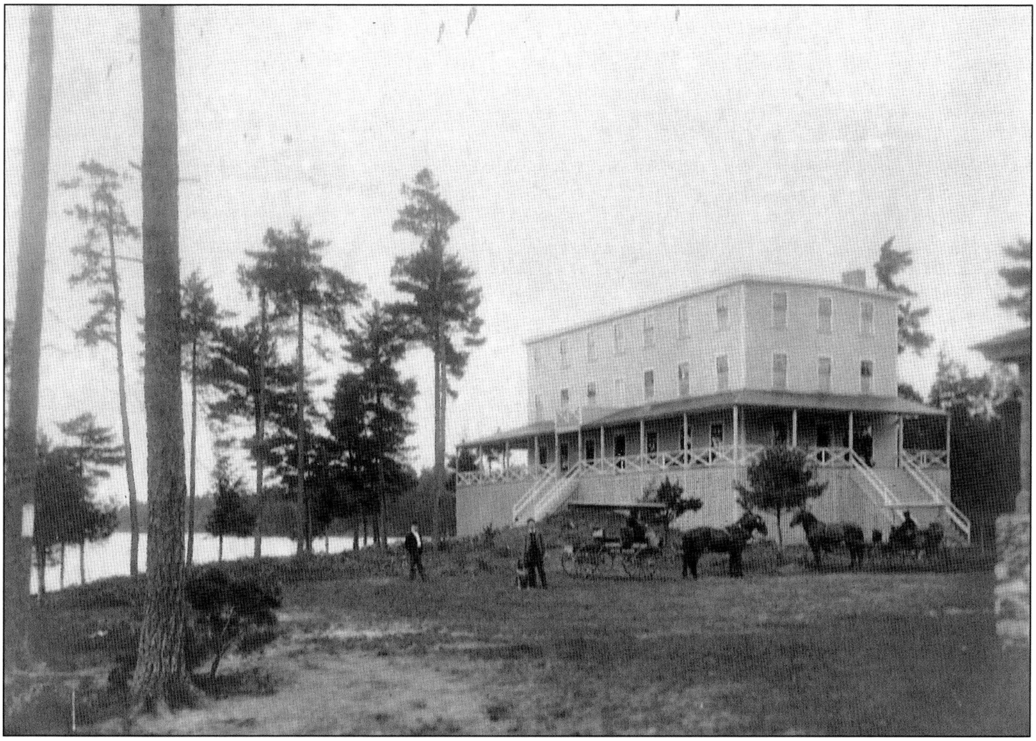

The Long Way Inn, built in 1904, was situated on the eastern shore of Mousam Lake. Three sides of this three-story hotel faced the water, which gave all guests the best possible views. The Long Way Inn could provide up to 50 guests with the most modern conveniences at the time at a rate of $10 per person. The inn was torn down and a summer cottage built in its place. In the bottom picture, a portion of the Long Way Inn can be seen on the extreme left. This cottage was built by Reverend Lowell of the Shapleigh Baptist Church and later sold and used as part of the Long Way Inn. The water level is much lower than it is today, providing more sandy beach areas.

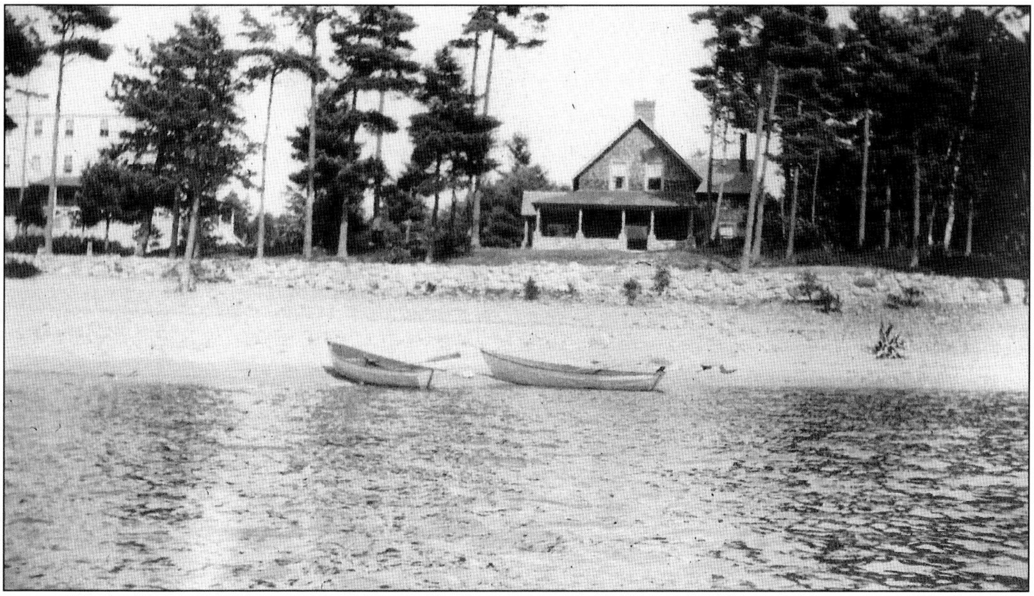

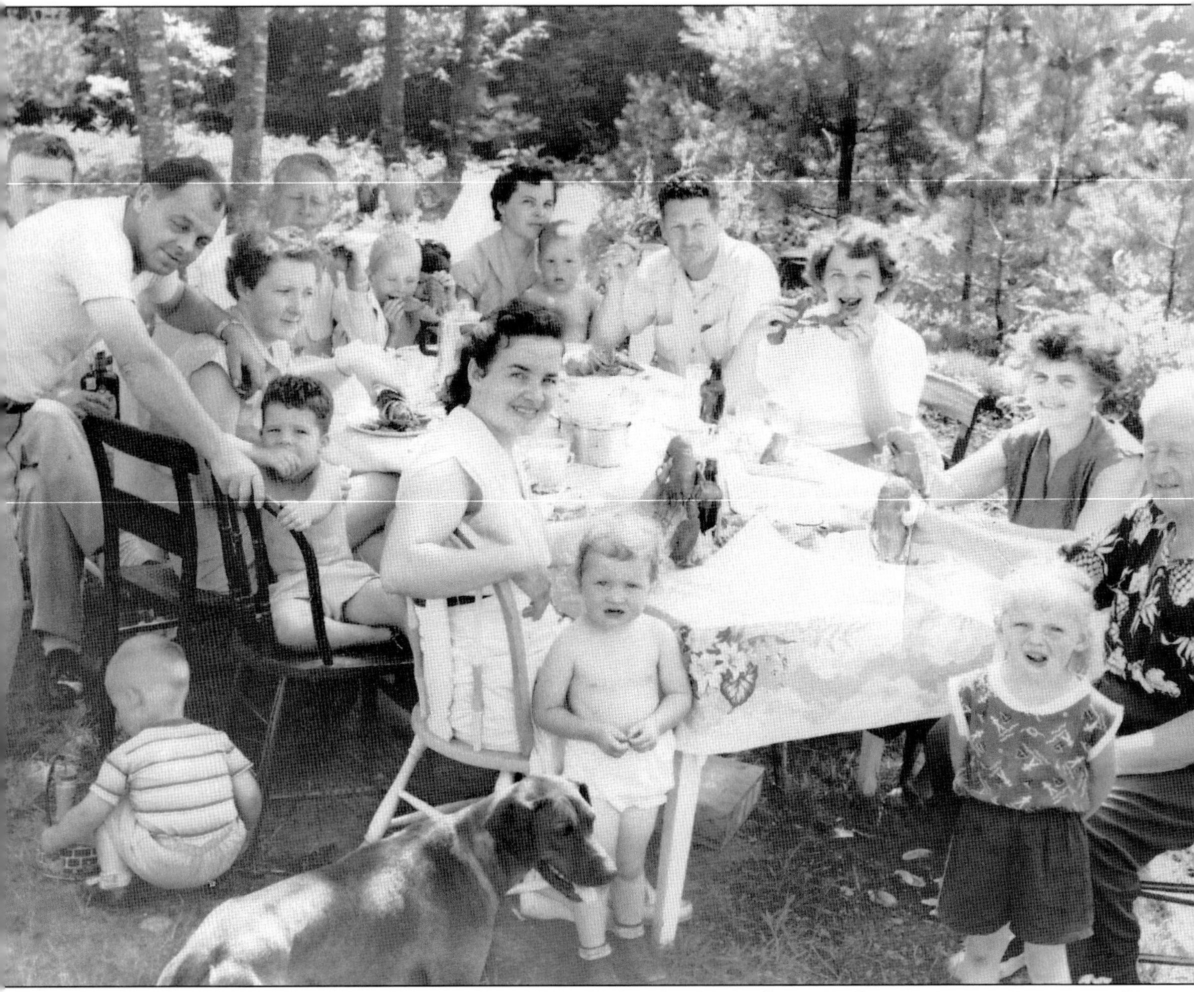

Benjamin Webber was one of the first settlers in Shapleigh. At the time the town was incorporated in 1785, those families already settled were gratuitously awarded the property they occupied. Almost 200 years later, in 1954, Webber's descendants gather for a lobster feast at Mousam Lake. This gathering represents four generations. Starting front center and continuing clockwise around the table are the following: Pamela Webber (child), Thelma Webber, Robert Webber (child on ground), Bryant Evans (child), Norma Webber Evans, Harold Evans, Fred Webber, Fred Gilbert Webber, Gilbert Webber (child), Linda Webber (child), Margaret Webber holding Irving Evans, Theodore Webber, Frances Webber, Marie Webber, Herbert Webber, Jacqueline Webber, and dog Trigger. Summertime is perfect for family reunions, and a New England clambake is always a favorite. Steamed clams, corn on the cob, lobster, cold drinks, and fresh strawberries atop homemade biscuits round out the menu of this Downeast feast. These summer reunions became traditions that are still carried on today in many families—and hopefully for many generations to follow. (Courtesy of Irving Evans.)

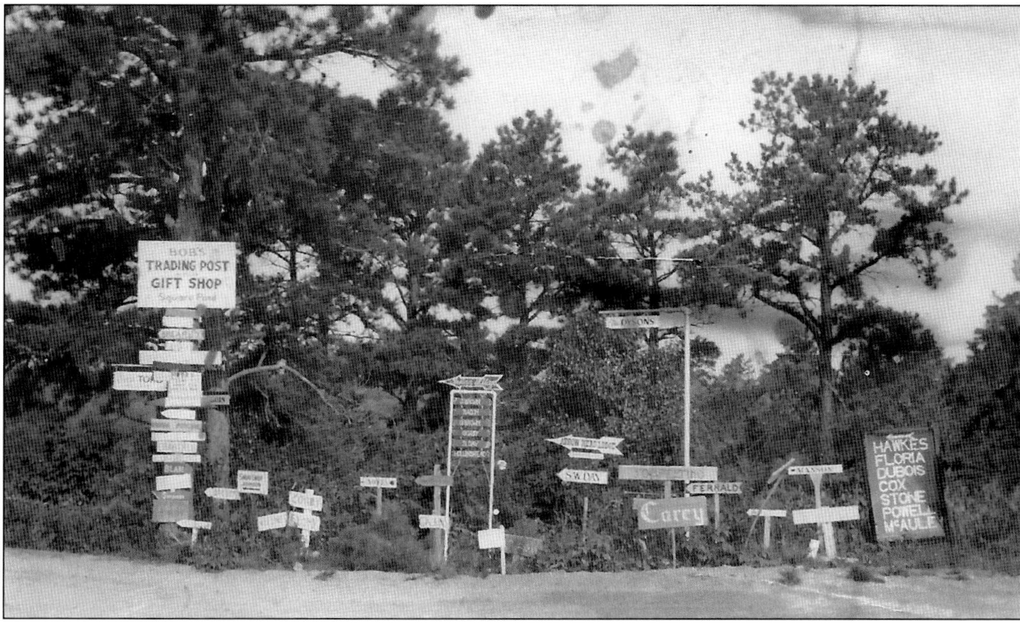

Camp signs dot the side of the road to assist travelers in finding their way through the maze of roads leading to the waters edge of the eastern shore of Square Pond. These signs are indicative of every camp road in Maine and can still be found while traveling in and around lakes and ponds today. (Courtesy of Robert Pike.)

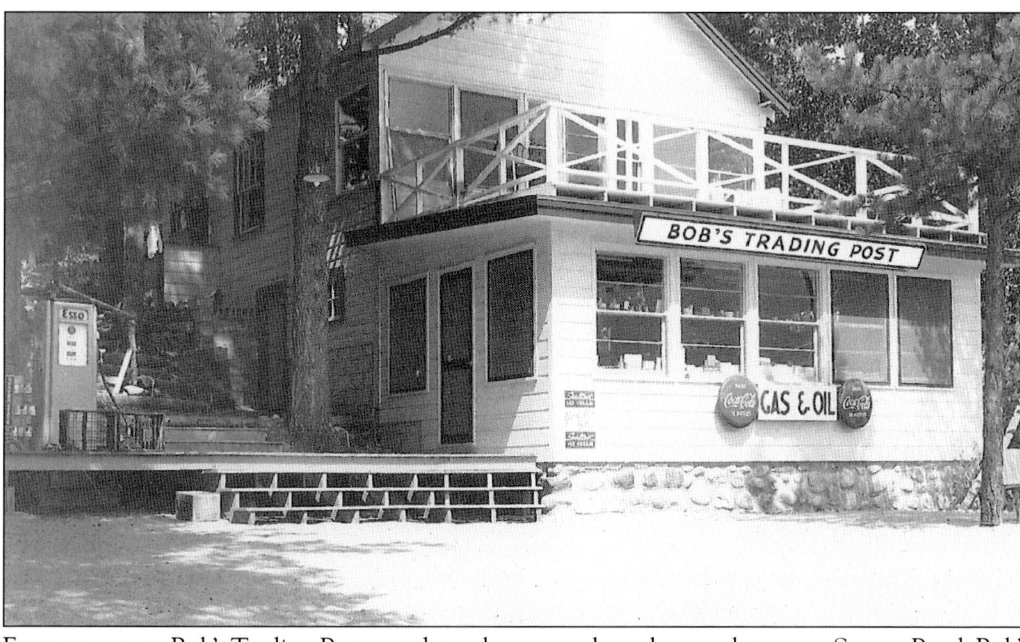

For many years, Bob's Trading Post was the only gas supply and general store on Square Pond. Bob's was a favorite for hamburgers, frappes, ice cream, penny candy, collectibles, and local souvenirs. (Courtesy of Robert Pike.)

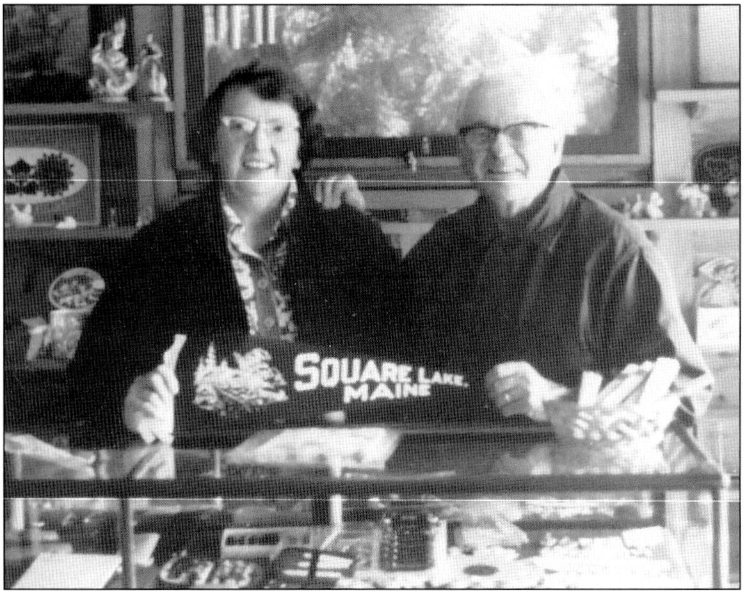

Carl and Catherine Pike are photographed inside Bob's Trading Post, Square Pond, Shapleigh. Although Carl's son, Bob, was the one who started the business in 1954, Carl and Catherine ran the store for more than 20 years. Pike was well known for his mechanical abilities. Although the pictured pennant states "Square Lake," the official name is Square Pond. (Courtesy of Robert Pike.)

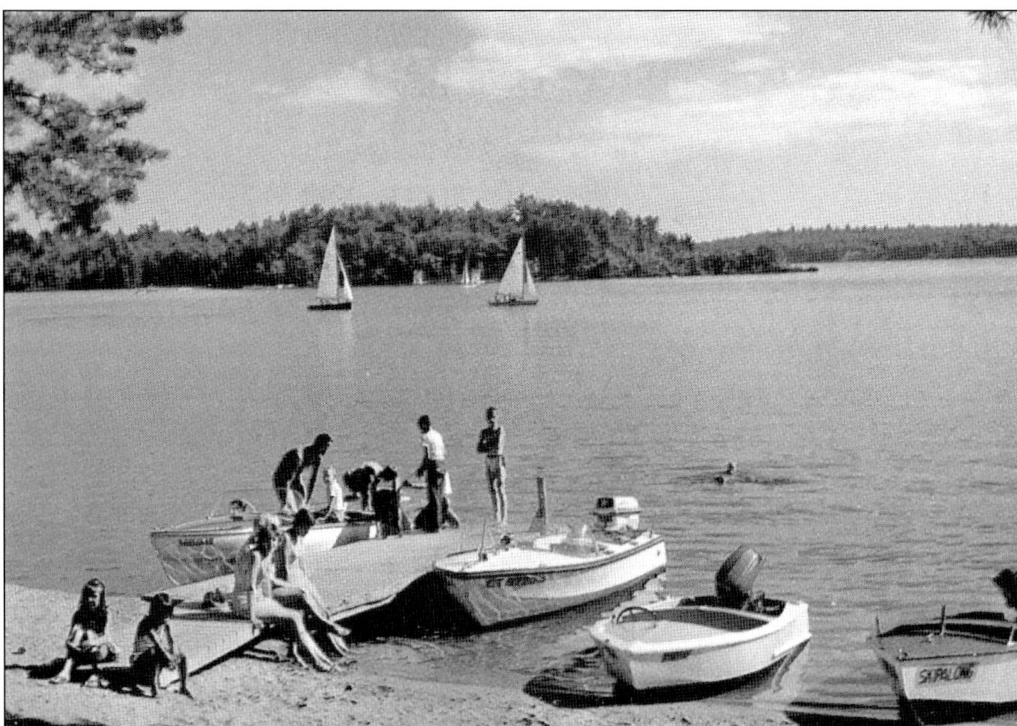

This view of Treasure Island on Square Pond is from Bob's Trading Post in Shapleigh. In the early 1900s, most of the land on the west shore was owned by Goodall-Sanford Mills, and the east shore was individually owned by local farmers and the town of Shapleigh. Square Pond was large enough to allow sailboats room to navigate freely.

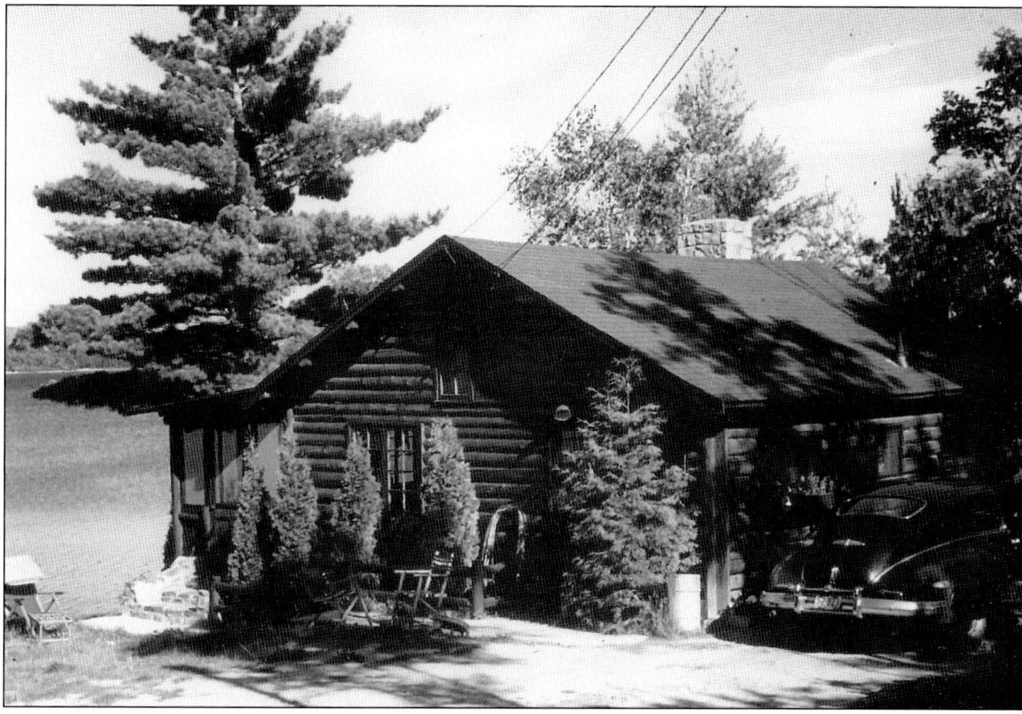

The summer home of Harold Evans Sr. and family, on West Shore Drive, was the first real log cabin to be built on Square Pond. Evans not only built this log cabin but he also had the foresight to install large granite slabs as erosion control to protect his shoreline. It is the only camp on the lake with this unique identifiable feature. (Courtesy of Norma Evans.)

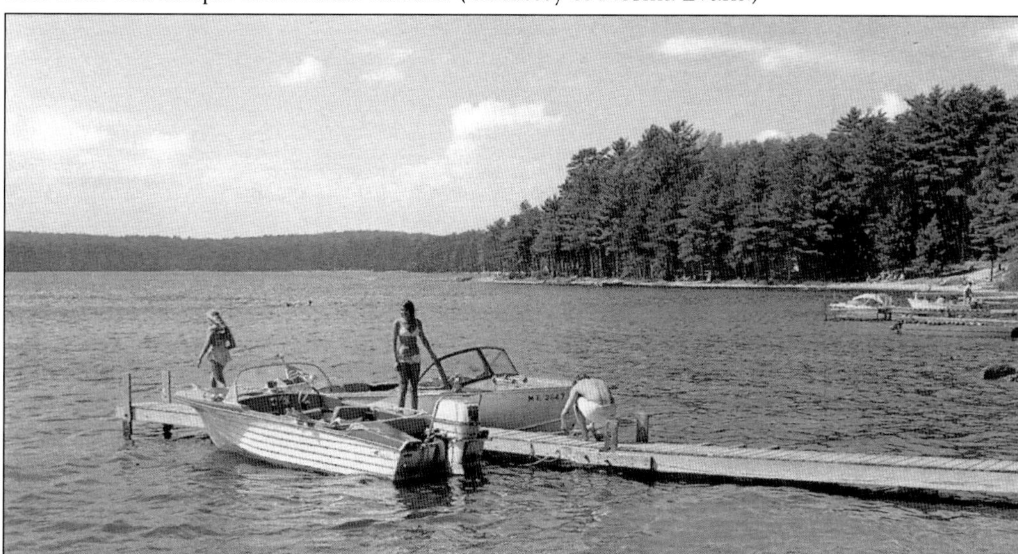

Square Pond was once called Crystal Lake, and the water level before 1900 was considerably higher than it is today. The pond is spring fed and has few other natural inlets or outlets. Because of Square Pond's secluded location, it allows residents to escape the hustle and bustle of urban life, making obtaining property nearly impossible. In fact, some camps and year-round cottages are still in the same families three and four generations later.

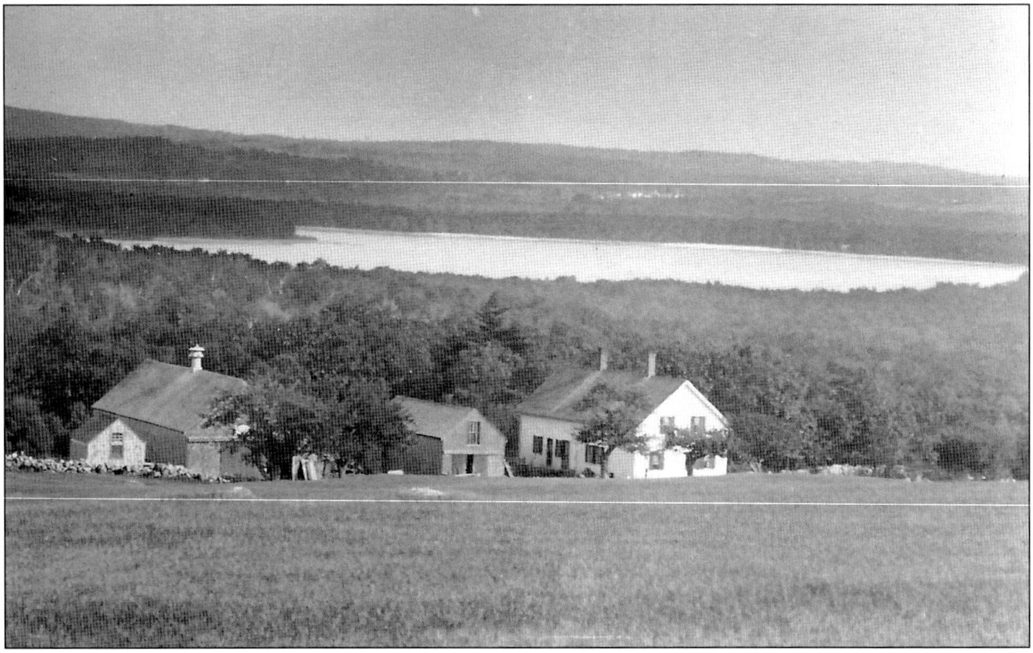

This is a view of Square Pond from Acton Ridge. Spanning two towns, Square Pond is nestled between Shapleigh on the western shore and Acton on the eastern shore. In the foreground, Oak Hill Farm is pictured. Almost centered in the background, one can faintly see the outcropping of Shapleigh Corner.

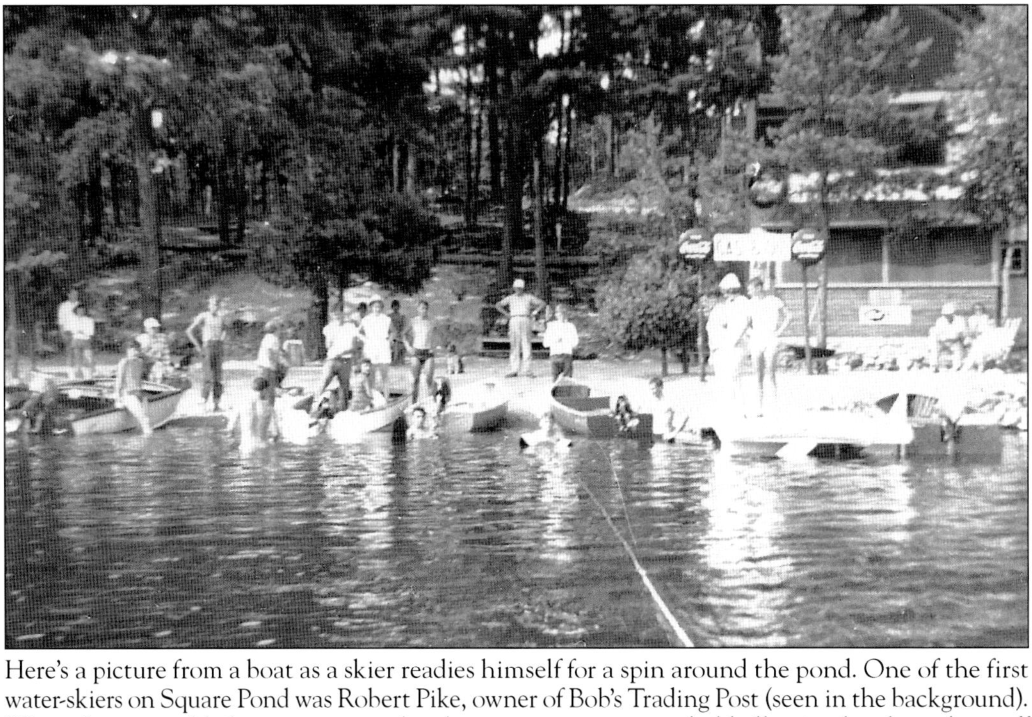

Here's a picture from a boat as a skier readies himself for a spin around the pond. One of the first water-skiers on Square Pond was Robert Pike, owner of Bob's Trading Post (seen in the background). Water-skiing quickly became so popular that tournaments were held allowing locals to show off their skills. (Courtesy of Robert Pike.)

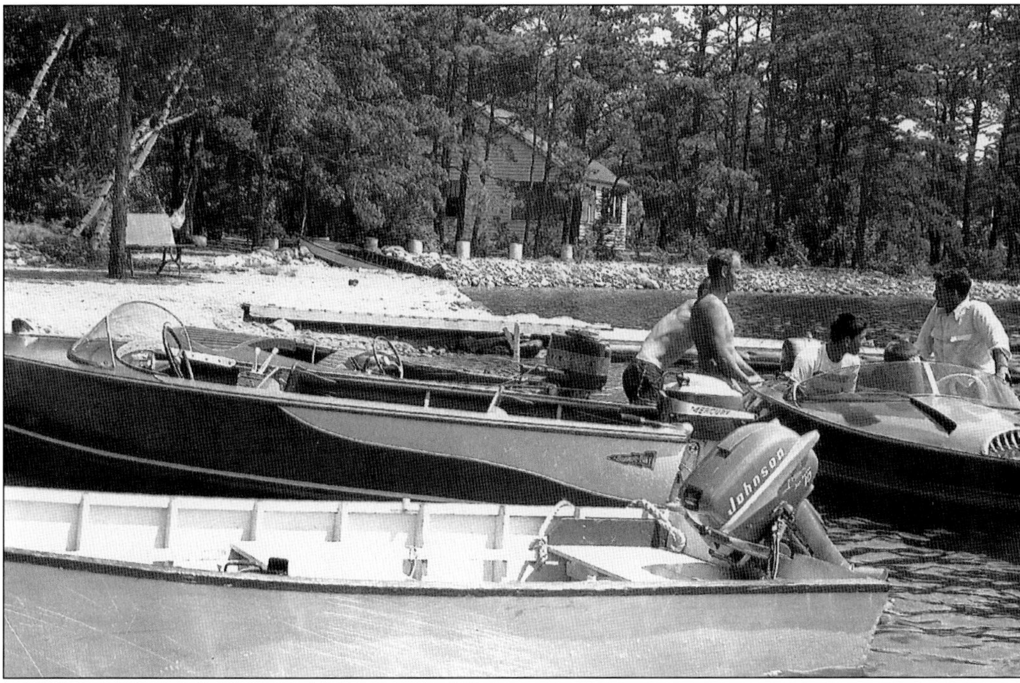

Teenagers gather at Bob's Trading Post for fuel and snacks before heading back out onto the lake. Prior to getting their driver's licenses, they would use the family boat like an automobile as a means of freedom to visit friends, water-ski, and hang out. It has always been a right of passage to drive a boat unsupervised. Upon careful observation, these same activities are just as popular as they used to be. (Courtesy of Robert Pike.)

Needing a place to cool off from the summer heat, Harry Wentworth had this building pulled across Wilson Lake in 1922. He then transformed it into a beautiful little summer camp, said to be the first on Wilson Lake. Wilson Lake is 3 miles long and 2 miles wide and surrounded by rolling hills and pine groves. (Courtesy of Joyce Cunningham.)

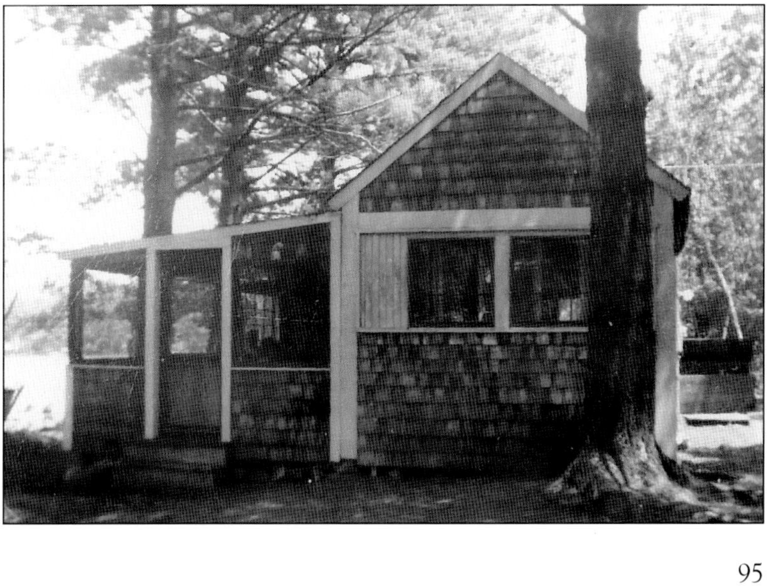

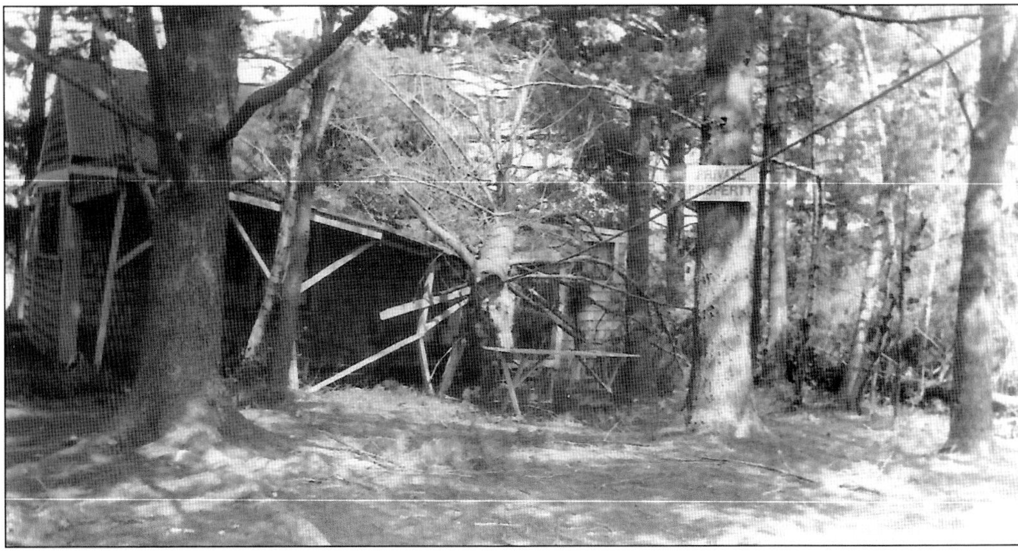

In 1954, the Wentworth camp suffered damage from Hurricane Carol, which uprooted several large pine trees. The camp was repaired and is still owned by the Wentworth family. For many years, the Acton–Milton Mills Free Baptist Church annual Fourth of July Sunday school picnic was held here. Hand-squeezed lemonade in a galvanized tub was always a favorite, as was a leisurely ride on the flat-bottom rowboat. (Courtesy of Joyce Cunningham.)

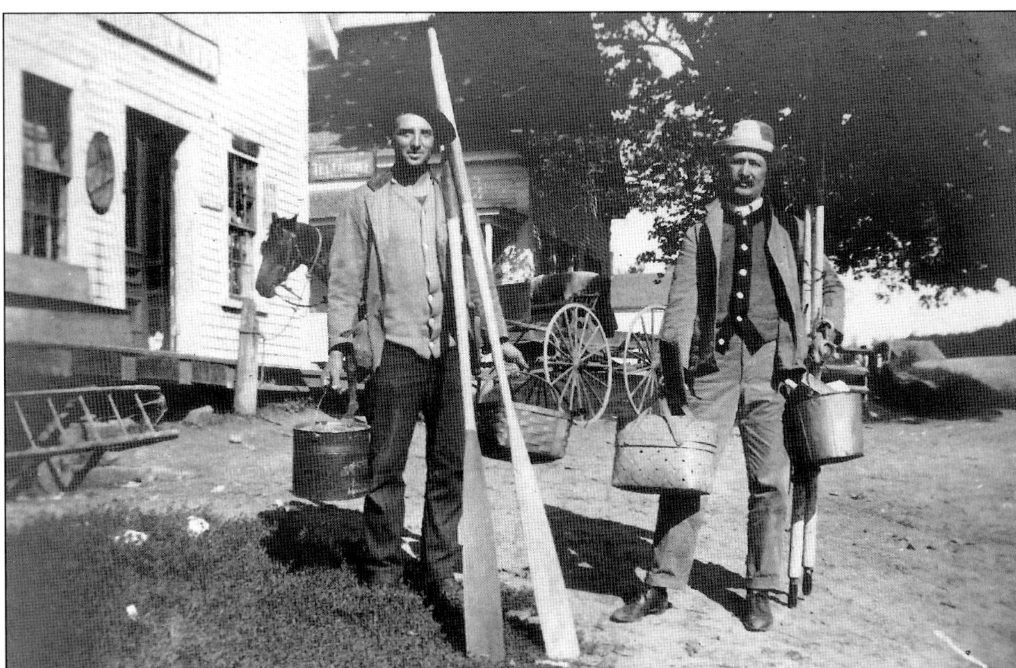

Armed with oars, lunch baskets, fuel, and fishing supplies, these men appear to be looking forward to a day of leisure on the lake. Making use of the lakes year-round, fishing is a popular activity in the winter. By day or night, ice fishing and snowmobiling are the most popular winter activities in this lakes region. With acres of lakes and hundreds of miles of groomed trails, there is no shortage of either.

Three

Acton and its Villages

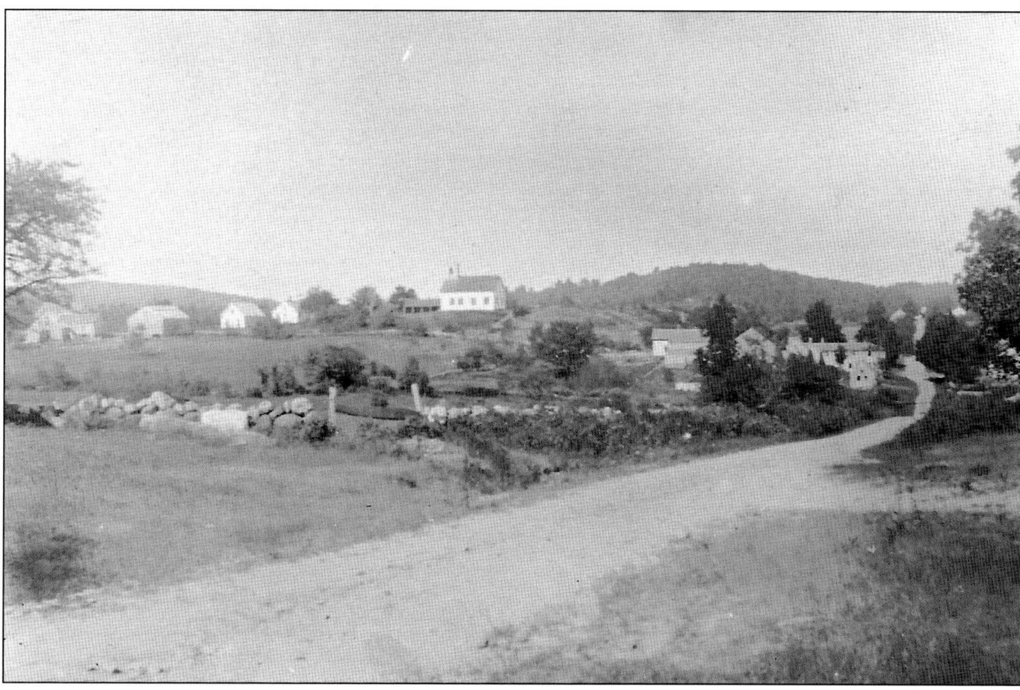

This is one of the earliest views of Acton Corner, before the state of Maine paved the way for the new Route 109. The Congregational church sits prominently atop the hill, with the town hall and school to its left. Due to its centralized location, this area became the focal point for the town and the seat of town government.

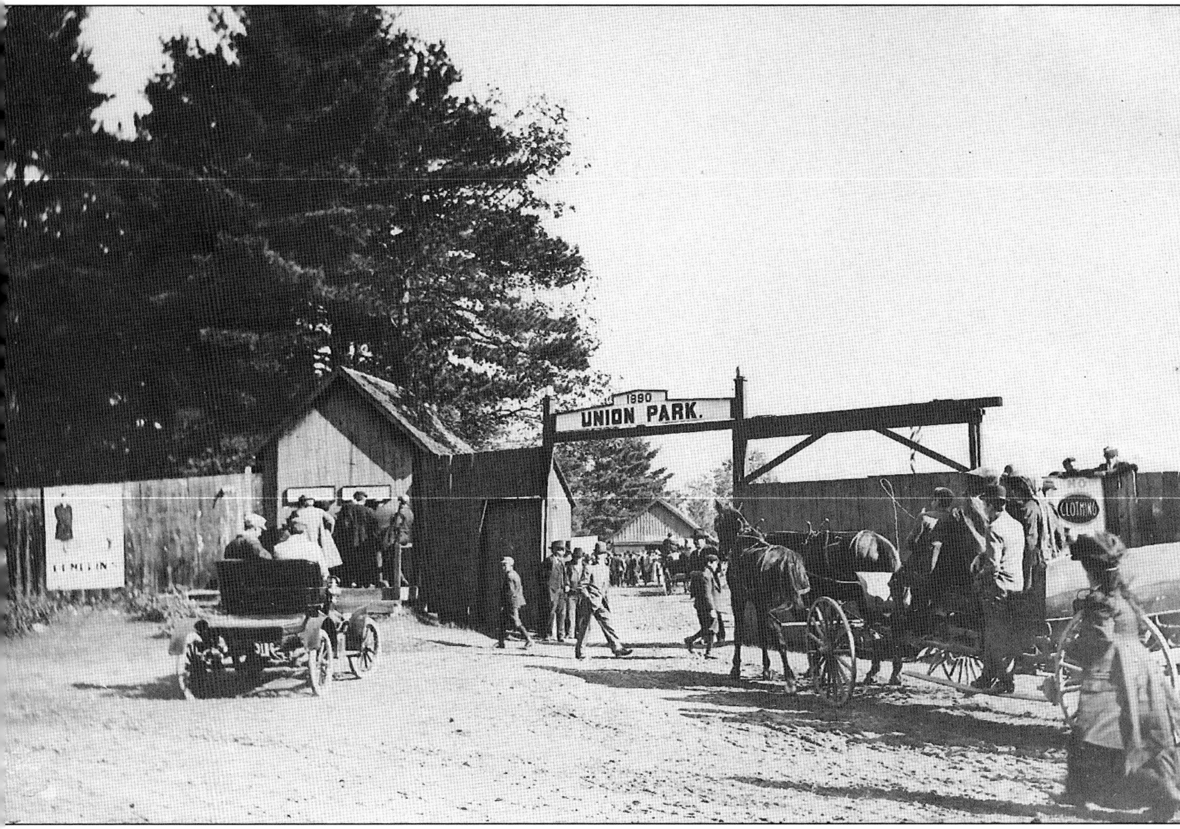

By the early 1820s, farmers wanted to be better informed, so they banded together and organized agricultural societies. As the societies took hold and to help stimulate interest in improved farming practices, they went one step further and organized what would become a statewide institution of agricultural fairs. The Shapleigh and Acton Agricultural Society, organized in 1866, held its very first fair in Acton in 1867. For over 20 years, the fair alternated between Shapleigh and Acton sites. In November 1889, the Lake Shore Park Association was organized, and permanent fairgrounds were established in Acton. The Acton Fair is still held on these premises annually in August. (Courtesy of Lista Staples.)

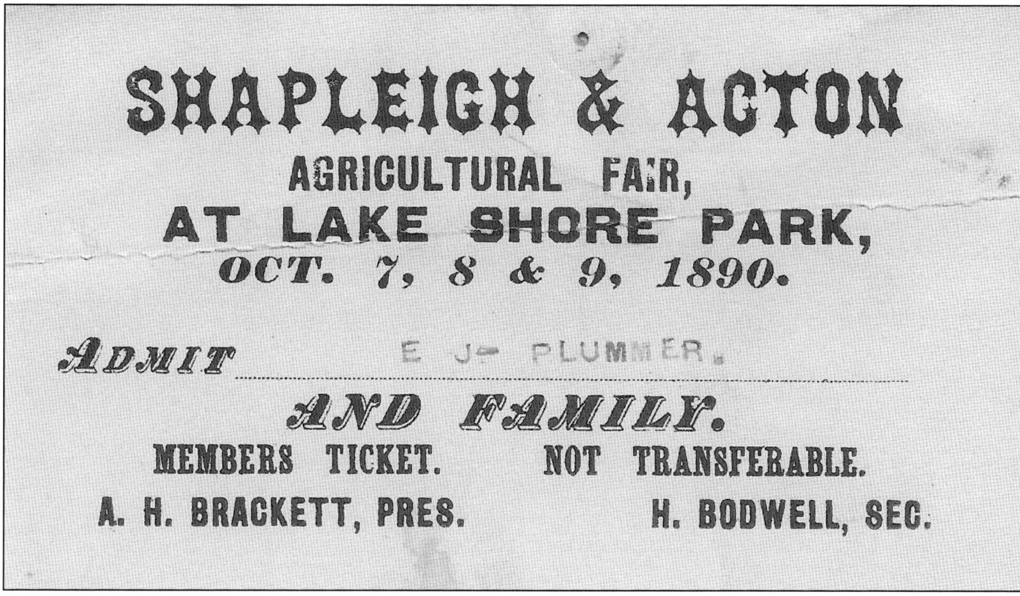

SHAPLEIGH & ACTON
AGRICULTURAL FAIR,
AT LAKE SHORE PARK,
OCT. 7, 8 & 9, 1890.

ADMIT E. J. PLUMMER.

AND FAMILY.

MEMBERS TICKET. NOT TRANSFERABLE.

A. H. BRACKETT, PRES. H. BODWELL, SEC.

One of the first tickets issued from the newly organized Lake Shore Park Association is shown. The Acton Fair is the single most attended event for the town. This annual fair is the largest gathering of the agricultural community in southern Maine, providing an economic boost and recognition to Acton.

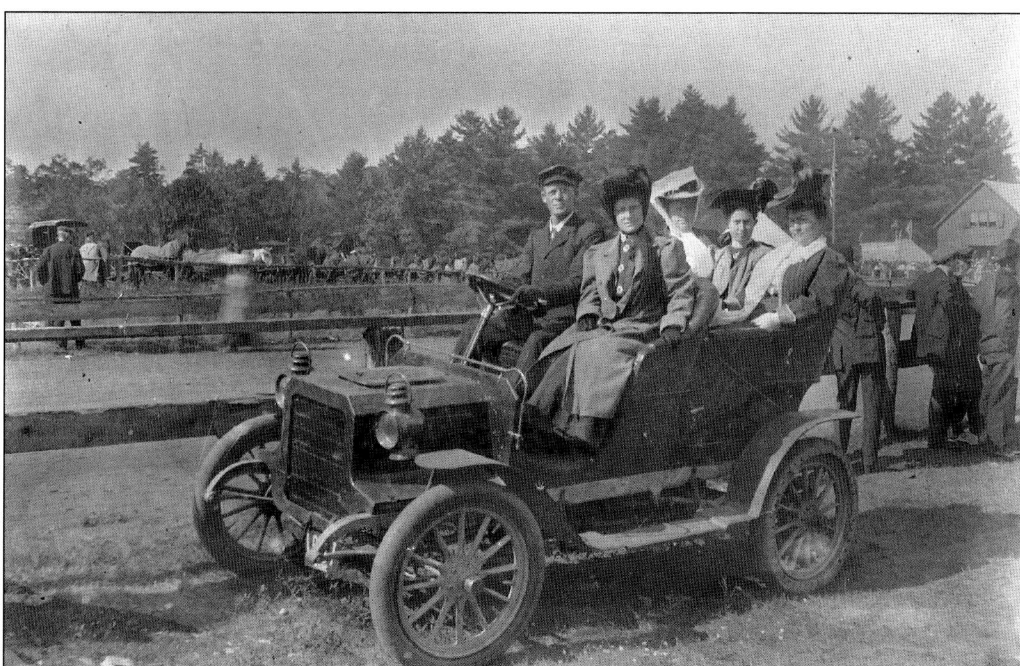

Friends and family attend the Acton fair on October 3, 1906. Early fair dates were held on Tuesday, Wednesday, and Thursday of the first week in October, but over the years, the date changed to the last full weekend in August, which still allowed farmers to show off their crops. Earlier in the summer of 1906, a new dining room was built to enhance the fair's appeal.

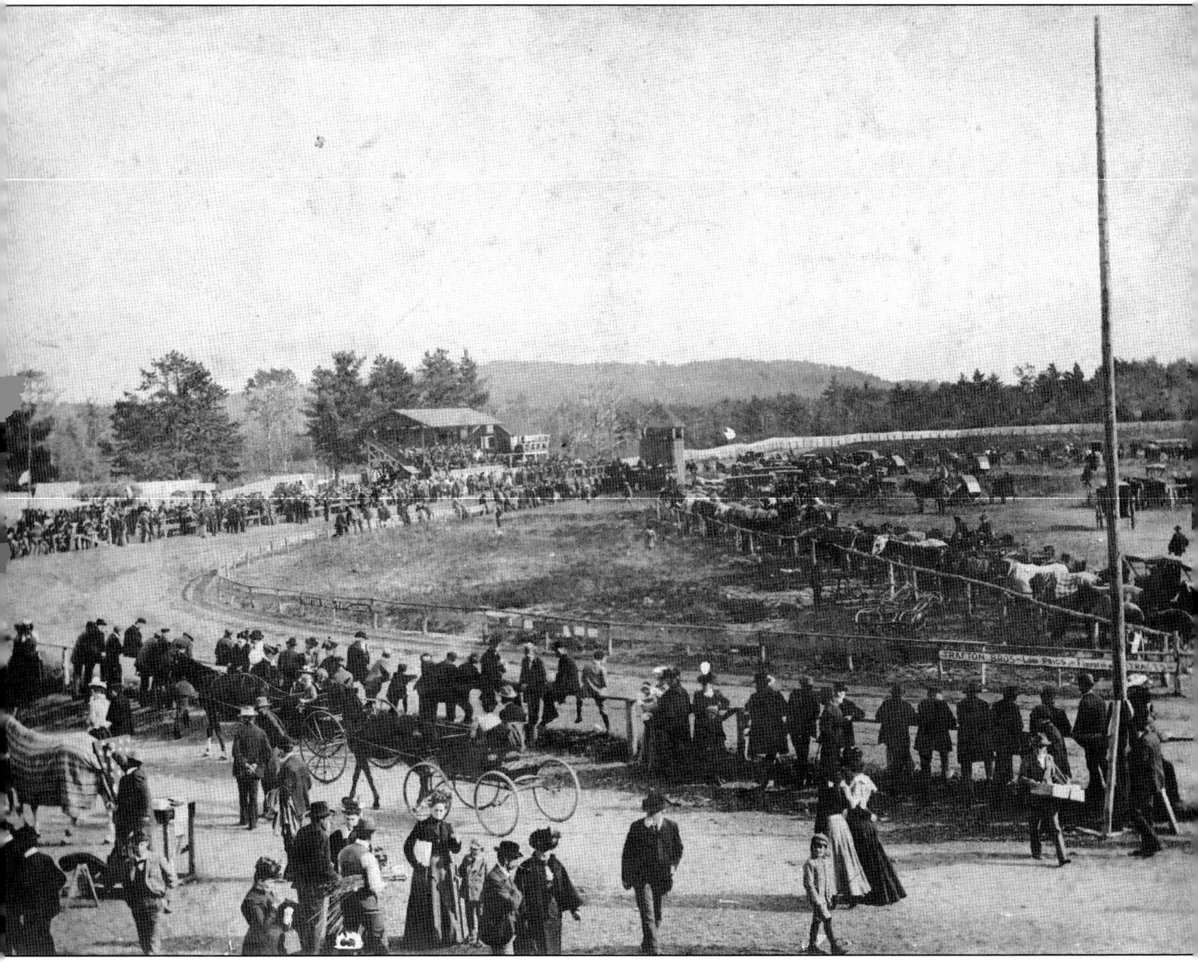

By 1825, harness racing was an institution at hundreds of fairs across the nation, and it reached its height of fame in the late 1800s. The sport began to decline in popularity after 1900, as the automobile replaced the horse and the United States became more urbanized. Besides livestock competitions and horse and oxen pulls, harness racing was another source of pride for local farmers. Harness racing was a major attraction at this fair until it was stopped in 1945. This half-mile track was built in 1890 at a cost of $620 on land donated by B. C. and Freeman Jordan. A stipulation in the agreement stated that all Jordan families would receive free passes to all fairs held on this land. (Courtesy of Melissa Conner.)

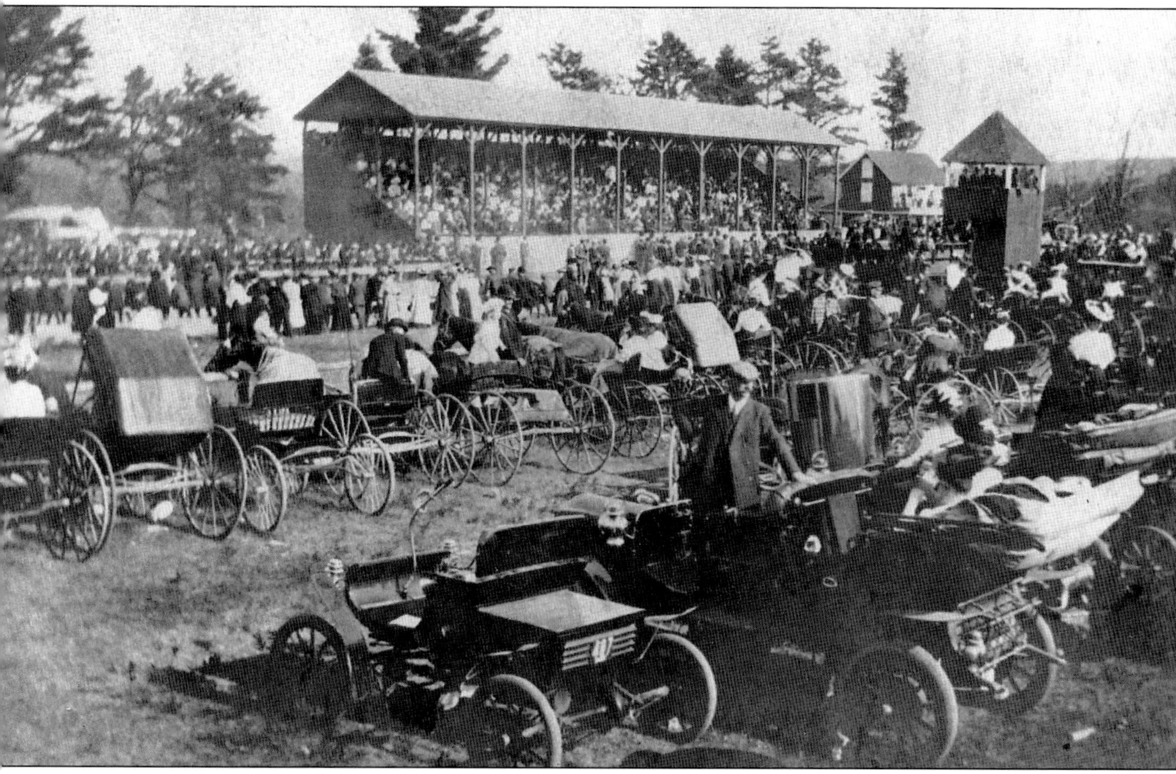

This picture, taken at the Acton Fair in 1908, shows the various means of transportation used by fairgoers. Then as now, fairgoers were allowed to drive onto the premises and park in designated areas. The area depicted here currently houses two metal exhibition halls and many food vendors. In 1976, the oldest wooden exhibition building burned to the ground during the fair. The building housed the main office, and many exhibits were on display. In the background is the relatively new grandstand (built 1905), where spectators would watch the horse and oxen pulling as well as the start and finish of the harness racing. (Courtesy of Lista Staples.)

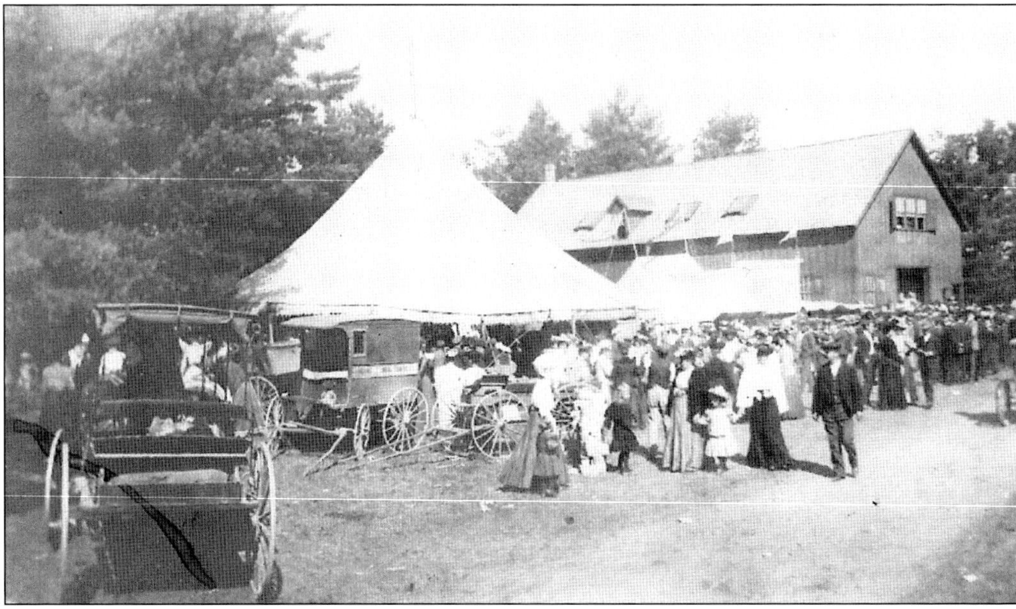

The Acton Fair is pictured in 1909. Fairgoers mill about the vendor displays and food tents. Providing cotton candy, ice cream, and fried foods plus other delights that many could not enjoy at home, fair food is always a treat for both children and adults. 4-H exhibits, demonstrations, and competitions are still huge attractions at the Acton Fair. (Courtesy of Melissa Conner.)

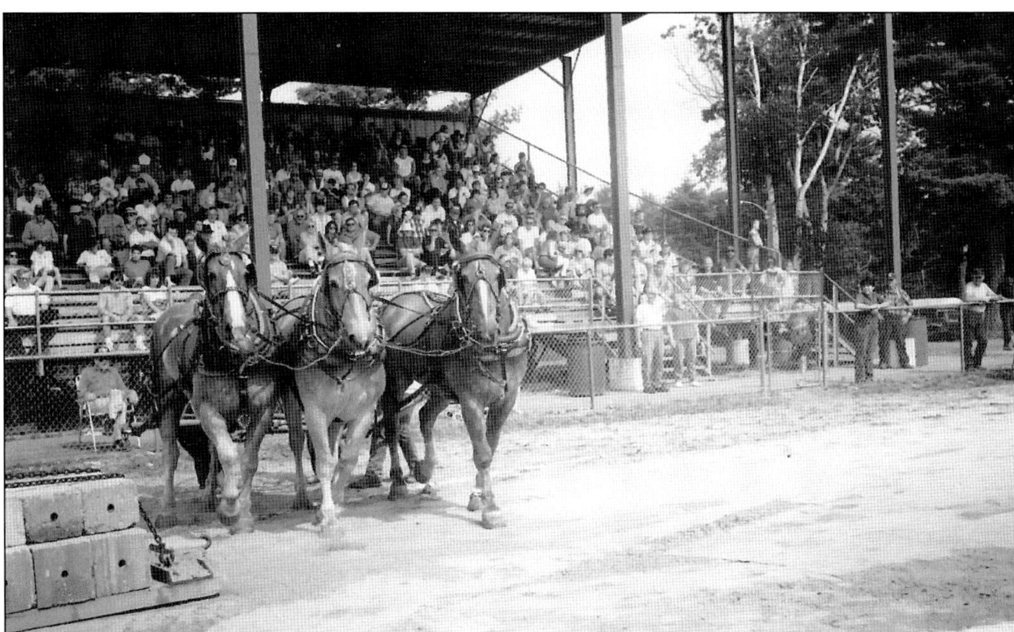

Horse pulling was originally a competition to determine which farmer had the strongest team and also provided year-long bragging rights. A beautiful team of three draft horses prepares to be hitched to a drag at the Acton Fair in the early 1970s. (Courtesy of Donald Morrill.)

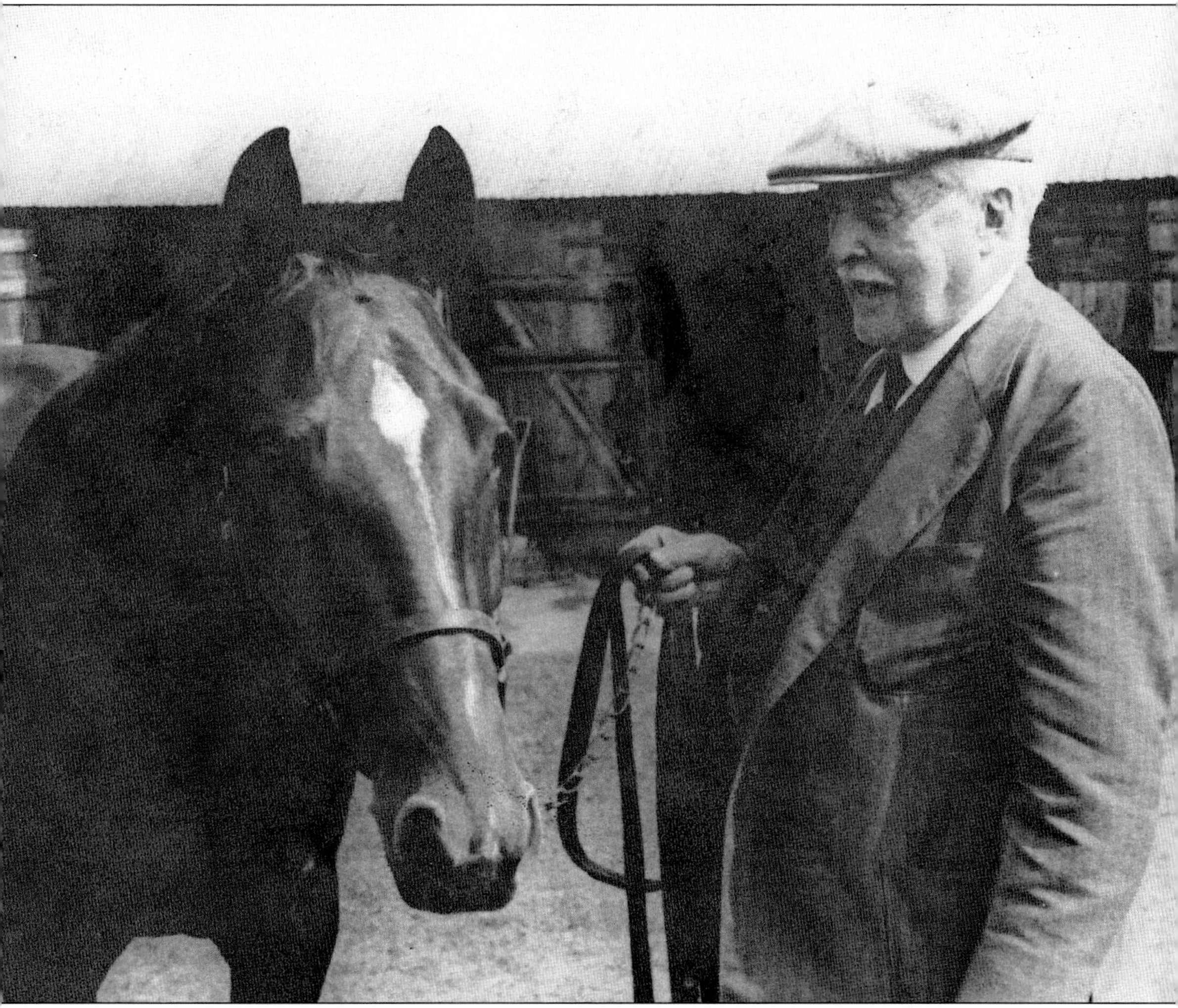

Dr. Frederick Bragdon was honored by 10,000 attendees on "Doc Bragdon Day" at the Acton Fair in 1937. Bragdon graduated with a medical degree with honors from Bowdoin College in 1883. The following year, he started a practice in Shapleigh, where he made his home for the next 10 years before moving to the neighboring town of Springvale. Bragdon was a familiar figure on the ovals throughout Maine and on many New England tracks. He loved harness racing almost as much as he loved practicing medicine. Over the course of 40 years, he would own an estimated 75 racing horses. Bragdon continued to practice up to the time of his death at the age of 80, after more than 55 years of service to the medical profession. Those who remembered him said he was the last of the old-school family doctors, and he left behind a record of love for humanity that all would do well to emulate.

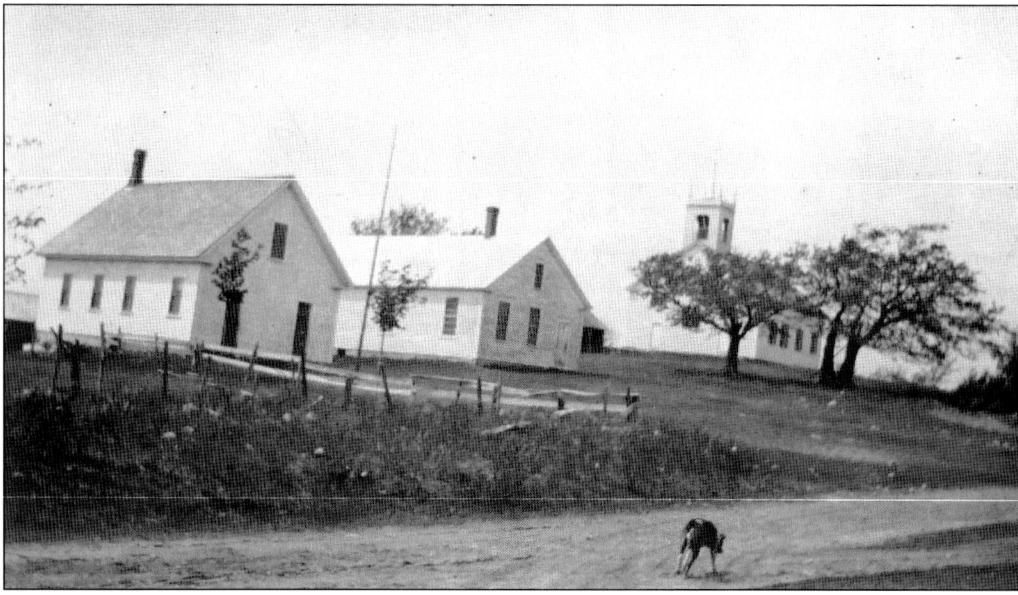

In the top picture, from left to right, are the Acton Corner School, the Acton Town Hall, and the Acton Corner Congregational Church. The town hall was built in 1842 at a cost totaling $217, which included the land. The Acton Corner Congregational Church (below) was built in 1827. At some point, the bell tower design changed from its original style. But in 1981, a major leak was found that required reconstruction, and it was decided to replicate the original tower's design. For many years, this church held summer services only. Since 1979, year-round services have been held, and the church continues to grow.

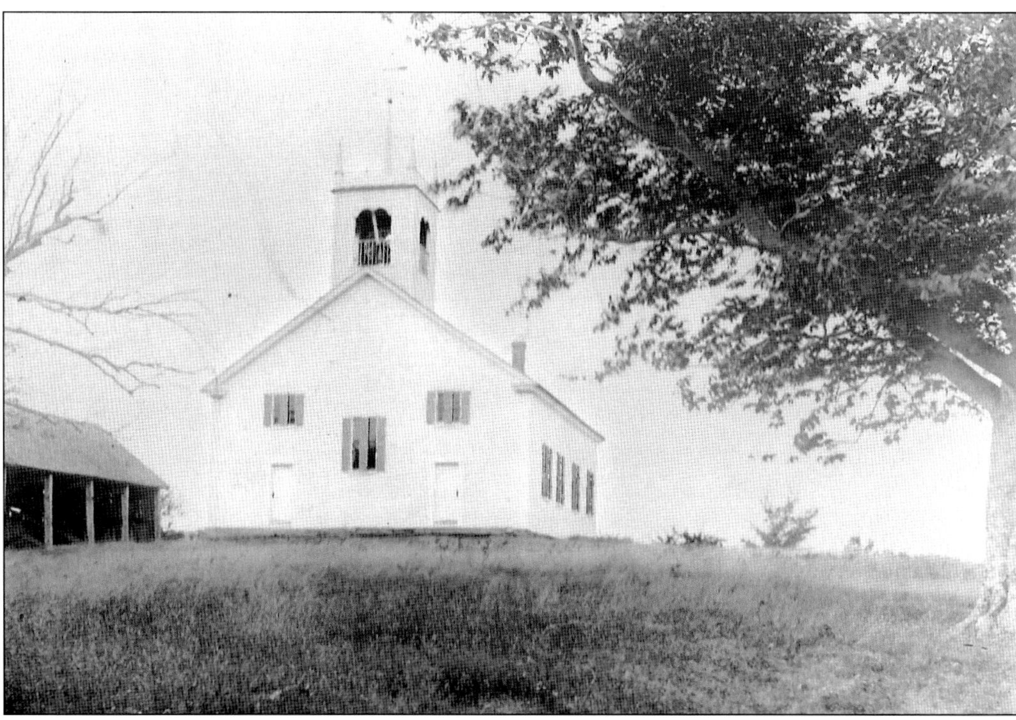

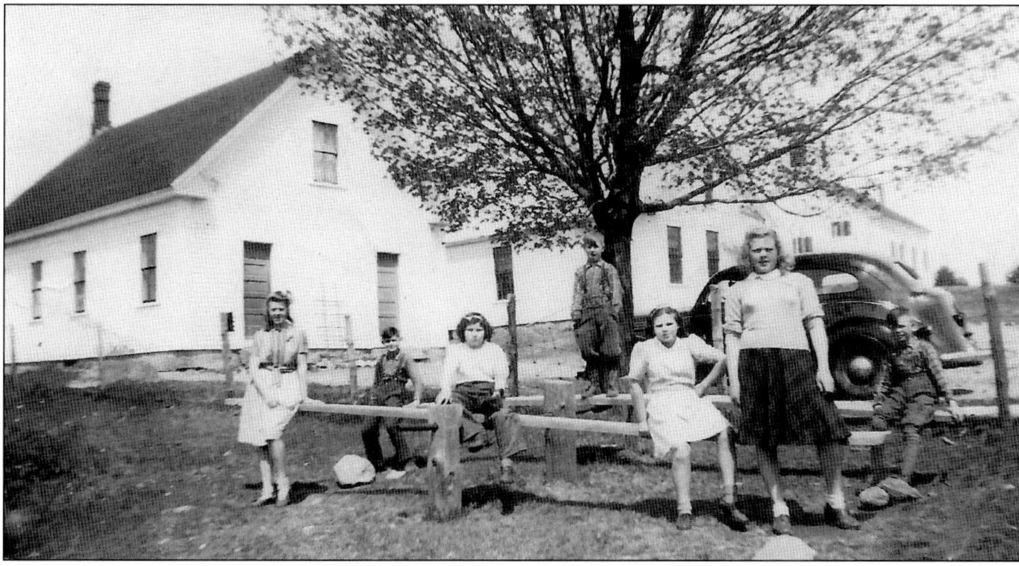

Built in 1866, the Acton Corner School was a typical one-room schoolhouse. Pictured are schoolchildren at recess time in 1944. They are, from left to right, Arlene Brulotte, Raymond Bouchard, Aleta Wilson, Irvin Pillsbury, Barbara Wilson, Eva Meyer, and Carl Pillsbury. The town hall and Congregational church are also visible. The school building was converted to the present-day Acton Public Library in 1957. (Courtesy of Eva Morrill.)

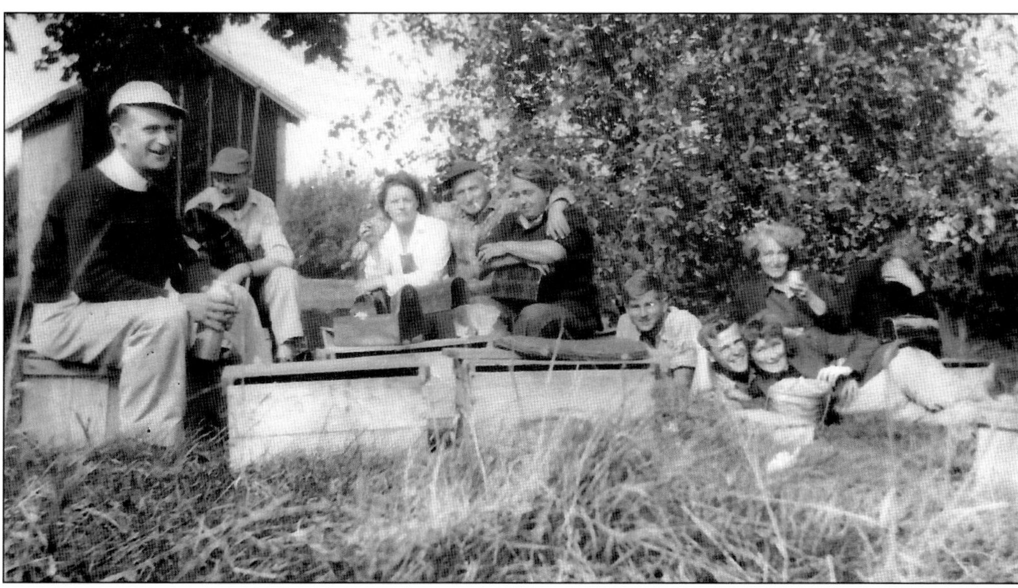

Employees take a break from packing apples at Lovejoy orchard in 1945. From left to right are Clifford Hannaford, Cory Goodwin, Gladys Yuill, Donald Bodwell, Mildred Grant, Merle Treadwell, Charlie Swett, Bernadine Webber, Gladys Ridley, and Lena Hooper. (Courtesy of Bernadine Dunnells.)

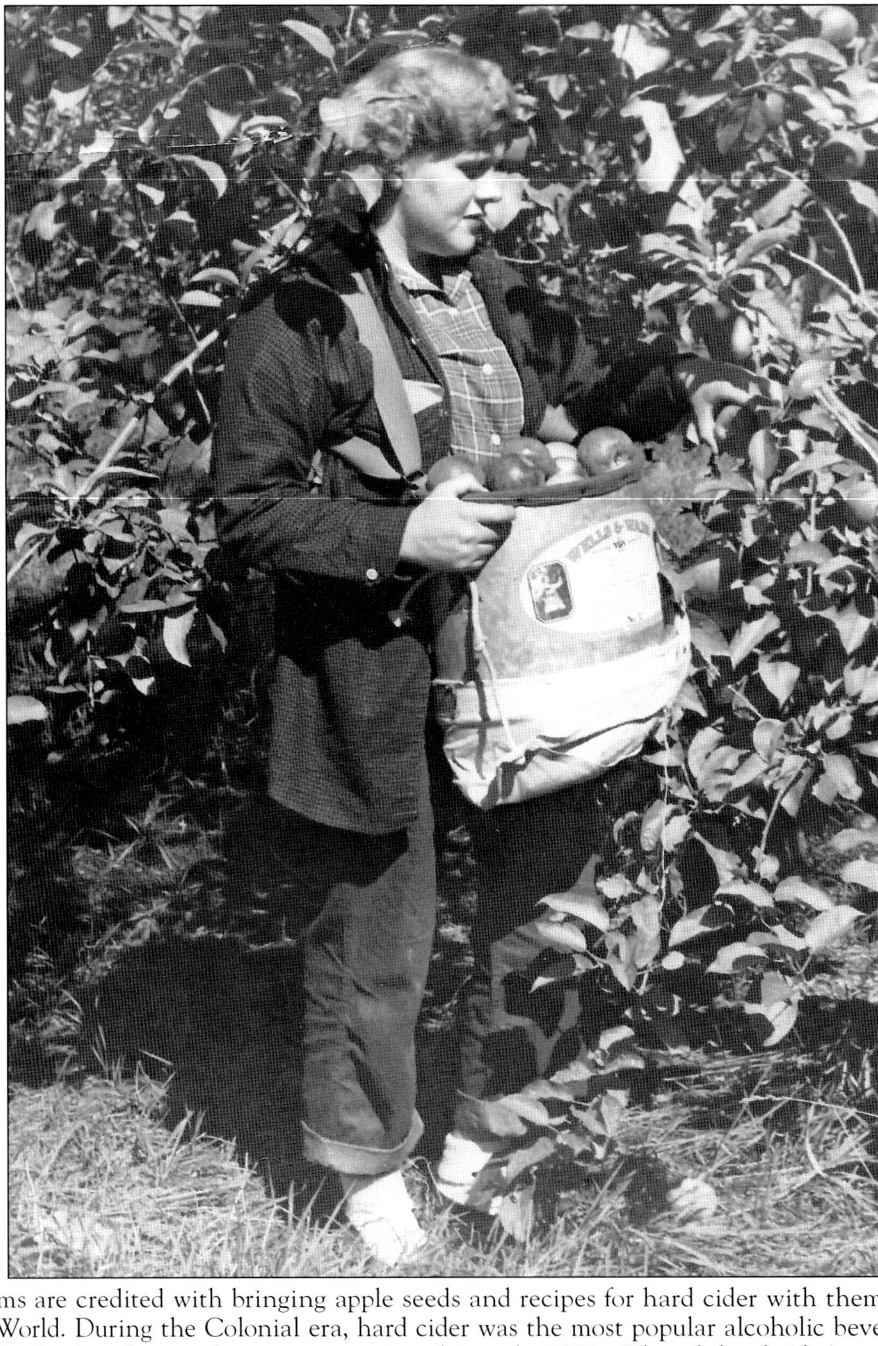

Pilgrims are credited with bringing apple seeds and recipes for hard cider with them to the New World. During the Colonial era, hard cider was the most popular alcoholic beverage in New England, and its predominance continued into the 1800s. Though hard cider's popularity dwindled over time, the growing popularity of microbreweries and home brewing in the past 20 years or so has brought about a resurgence of this beverage considered to be so much a part of Americana. Apples are still one of the most abundant crops of this region, providing a unique blend of flavors due to the warm summer days and cool fall nights. Acton celebrates the apple each autumn with its Apple Festival Day. Eva Meyer is photographed picking apples at Lovejoy Orchard in 1952. (Courtesy of Eva Morrill.)

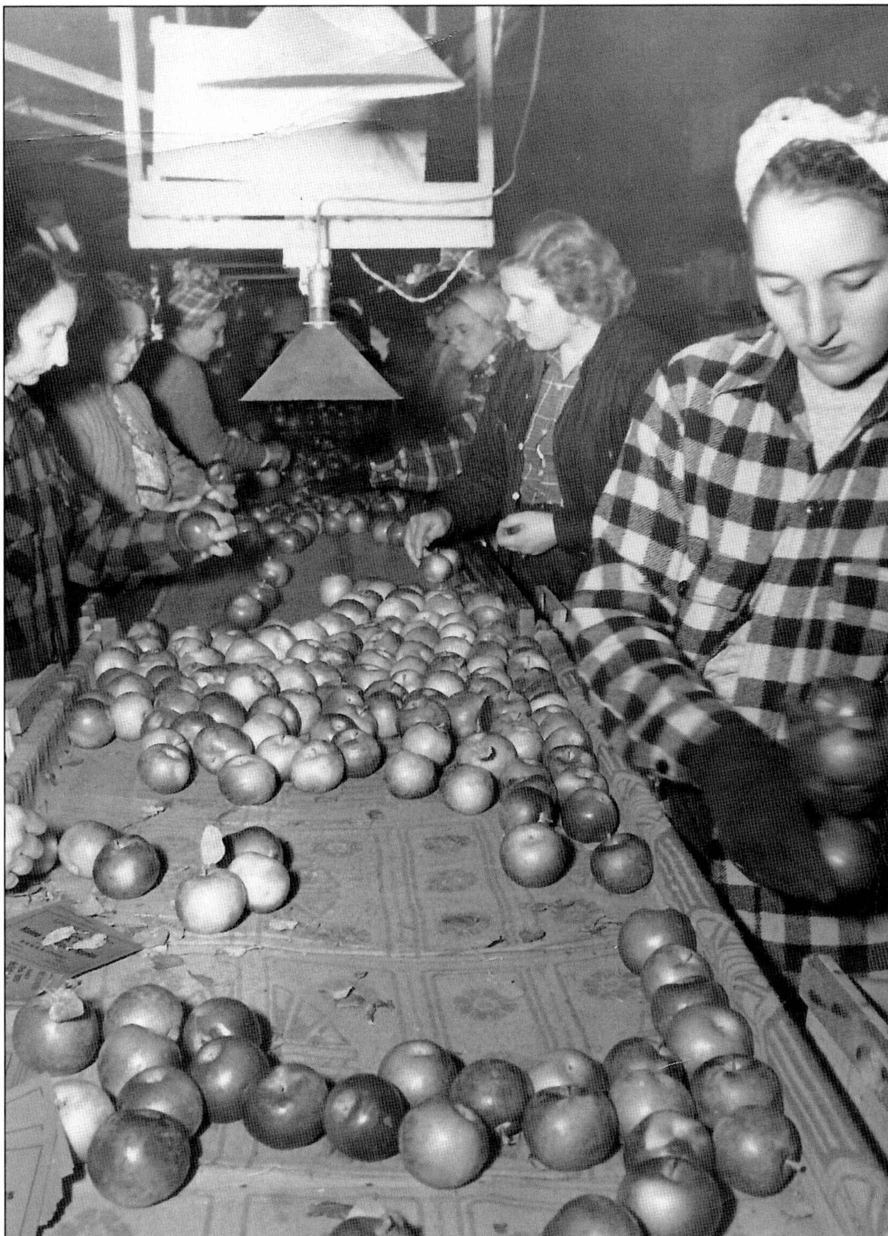

Raymond Lovejoy began the first commercial apple orchard in Acton in 1928 with a total acreage of 120. In just two years, 4,000 apple trees were planted. Almost everyone who grew up in Acton back then worked at one time or another in either the orchards or the packinghouse. In the 1930s, salaries ranged between 30¢ and 50¢ per hour, with various jobs available to men and women. Pictured here, local women hand grade apples for Lovejoy orchard in 1952. All apples were hand graded for packing until 1978, when new machinery assisted workers with the task. Many locals believe the best apples one will ever taste are grown on New England's rocky soils. About 40 varieties of apples are commonly grown in New England. Apple pie, apple juice, candied apples, applesauce, and apple jelly are just a few favorites that people everywhere enjoy. (Courtesy of Eva Morrill.)

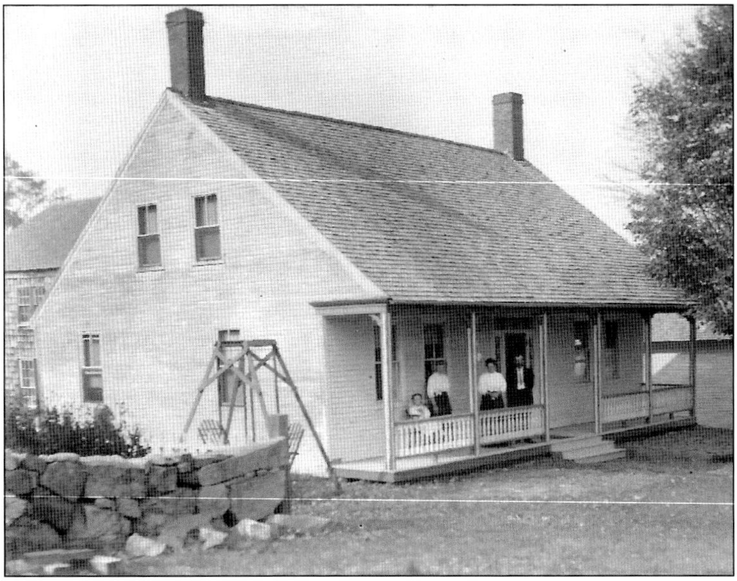

In the days before telephones, radios, or televisions were common, rural farmers' main links to the outside world were the mail and newspapers that came to the nearest post office. Rural free delivery (RFD) was established in Acton in 1902 and is still a vital link between industrial and rural America. This house was built about 1856 at Acton Corner and was home to the Acton post office for over 45 years.

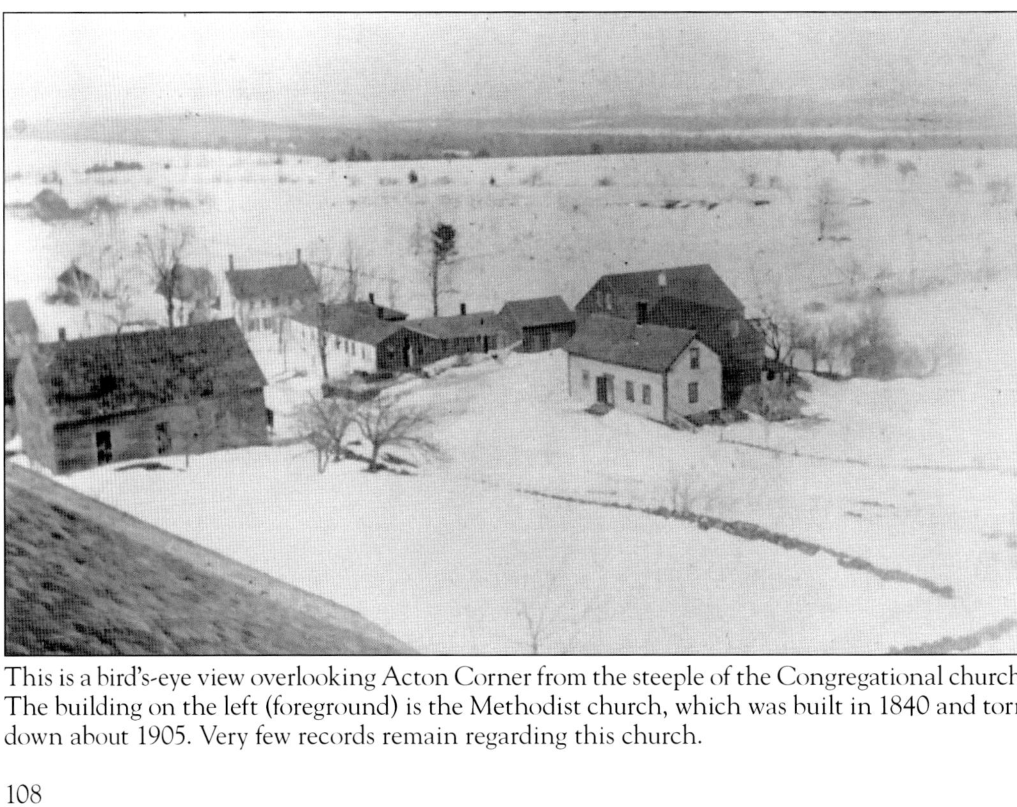

This is a bird's-eye view overlooking Acton Corner from the steeple of the Congregational church. The building on the left (foreground) is the Methodist church, which was built in 1840 and torn down about 1905. Very few records remain regarding this church.

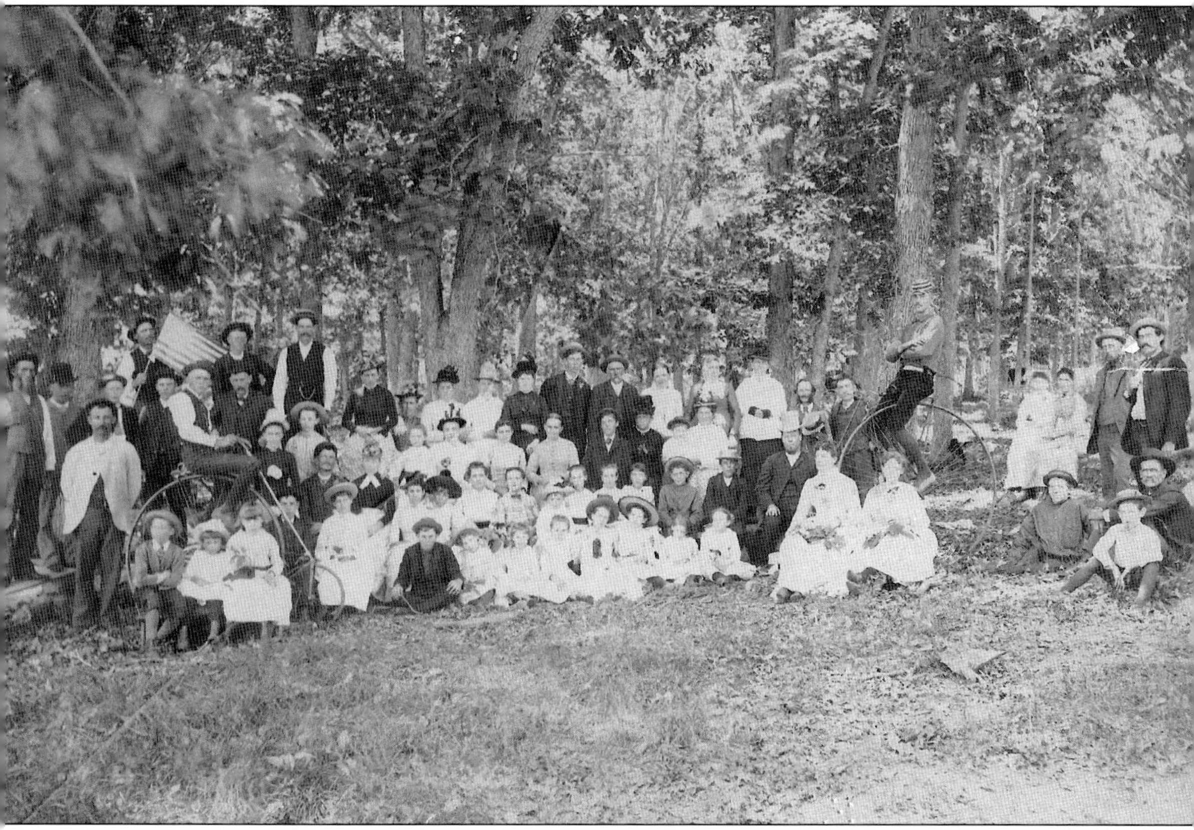

A long-standing tradition and popular event with families was attending the annual church picnic. These gatherings were a good time to enjoy each other's company, sing songs, play games and, of course, share home-baked goods. Pictured here are parishioners of the Acton Methodist Church during a picnic at Young's Grove on July 4, 1888. It is interesting to note both large rear-wheeled bicycles. In some cases, these bicycles could cost the owners up to six months' wages. More times than not, the church picnic would coincide with the Fourth of July holiday, as most businesses would close for that day. Even today, the tradition continues, as the Fourth of July is synonymous with picnics and barbecues between friends and family. If the stars on this flag were visible, one would be able to detect 38 of them.

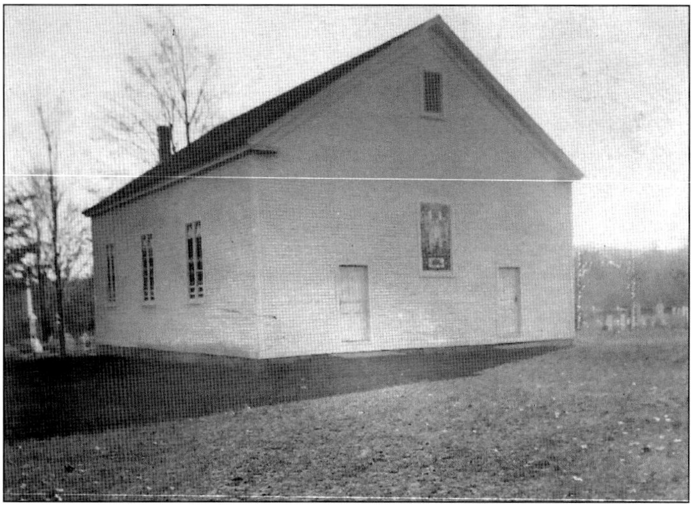

The South Acton Baptist Church is a unique "back-end-to" church built in 1841. Upon entering one of the two front doors and stepping through the entryway, instead of gazing down the length of the interior of the pulpit, visitors are immediately met with pews that face forward. One seat is just as good as another since the floor is laid in theater style, being inclined at an angle from the platform upward to the rear of the room.

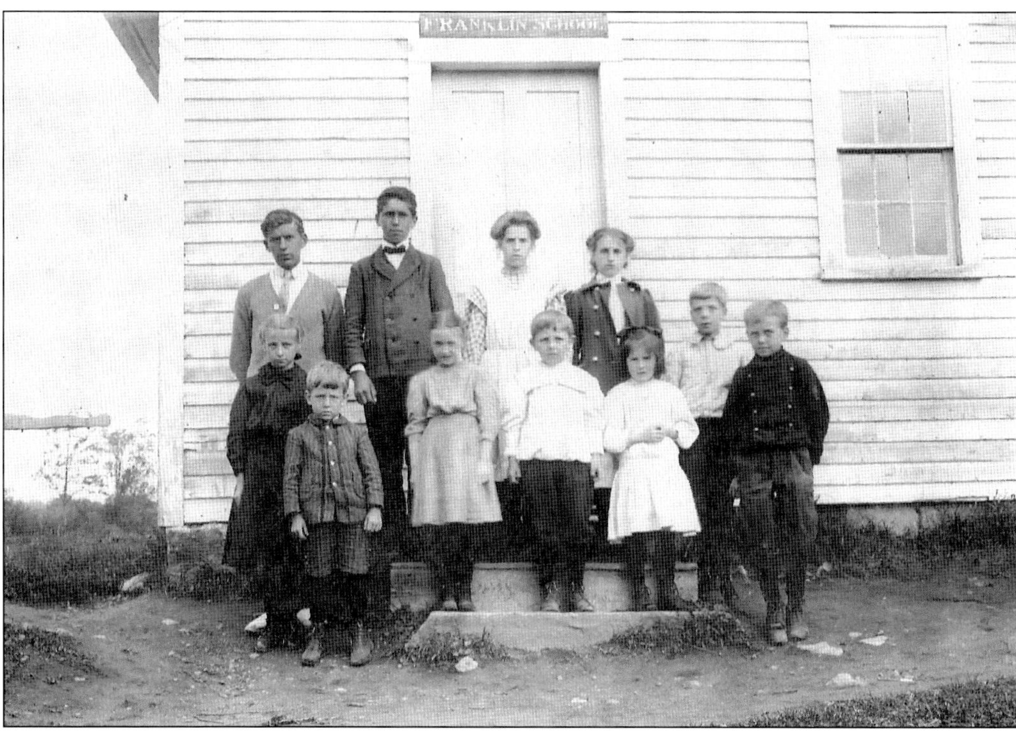

Teacher Harry Goodwin (back row, left) is shown with his class of 1914 from Franklin School at Hubbard's Corner. In 1876, Acton had 14 school districts. Franklin, located in District Three, closed about 1921.

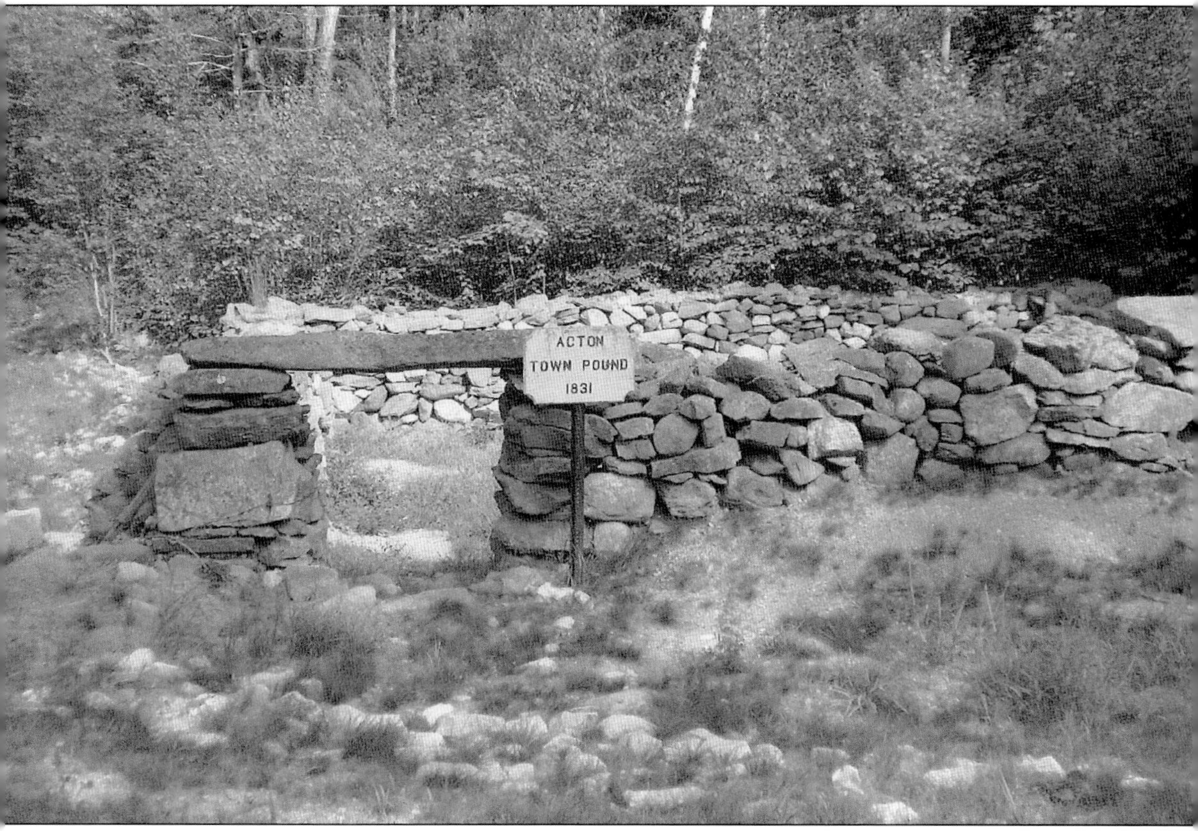

In 1831, the town of Acton paid $35.50 for the building of this pound. Town pounds were a very important part of the agricultural life because it was in these enclosures that farm animals that strayed were kept until claimed by their owners, for a fee that depended on the type of animal and length of time it had been cared for by the pound keeper, or "pinder." With the advent of barbed wire and electric fences, farmers enclosed their own pastures. The pound, once an important part of the farming community, gradually became obsolete. Animal pounds are today a scarce survivor from days gone by as modern culture becomes removed from an earlier farming focus. Acton is proud to have such a perfectly preserved example, of which there are only 19 left in the state.

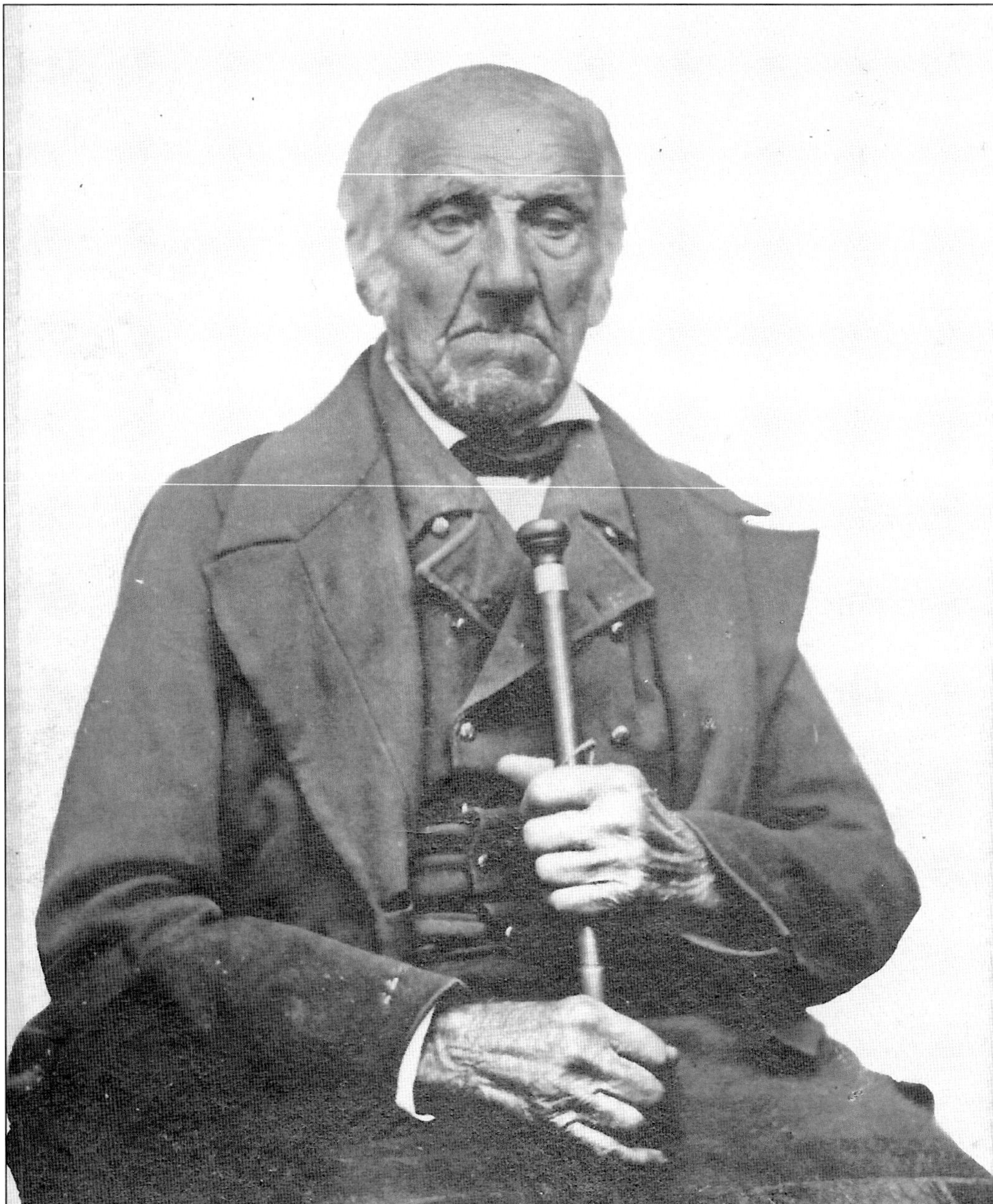

Ralph Farnham, born on July 7, 1756, was one of the most notable citizens of Acton. When he died at the age of 104, he was the last known survivor of the Battle of Bunker Hill. Ralph enlisted in the military at the age of 18 and shortly thereafter marched to Boston with fellow enlistees. They arrived just in time to participate in the battle, on June 17, 1775. Ralph married and was blessed with seven children. He built his family a farmhouse on approximately 100 acres on Foxes Ridge. In 1832, Ralph applied for and received a Revolutionary War pension of $61.66 per year, which he received until his death in 1860. At the age of 104, Farnham was invited to a celebration in his honor in Boston, where he again visited Bunker Hill and shook hands with the Prince of Wales, later King Edward VII of England. He died at home shortly after and is buried on this farmland. This photograph was taken on his 102nd birthday.

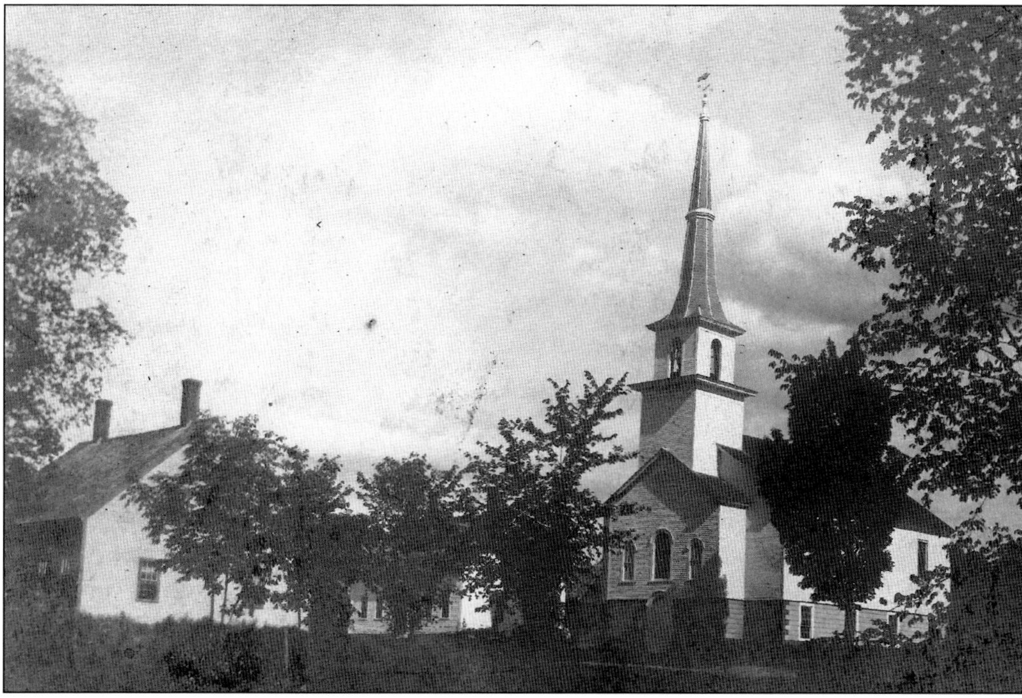

Acton–Milton Mills Free Baptist Church was built in 1840 and was moved to its present site by oxen in midwinter 1873. Ten years later, the building was raised and a vestry was built beneath the auditorium. The church officers and committee members of 1950 are, from left to right, (first row) Helen Wentworth, Beulah Maxfield, George Mee, Paul Gerrish, Rev. Buel Maxfield, Harry Wentworth, Jacob Stevens, Alfred Lewis, Herman Buck, and Irl Hurd; (second row) unidentified, Virginia Mee, Jennie Hurd, Della Ramsey, Abbie Anderson, Grace Venness, Agnes Hayes, Lucia Fox, Alice King, Farrand Hodgton, Carl Hurd, and Whitfield Beals; (third row) Ella Wentworth, two unidentified, Arthur Mee, Roy Hamm, Minnie Hamm, Violet Kimball, Roland Kimball, Helen Grant, and Grace Hodgton. (Both, courtesy of Joyce Cunningham.)

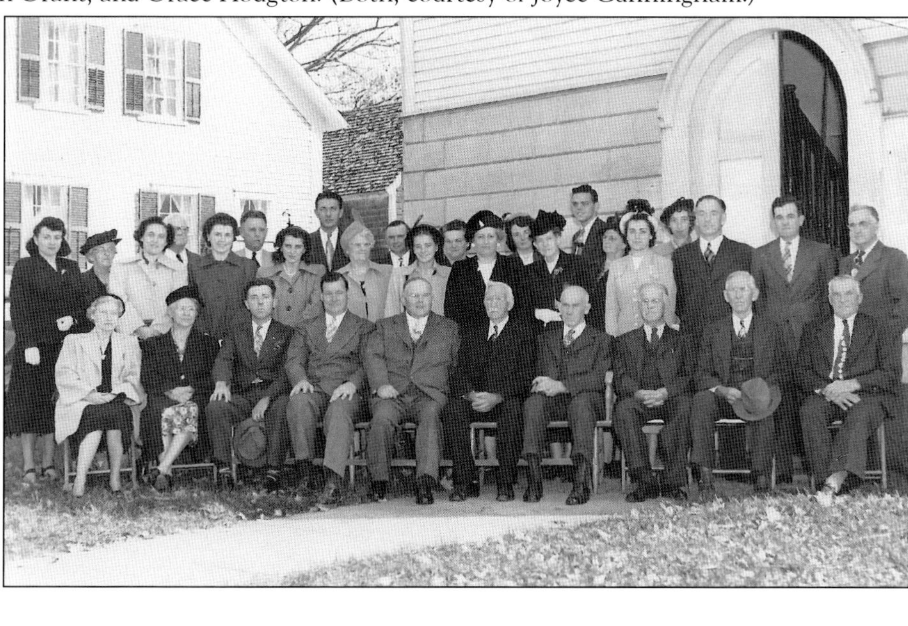

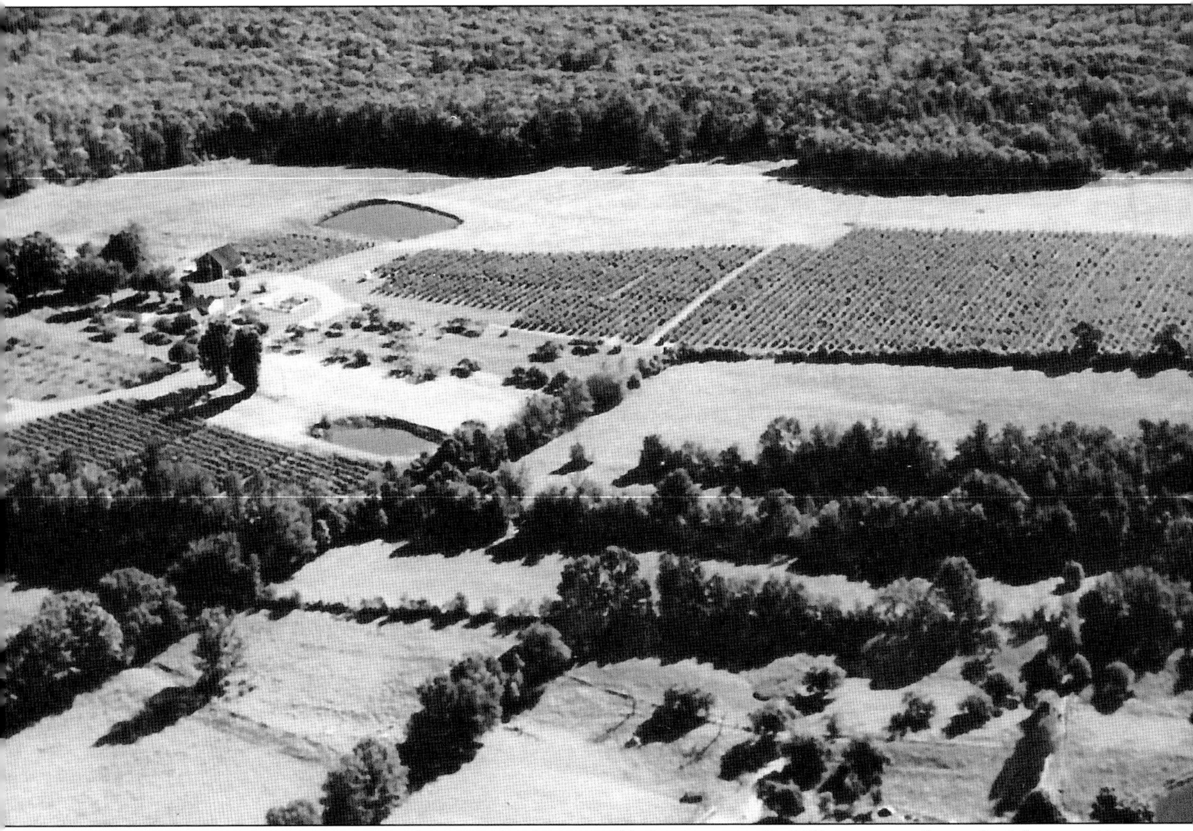

Frank and Virginia Robinson began Blueberry Hill Farm in 1962. What started as a hobby quickly turned into a thriving business, at one time employing up to 100 youngsters as pickers. For years, the farm provided cultivated berries to Shaw's Supermarkets and to Boston's Bay State Produce Company. Blueberry Hill Farm started with 2,000 high bush blueberries and now encompasses 10 acres of seven varieties that produce an average of 30 tons per season. Spreading across 111 acres at an elevation of 790 feet above sea level, Blueberry Hill offers beautiful views of the Atlantic Ocean on one side and the White Mountain foothills on the other. Since 1986, Keven Ham has owned and operated Blueberry Hill Farm along with his wife, Darlene. This panoramic location was even selected as the sight of a movie shoot. Roger Moore and Colleen Dewhurst shot a scene among the rows of blueberries for *Bed and Breakfast* here in 1991. (Courtesy of Darlene Ham.)

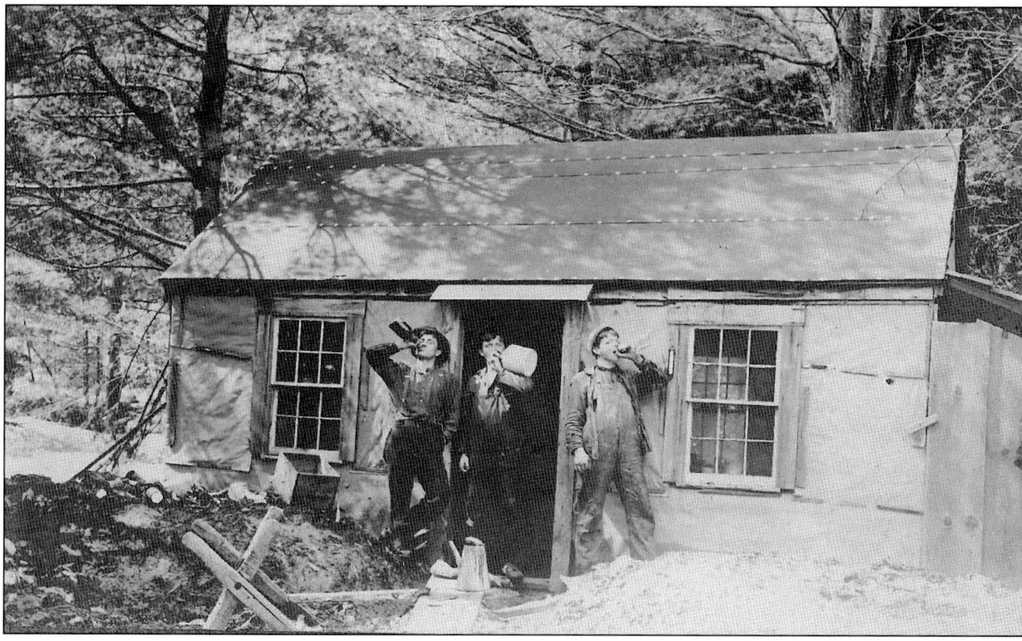

Because this region is quite rural, most women took to canning the fruits of their labor, which provided food during the long, harsh winters. The same can be said about alcohol. Many men folk brewed their own libations to be enjoyed throughout the year. Pictured above are three unknown locals having a little nip of what appears to be home brew. This tradition of fermenting sugars into alcohol continues today. Due to the popularity of the relatively recent microbrewing industry and the abundance of fresh fruit, there has been a resurgence of home brew activity in this area. In fact, there are quite a few people, including a local home brew club, who enjoy making, sharing, and drinking home-brewed creations such as wine, beer, mead, and cider. Pictured below are oak fermenting barrels, a sheave of grain, a couple boxes of bottle caps, and bottle cappers, which were used by early home brewers. (Below, courtesy of Steven Loignon.)

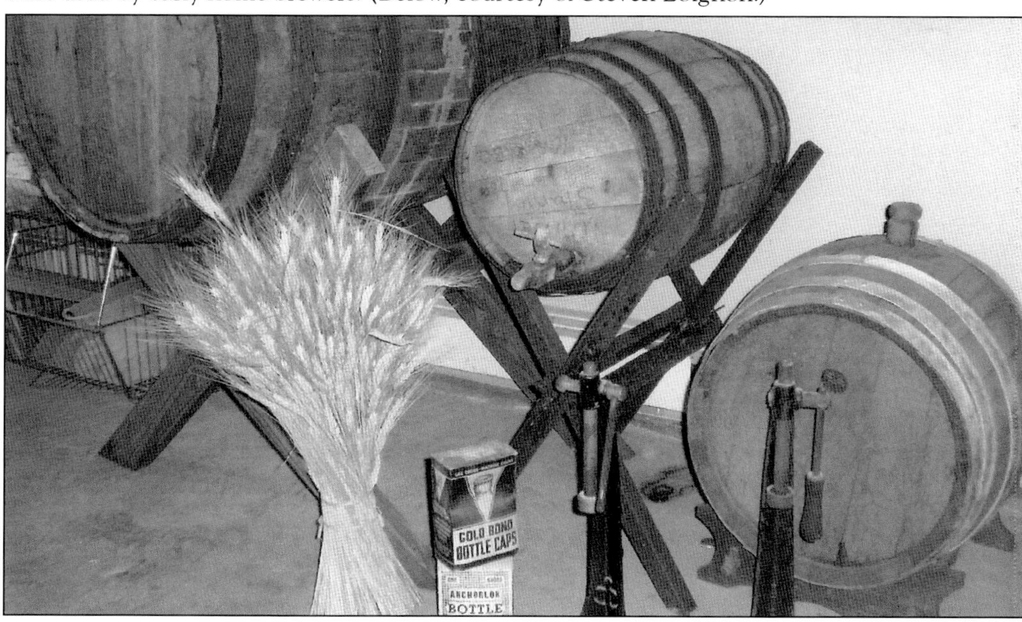

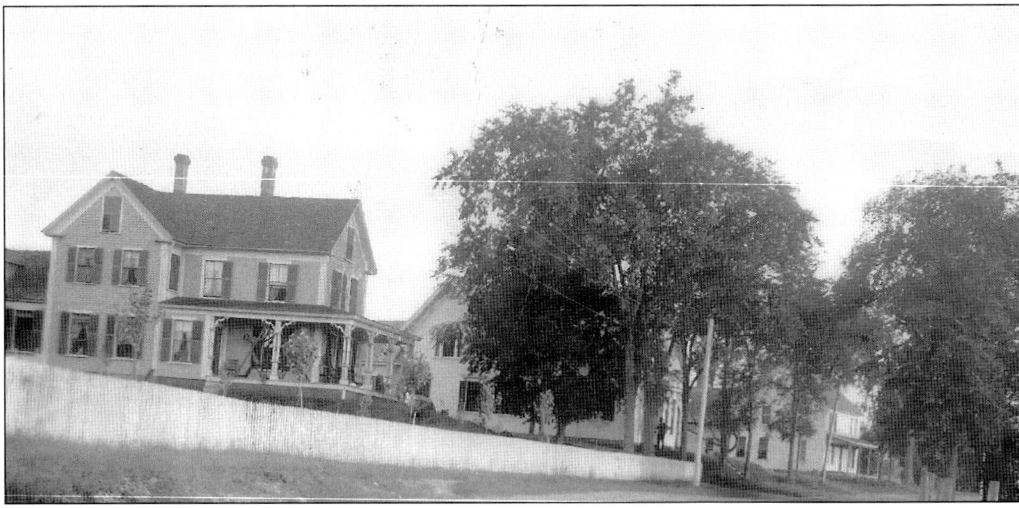

This picture was taken in 1923 from the bridge that joins Acton to Milton Mills, New Hampshire. The large, ornate home on the far left was owned by Harry Wentworth, and the neighboring home was owned by George Marsh. These houses are located on the lower end of Foxes Ridge Road, just a few hundred feet from Milton Mills. (Courtesy of Joyce Cunningham.)

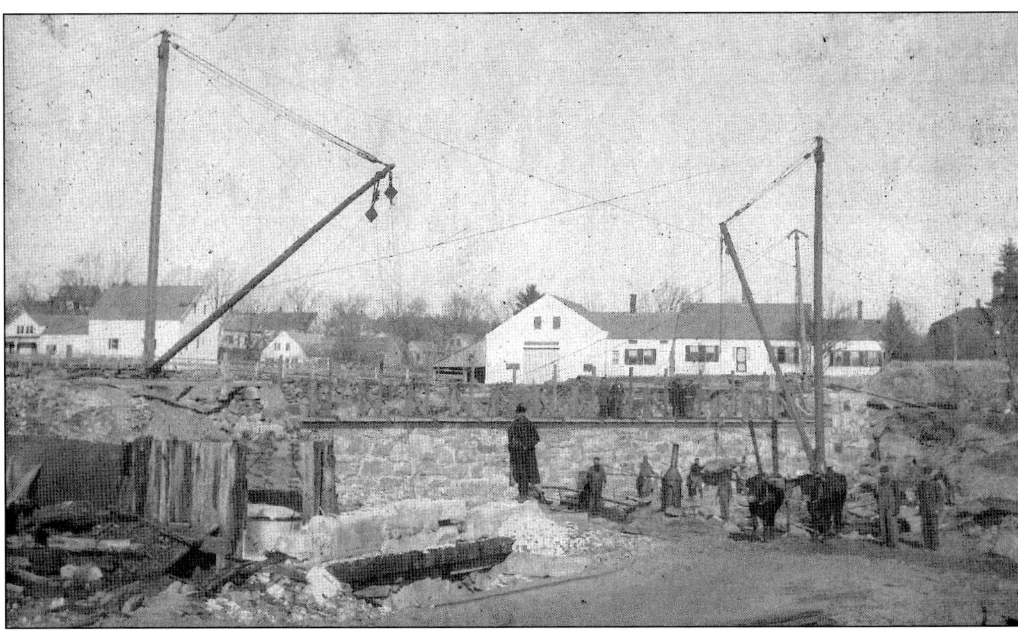

This faded photograph shows the ingenuity used in building the dam at the Acton–Milton Mills line. Booms were erected to lift the heavy stones into place. This was done with the help of a team of oxen and the use of block and tackle. (Courtesy of Eva Morrill.)

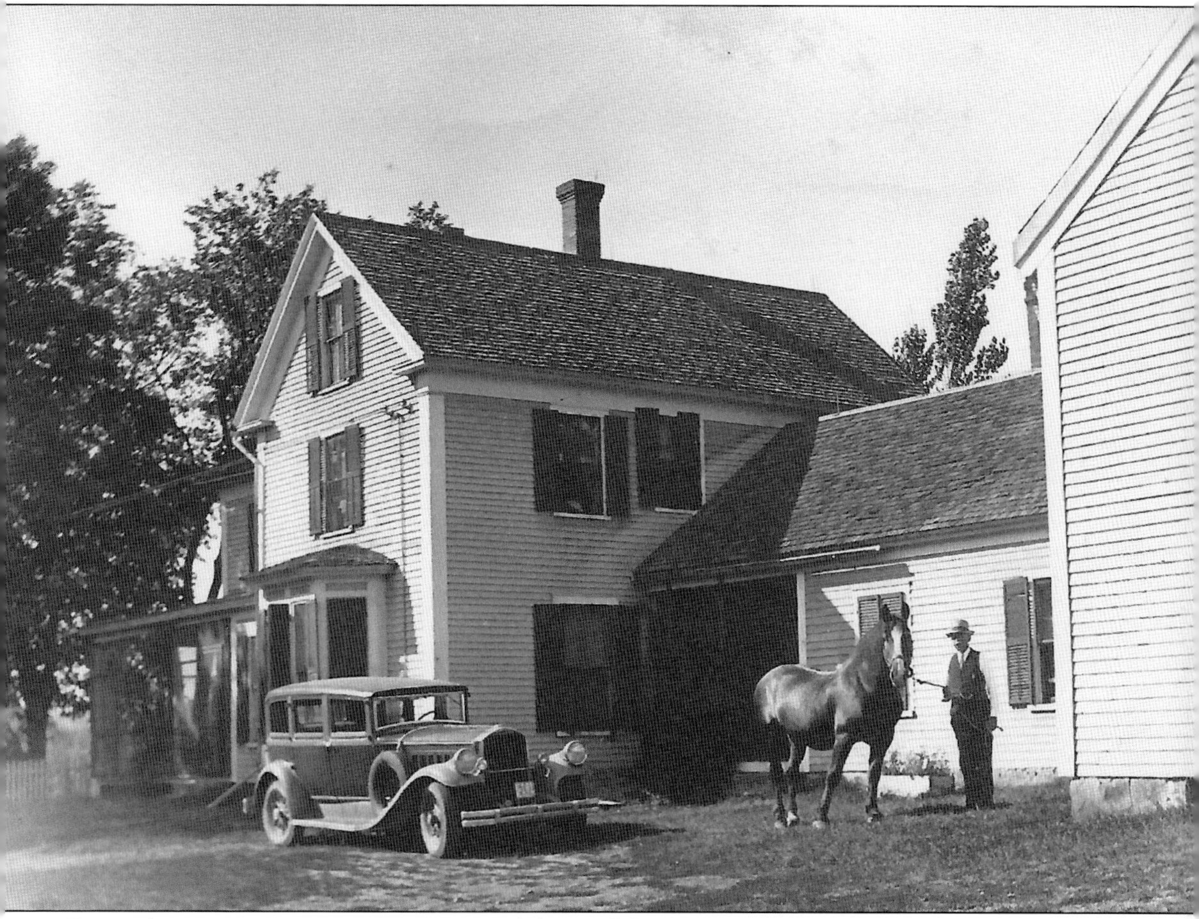

Pierce-Arrows were very expensive automobiles, and their owners were among the most influential and wealthy people of the time. Successful businessman and land baron Harry Wentworth stands outside his home on Foxes Ridge with two of his prized possessions—Chubby the horse and his Pierce-Arrow. Wentworth was a town father, highly regarded within the community, and served as the Acton town moderator from 1945 to 1948. Just a two-minute walk across the bridge takes one into Milton Mills, New Hampshire. (Courtesy of Joyce Cunningham.)

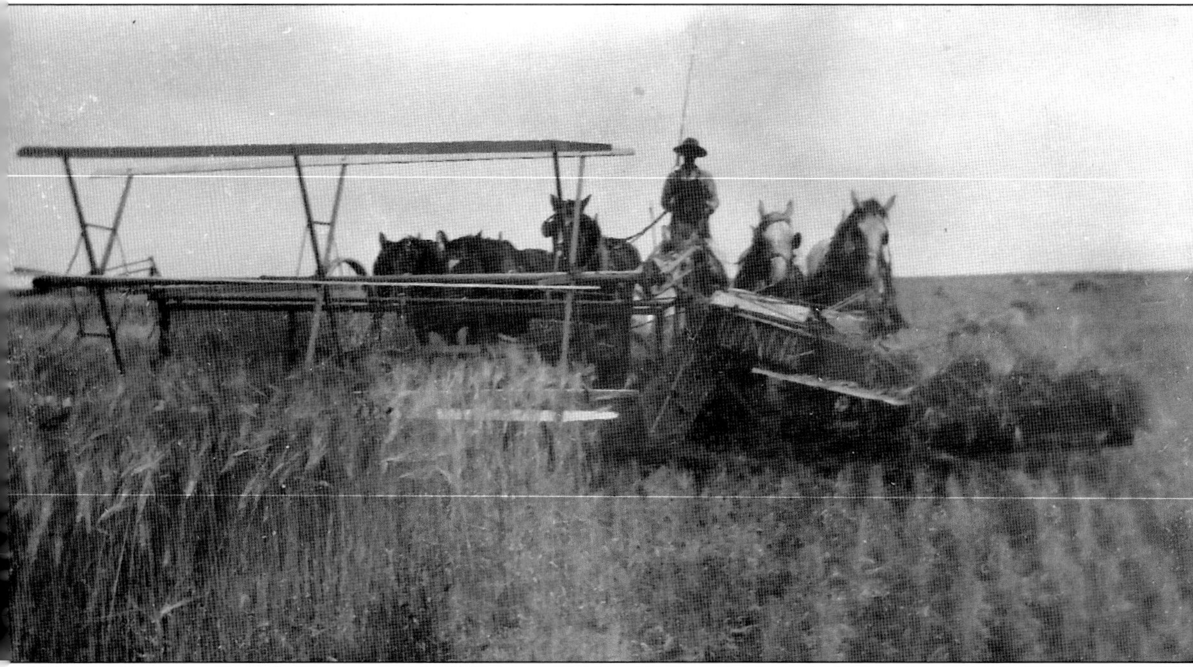

Until the middle of the 19th century, hay was cut by hand with sickles and scythes. By the 1860s, early cutting devices were developed that resembled those on reapers and binders like the one pictured here. Binders reduced the labor required to cut and shock the wheat, but considerable horsepower was required. Commonly, four horses were needed to pull a binder. One person drove the team of horses (later a tractor was used), while another rode the binder to stack the bundles as they came out. Farming and farm machinery have continued to evolve. Plows are not used nearly as extensively as before, due in large part to the popularity of minimum tillage to reduce soil erosion and conserve moisture. Today's farm machinery allows farmers to cultivate many more acres of land than the machines of yesterday. William Goding is seen here cutting wheat with his new 12-foot binder, which allowed him to easily cut 30 acres in eight hours, quite a feat for the times.

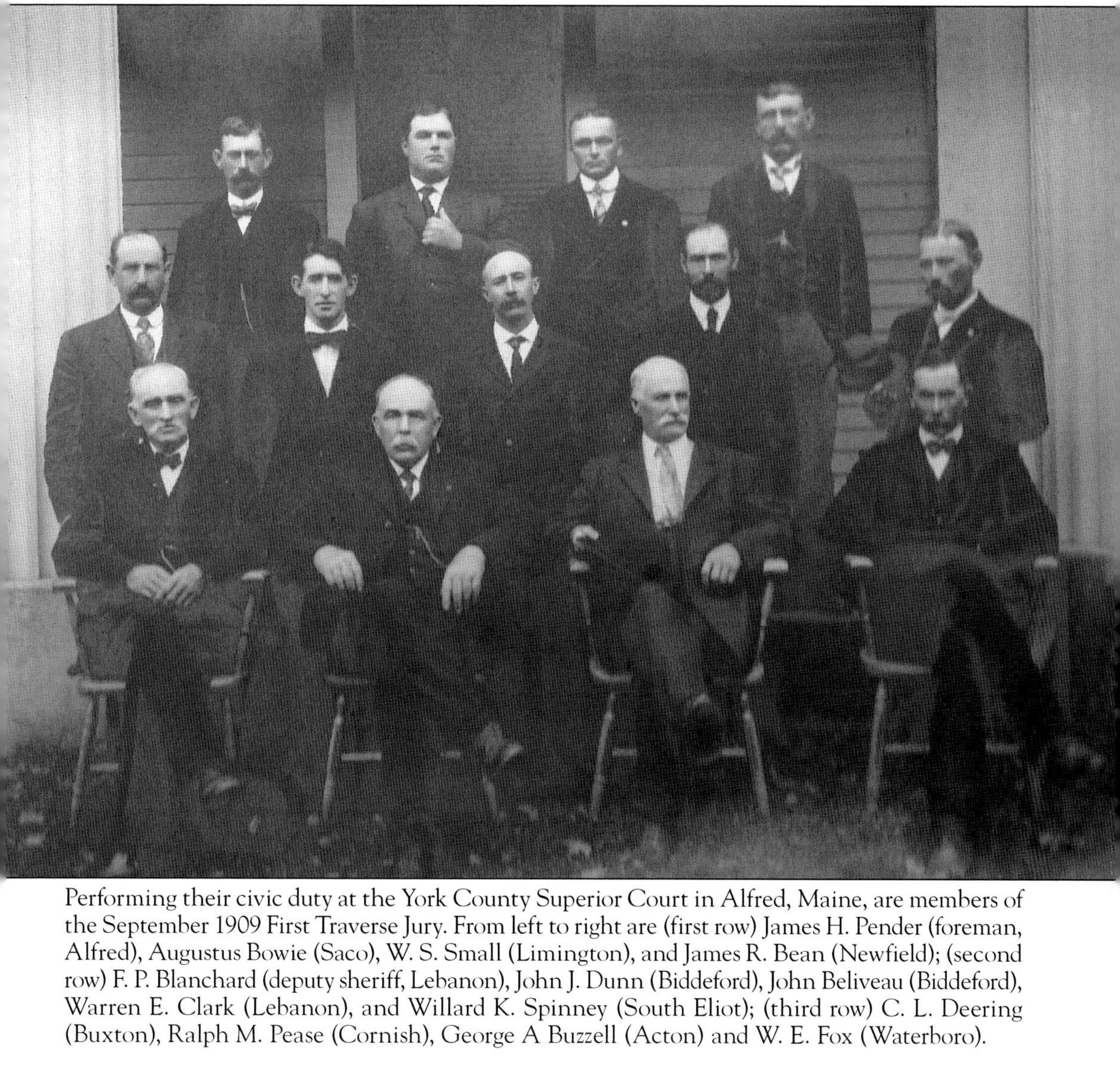

Performing their civic duty at the York County Superior Court in Alfred, Maine, are members of the September 1909 First Traverse Jury. From left to right are (first row) James H. Pender (foreman, Alfred), Augustus Bowie (Saco), W. S. Small (Limington), and James R. Bean (Newfield); (second row) F. P. Blanchard (deputy sheriff, Lebanon), John J. Dunn (Biddeford), John Beliveau (Biddeford), Warren E. Clark (Lebanon), and Willard K. Spinney (South Eliot); (third row) C. L. Deering (Buxton), Ralph M. Pease (Cornish), George A Buzzell (Acton) and W. E. Fox (Waterboro).

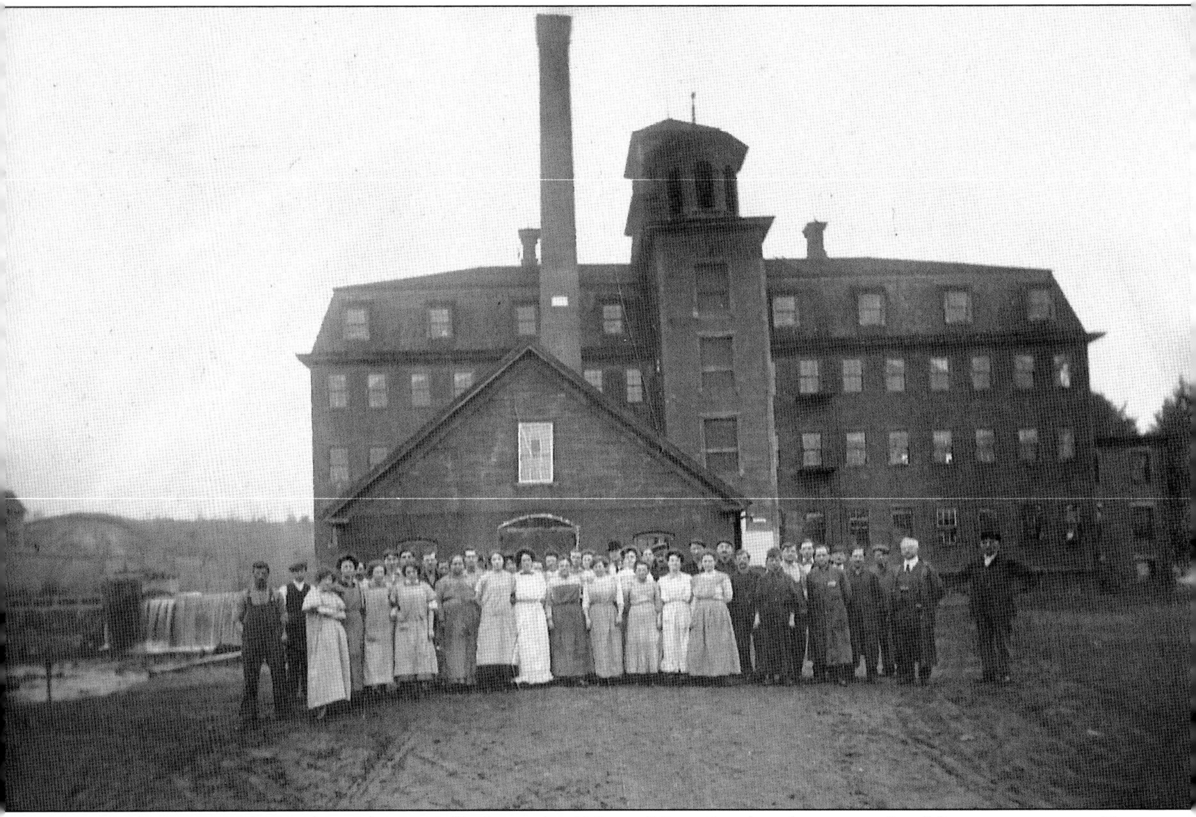

Built in 1893 along the Salmon Falls River by Edward Brierly, this four-story building was originally a felt mill. Due to the abundant source of power, many mills sprang up in rural towns located along rivers and waterways. Eventually, mills were relocated as water power was replaced by steam, and many riverside towns felt the effects of an economic downturn. Throughout its years of operation, this mill changed hands and names several times, and the nature of business evolved to shoe manufacturing and then to the manufacturing of cloth. Seized for nonpayment of taxes, the building was torn down around 1930. (Courtesy of Eva Morrill.)

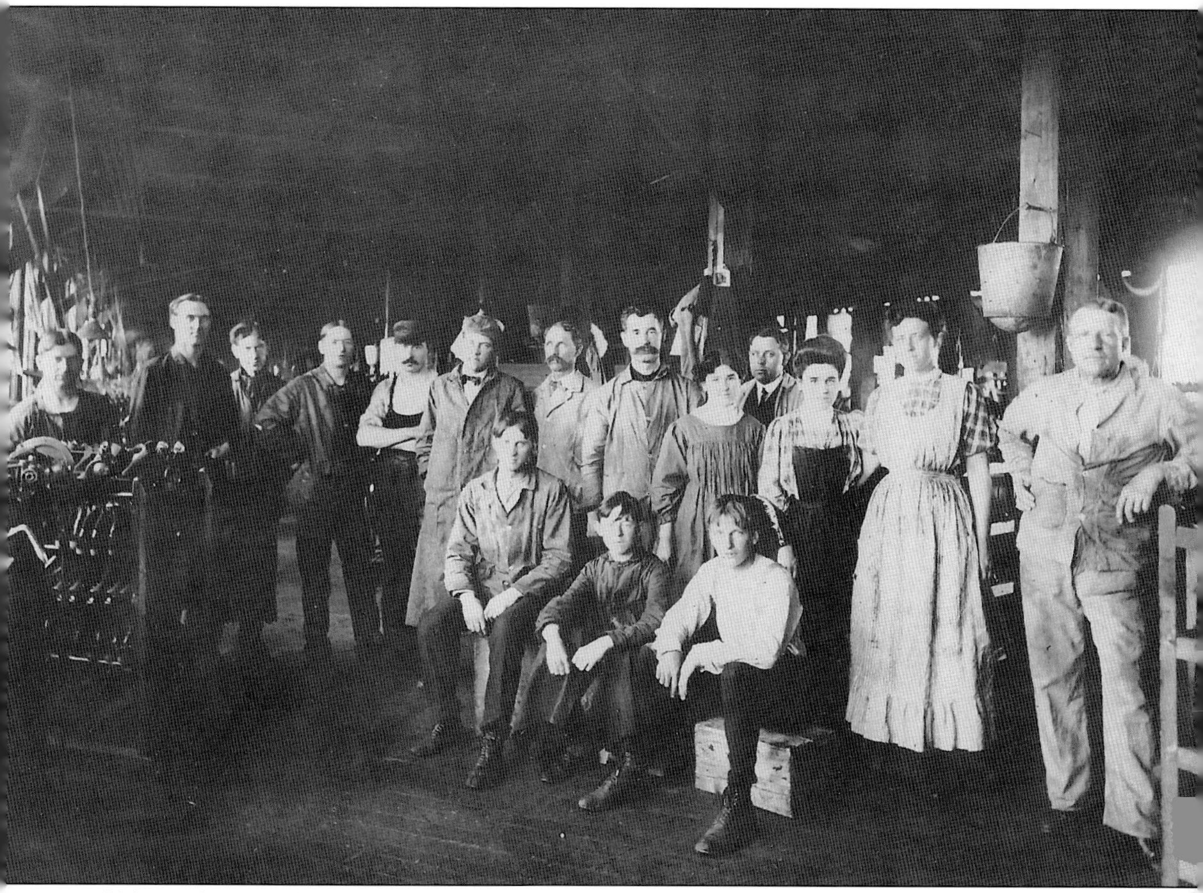

Cobblers, who provided early colonists with much needed footwear, practiced one of the earliest professions in the New World. After acquiring leather from nearby tanneries, these shoemakers, who frequently worked at home, used hand tools and centuries-old techniques to cut out the various parts, sew together the pieces, and shape each shoe over a wooden last, or form. With the advent of the industrial revolution, changing manufacturing from hand-and-home production to machine-and-factory, many rural villages became industrial sites, where large machines mass-produced items such as textiles and shoes, as depicted in this early photograph from the late 1880s. During this period, it was common to employ entire families, from youths to adults. For some youngsters, this was the primary reason for leaving their education behind and replacing it with a paycheck. The number of workers at the Gale Shoe factory, shown here, ranged over time from 200 down to 50 before the mill closed its doors in the 1900s. (Courtesy of Eva Morrill.)

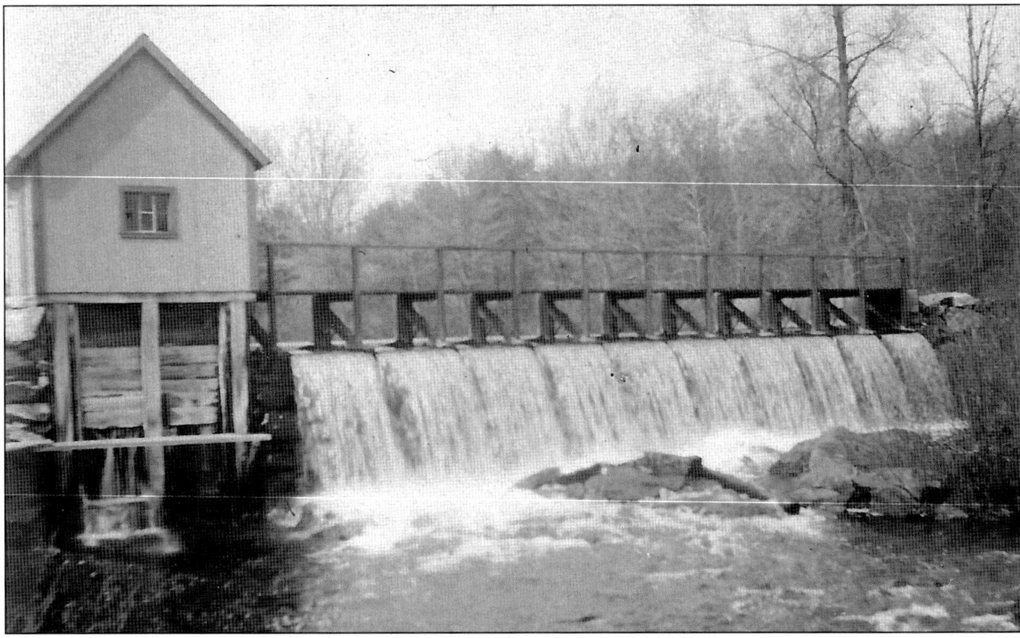

Rowe Dam is located on the Hopper Road and borders Acton and Milton Mills, New Hampshire. In the bottom picture, Robert Meyer of Acton is standing on frozen water at Rowe Dam in 1943. This dam was one in a series that controlled water flow on the Salmon Falls River. (Both, courtesy of Eva Morrill.)

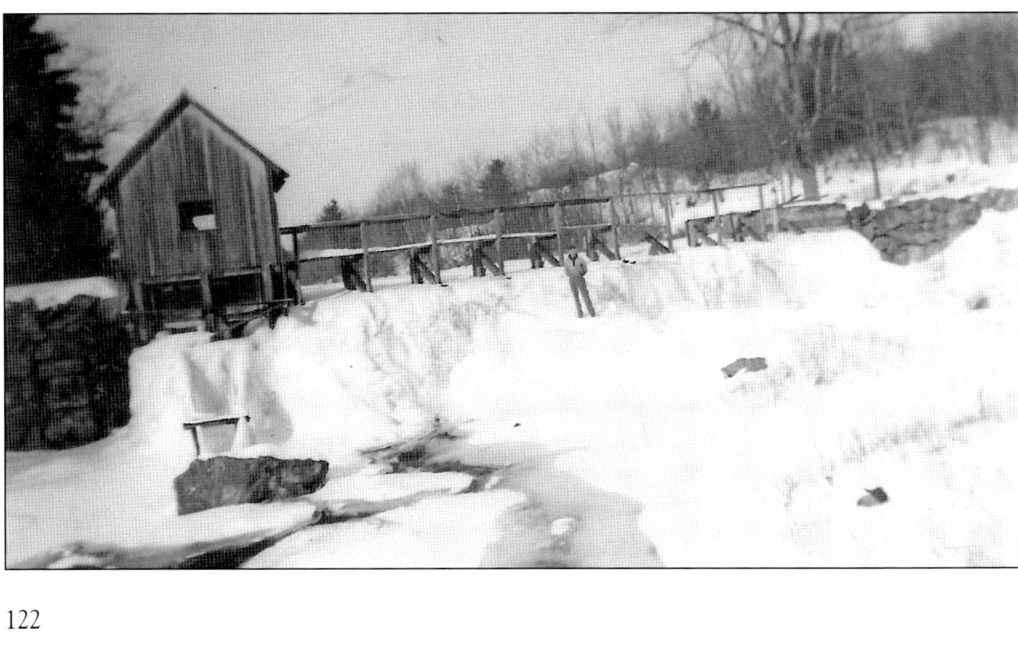

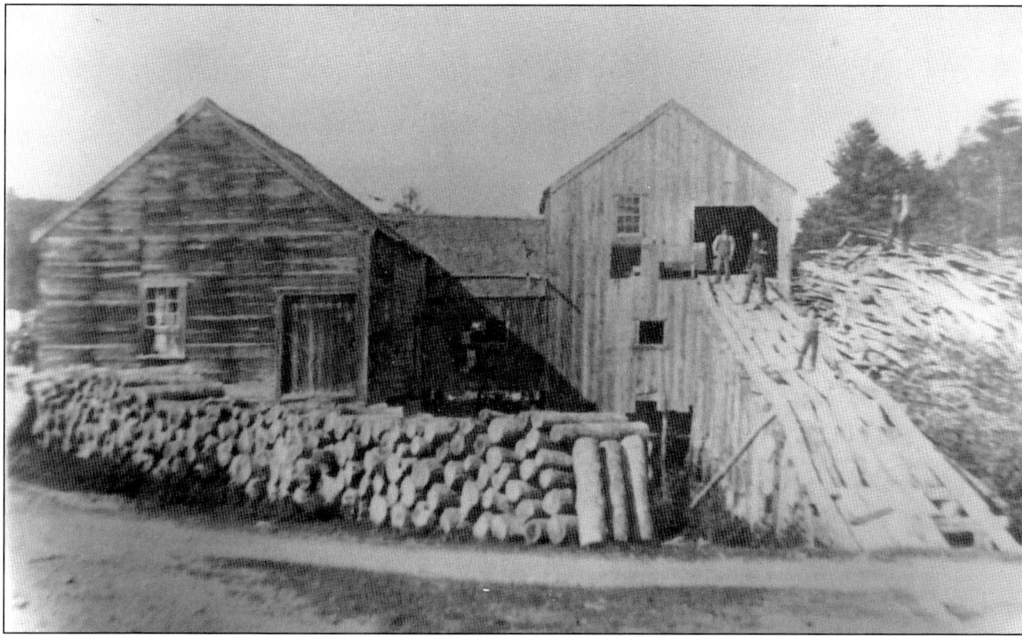

Forest products and textiles dominated Maine's production from 1860 to 1900. Logs were driven to mills, debarked, cut to length, and sometimes cut into boards. In 1976, Maine passed a law banning river driving of logs. Although the days of log drives are over, the mystique will always be a part of Maine's history. Pictured here is Balch Lumber Mill as it looked in 1884, with (from left to right) employees Fred Walls, Freeman Horn, Julian Horn, and Ben Horn.

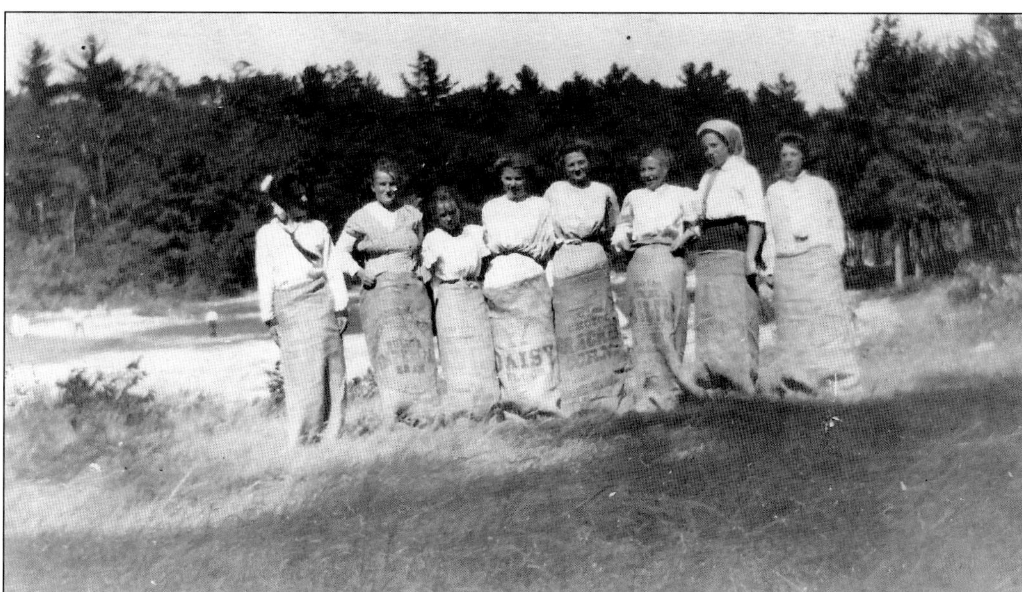

A group of young women await the whistle to start a sack race, a favorite activity at church picnics and community outings. Traditionally an activity for children, adults often found it amusing as well as challenging. It is interesting to note the different types of burlap sacks used.

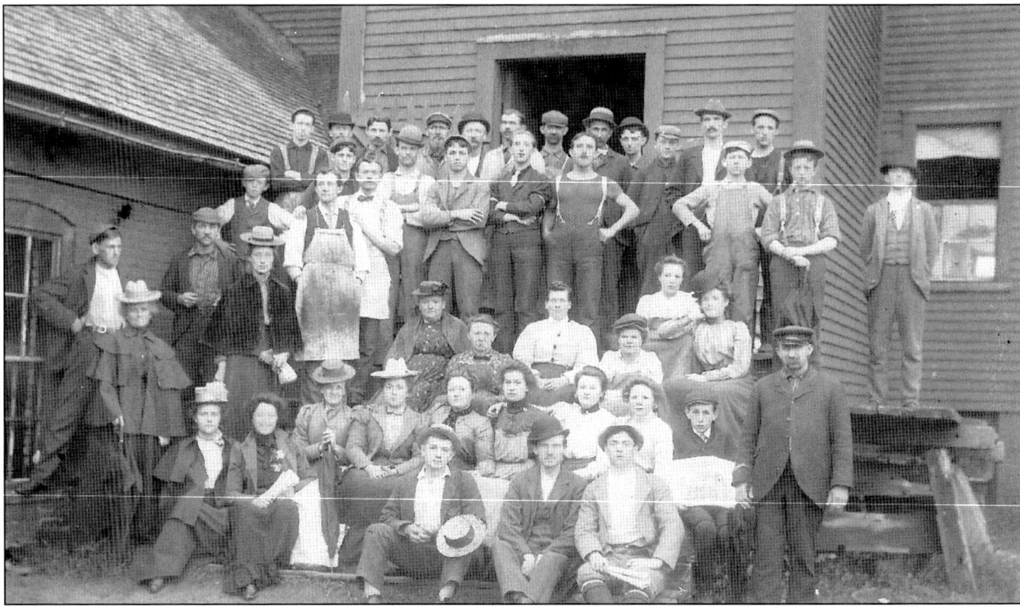

A group of shoe shop employees takes a break from working to pose outside for this photograph. Again, one can see the range in ages of workers and also the inclusion of women in the workforce. During this era, factory work was believed to be more suited for women because it was less physical and allowed for some independence.

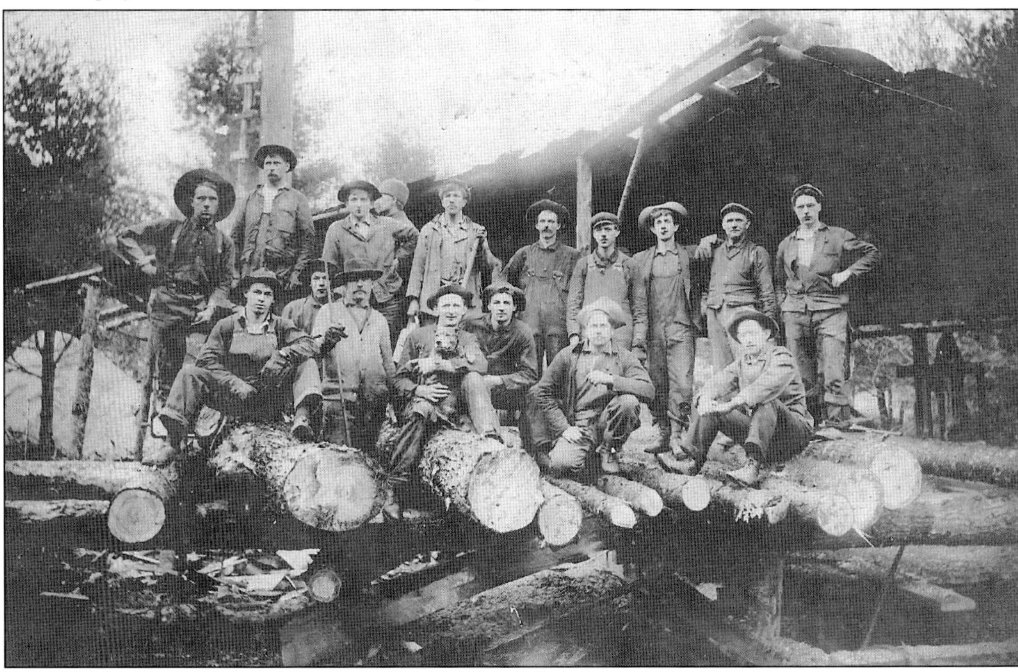

Pictured here are local lumber mill workers. Early loggers and sawmill owners who cut forests with little thought to future timber production and the environment were forced to follow the timber supply west and south. Sawmills, like farming, have since evolved into large technological and highly efficient mills. As with farming, the larger, more productive mills drove the price of wood down so far that many small local sawmills were forced to shut down.

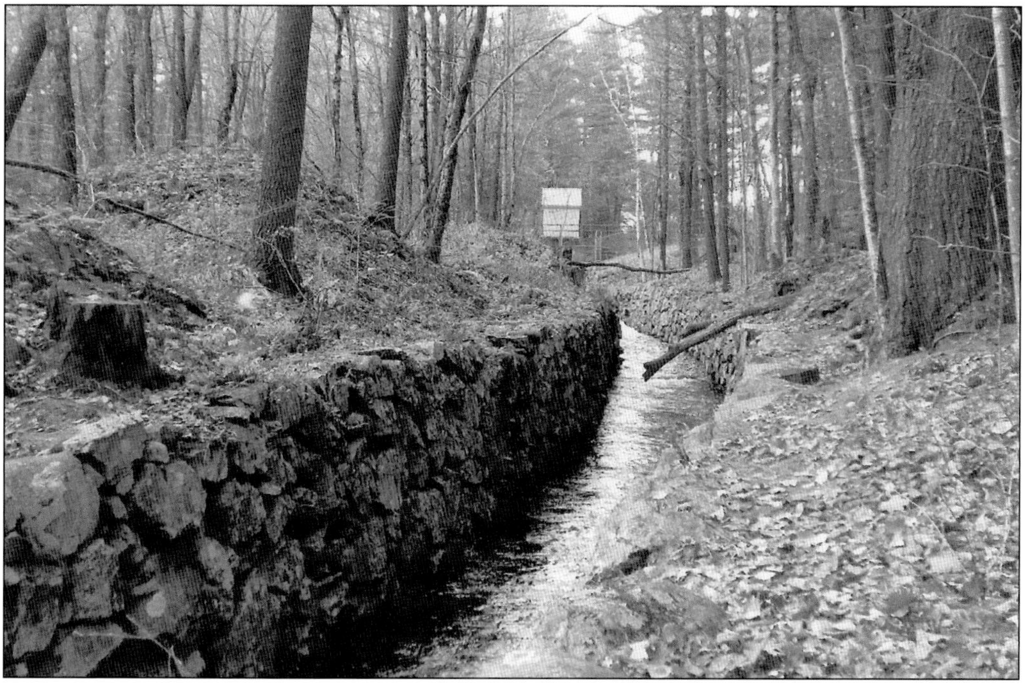

Great East Canal was an engineering marvel of the 1800s. There was no cement or mortar used in either the archway, which supports a two-lane road crossing the canal, or the canal itself. The archway was built on a diagonal, because the road crosses at a decided angle. The large granite stones were hauled into place by men and oxen. Excavation of the canal started in the 1850s. Construction was delayed due to the outbreak of the Civil War in 1861 and was finally completed a few years later. The canal is three-quarters of a mile long, 16 feet deep, and 13 feet wide. It forms the boundary between Acton and New Hampshire near Great East Lake. Part of a system of dams that controlled water flow on the Salmon Falls River, the canal provided water power for many industries along the river as far south as Dover, New Hampshire.

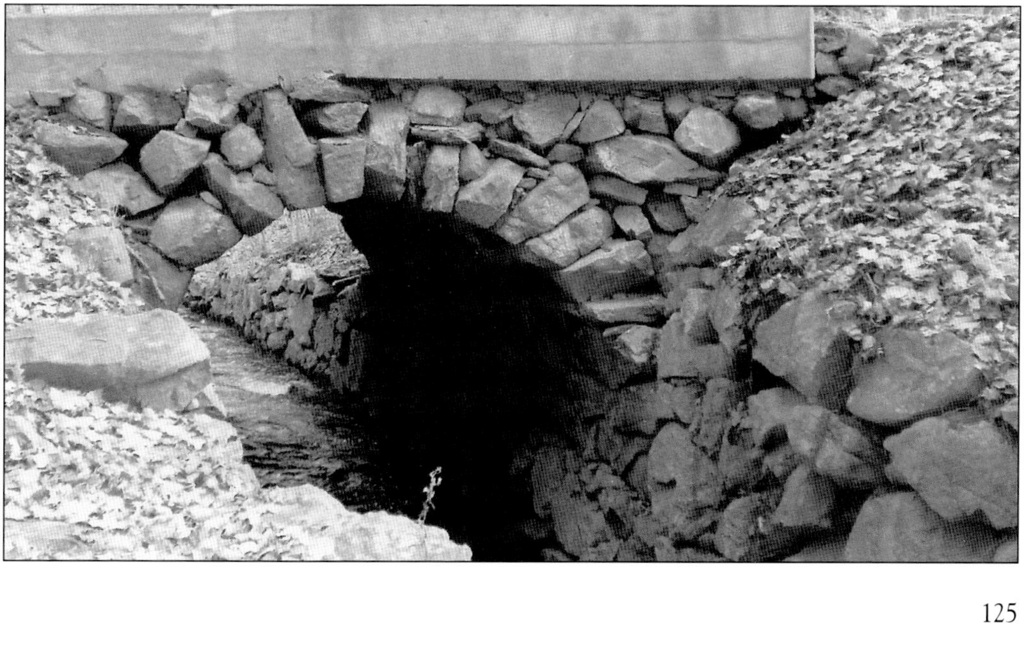

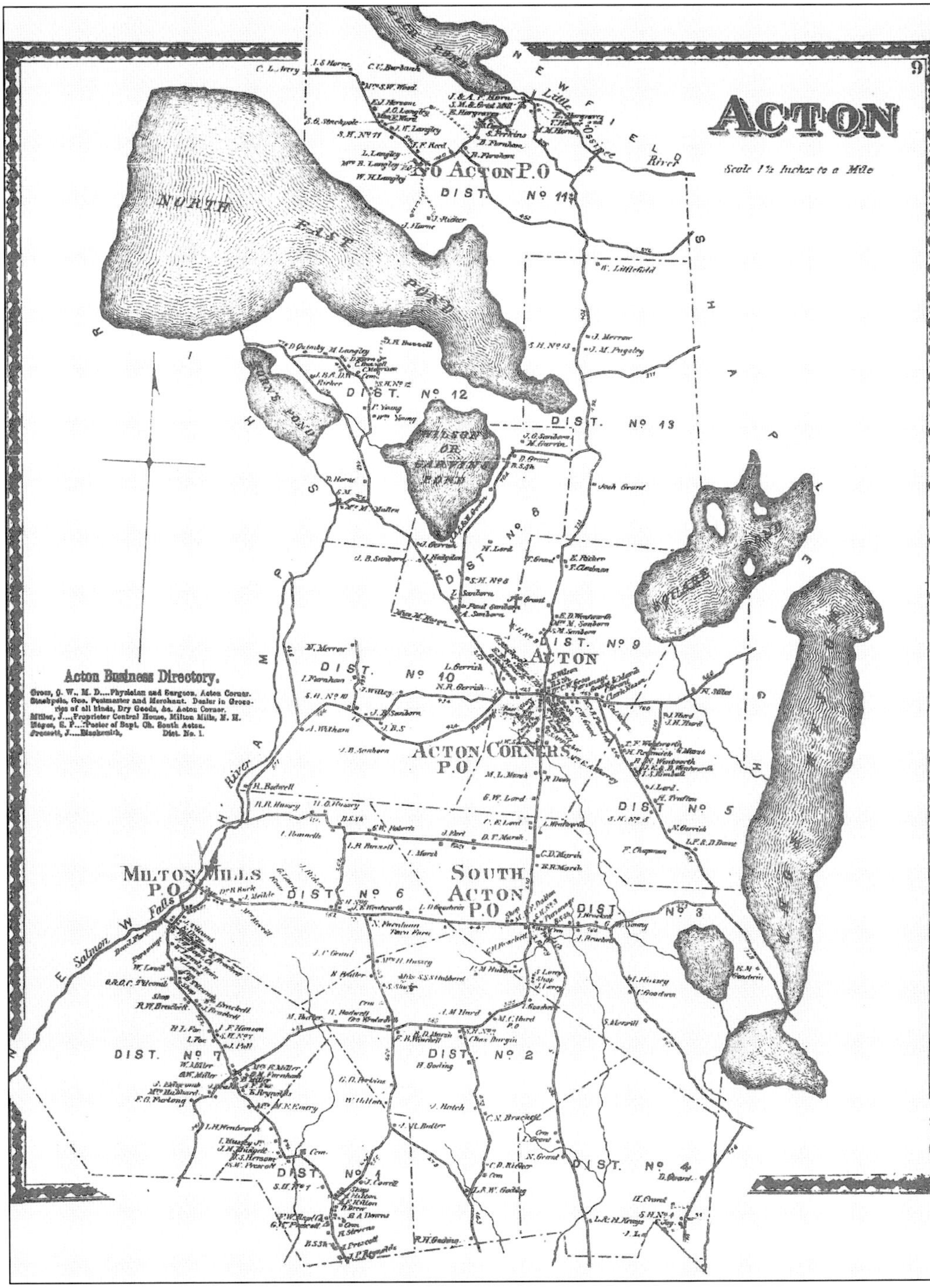

Pictured here is an 1872 map of Acton.

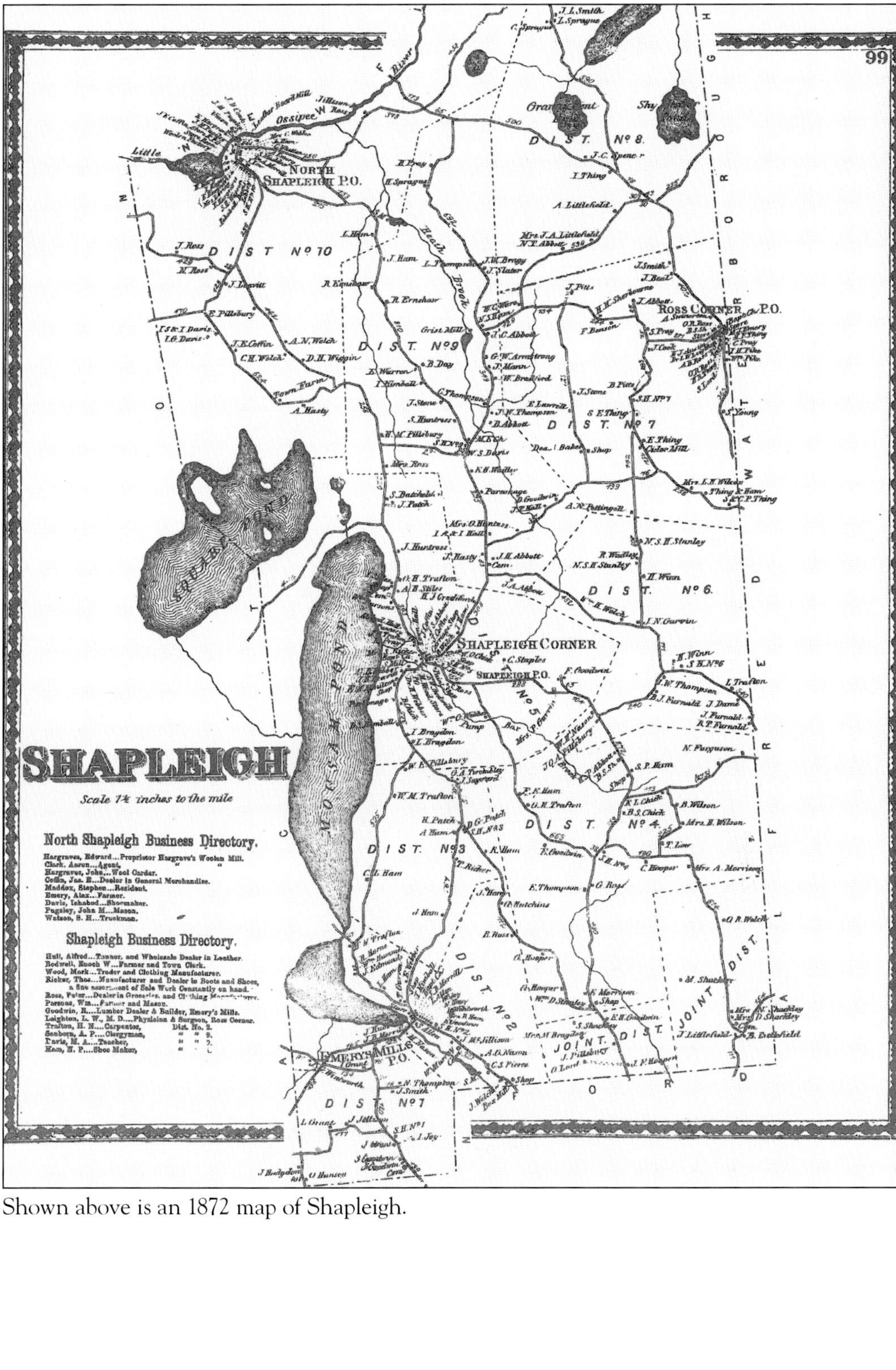

Shown above is an 1872 map of Shapleigh.